POWERS OF HORROR
An Essay on Abjection

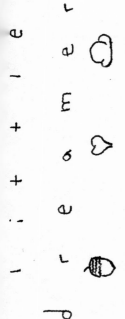

EUROPEAN PERSPECTIVES
A Series of the Columbia University Press

Other works by Julia Kristeva
published by Columbia

*Desire in Language: A Semiotic Approach
to Literature and Art*

Revolution in Poetic Language

Powers of Horror: An Essay on Abjection

The Kristeva Reader

Tales of Love

In the Beginning Was Love: Psychoanalysis and Faith

Language: The Unknown

Black Sun: Depression and Melancholia

POWERS OF HORROR

An Essay on Abjection

☙ JULIA KRISTEVA

Translated by
LEON S. ROUDIEZ

COLUMBIA UNIVERSITY PRESS
New York

Library of Congress Cataloging in Publication Data

Kristeva, Julia, 1941–
  Powers of horror.

  (European perspectives)
  Translation of: Pouvoirs de l'horreur.
    1. Céline, Louis-Ferdinand, 1894–1961—
  Criticism and interpretation.   2. Horror in
  literature.   3. Abjection in literature.
  I. Title.   II. Series.
  PQ2607.E834Z73413   843'.912   82-4481
  ISBN 0-231-05346-0   AACR2
  ISBN 0-231-05347-9   (pbk.)

Columbia University Press
New York   Oxford

p 10 9 8 7 6
c 10 9 8 7 6 5 4 3 2

Contents

Translator's Note

When the original version of this book was published in France in 1980, critics sensed that it marked a turning point in Julia Kristeva's writing. Her concerns seemed less arcane, her presentation more appealingly worked out; as Guy Scarpetta put it in *Le Nouvel Observateur* (May 19, 1980), she now introduced into "theoretical rigor an effective measure of seduction." Actually, no sudden change has taken place: the features that are noticeable in *Powers of Horror* were already in evidence in several earlier essays, some of which have been translated in *Desire in Language* (Columbia University Press, 1980). She herself pointed out in the preface to that collection, "Readers will also notice that a change in writing takes place as the work progresses" (p. ix).

One would assume such a change has made the translator's task less arduous; in one sense it has, but it also produced a different set of difficulties. As sentences become more metaphorical, more "literary" if you wish, one is liable to forget that they still are conceptually very precise. In other words, meaning emerges out of both the standard denotation(s) and the connotations suggested by the material shape of a given word. And it emerges not solely because of the reader's creativity, as happens in poetic language, but because it was put there in the first place. For instance, "un être altéré" means either a changed, adulterated being or an avid, thirsty being; mindful, however, of the unchanged presence of the Latin root, *alter*, Kristeva also intends it to mean "being for the other." This gives the phrase a special twist, and it takes a reader more imaginative than I am to catch it.

As Kristeva's writing evolves, it also displays a greater variety in tone. In this essay it includes the colloquial and the formal, the lyrical and the matter-of-fact, the concrete and the abstract. I resisted the temptation to unify her style and tried as much as possible to preserve the variety of the original. Only in a few instances, when a faithful rendition would in my opinion have sounded incongruous (e.g., translating *pétard*, which she borrows from the text of a Céline novel, as "gat" or "rod"), did I consciously neutralize her prose.

A particularly vexing problem stems from the nature of the French language and its limited vocabulary as compared to English; words tend to point in a greater number of different directions. Usually, in expository prose, the context removes the ambiguities that poetic language thrives on. Kristeva is not averse to using polysemy to her advantage, as other French theorists like Derrida and Lacan have also done. The French word *propre*, for instance, has kept the meaning of the Latin *proprius* (one's own, characteristic, proper) and also acquired a new one: clean. At first, in *Powers of Horror*, the criteria of expository prose seemed to apply, but in several instances I began to have my doubts about this. When I asked Kristeva which meaning she intended the answer was, both. As a result I decided to use the rather cumbersome "one's own clean and proper body" to render the French *corps propre*, sacrificing elegance for the sake of clarity and fullness of meaning.

Examining my translation carefully, one is apt to notice anomalies in the text of the quotations. There are two reasons for this. When the original is not in French, Kristeva cites a published French translation and I refer to a published English one when available. Discrepancies are inevitable and for the most part inconsequential. In the case of Freud's *Totem and Taboo*, however, the French version, in the excerpts quoted here, contains a couple of mistranslated words: *Inzestscheu* becomes "phobie de l'inceste" instead of the more accurate "incest dread," and *Genussgefähig* gets afflicted with the connotation of "objets comestibles" that belongs to *Geniessbar* instead of the more general and accurate "capable of enjoyment" of the English version. While this has required some vocabulary adjustment, it does not affect Kristeva's argument. Where Hegel's works are concerned the situation is even more troublesome, for discrepancies between French and English translations are considerable. Referring back to the German text of *Vorlesungen über die Philosophie der Religion* I find that the English text is faithful to it. What apparently happened is that the French translation was made from an earlier version of the *Lectures*, which, like Saussure's famous *Cours de linguistique générale*, was published by Hegel's students after his death. The second edition, on which the English version is based, is presumably an improved one—but that need not concern us here. In the excerpts quoted by Kristeva, the meaning is essentially the same even though the wording differs and in one instance a metaphorical development has been eliminated.

When several translations are available, as they are for Sophocles, I used the one that seemed closest to the one used by Kristeva. For the Bible, I relied on the King James version; minor differences between biblical and anthropological terminology should pose no problem, and the reader will readily see that the latter's pure/impure distinction corresponds to the biblical contrast between clean and unclean.

For an original quotation from the French, I have also used available published translations. Working with Céline's novels, however, translators have endeavored to produce effective English-language fiction. As a result they were occasionally led to stray from a literal version of the text—and rightly so. On the other hand, for the purpose of Kristeva's analysis, there are times when close attention to material details of the text is essential. I have therefore, in a number of instances, had to modify the published translation—but that should not be seen as a reflection on their quality. On a few occasions, though, especially where the early novels are involved, translators have tended to be squeamish; thus, in *Journey to the End of the Night*, the statement pertaining to women in wartime, "la guerre porte aux ovaires," becomes, "war goes straight to their tummies." I naturally put the ovaries back in.

Throughout this essay, Kristeva plays with the titles of Céline's novels (and a few others: Robert Musil's *The Man Without Qualities* makes a fleeting appearance toward the end).

Journey to the End of the Night is easily recognizable; the title *From Castle to Castle*, in this connection, needs to be changed to the more literal, "From One Castle to an Other," which produced the title of an earlier essay, "From One Identity to an Other" (collected in *Desire in Language*); I have rendered the untranslated *Féerie pour une autre fois* as "Enchantment for Some Other Time." For some features of her terminology, readers should consult the "Notes on the Translation and on Terminology" that appeared in *Desire in Language*. Here, however, instead of invariably rendering "écriture" as "writing," I have attempted to distinguish between the weak and the strong meanings of the French word. For the latter I used the term "scription," which I had introduced in my *French Fiction Today* (Rutgers University Press, 1972). There are in *Powers of Horror* a few additional items of Lacanian vocabulary that the context should clarify. The object *a* is mentioned twice, and it could be puzzling. A few lines from Stuart Schneiderman's *Returning to Freud* (Yale University Press, 1980) might prove helpful: "For the psychoanalyst the important object is the lost object, the object always desired and never attained, the object that causes the subject to desire in cases where he can never gain the satisfaction of possessing the object. Any object the subject desires will never be anything other than a substitute for the object *a*."

I should like to thank those who have given assistance in areas I am less familiar with: Stuart Schneiderman for the vocabulary of psychoanalysis, Robert Austerlitz for that of linguistics, Marvin I. Herzog for Hebrew terms, Robert D. Cumming for philosophy, and of course Julia Kristeva herself for clarifying a number of difficulties. I should point out, however, that while I sought assistance whenever I realized I had met with a problem, there may well have been problems I did not identify and on which I foundered. In such instances and in all others where mistranslations occur the responsibility is mine alone.

POWERS OF HORROR
An Essay on Abjection

§∞ I

APPROACHING ABJECTION

No Beast is there without glimmer of infinity,
No eye so vile nor abject that brushes not
Against lightning from on high, now tender, now fierce.
Victor Hugo, *La Légende des siècles*

NEITHER SUBJECT NOR OBJECT

There looms, within abjection, one of those violent, dark re-
volts of being, directed against a threat that seems to emanate
from an exorbitant outside or inside, ejected beyond the scope
of the possible, the tolerable, the thinkable. It lies there, quite
close, but it cannot be assimilated. It beseeches, worries, and
fascinates desire, which, nevertheless, does not let itself be seduced. Apprehensive, desire turns aside; sickened, it rejects. A
certainty protects it from the shameful—a certainty of which
it is proud holds on to it. But simultaneously, just the same,
that impetus, that spasm, that leap is drawn toward an elsewhere
as tempting as it is condemned. Unflaggingly, like an inescapable boomerang, a vortex of summons and repulsion places the
one haunted by it literally beside himself.

When I am beset by abjection, the twisted braid of affects
and thoughts I call by such a name does not have, properly
speaking, a definable *object*. The abject is not an ob-ject facing
me, which I name or imagine. Nor is it an ob-jest, an otherness
ceaselessly fleeing in a systematic quest of desire. What is abject
is not my correlative, which, providing me with someone or
something else as support, would allow me to be more or less
detached and autonomous. The abject has only one quality of
the object—that of being opposed to *I*. If the object, however,
through its opposition, settles me within the fragile texture of

a desire for meaning, which, as a matter of fact, makes me ceaselessly and infinitely homologous to it, what is *abject*, on the contrary, the jettisoned object, is radically excluded and draws me toward the place where meaning collapses. A certain "ego" that merged with its master, a superego, has flatly driven it away. It lies outside, beyond the set, and does not seem to agree to the latter's rules of the game. And yet, from its place of banishment, the abject does not cease challenging its master. Without a sign (for him), it beseeches a discharge, a convulsion, a crying out. To each ego its object, to each superego its abject. It is not the white expanse or slack boredom of repression, not the translations and transformations of desire that wrench bodies, nights, and discourse; rather it is a brutish suffering that "I" puts up with, sublime and devastated, for "I" deposits it to the father's account [*verse au père—père-version*]: I endure it, for I imagine that such is the desire of the other. A massive and sudden emergence of uncanniness, which, familiar as it might have been in an opaque and forgotten life, now harries me as radically separate, loathsome. Not me. Not that. But not nothing, either. A "something" that I do not recognize as a thing. A weight of meaninglessness, about which there is nothing insignificant, and which crushes me. On the edge of non-existence and hallucination, of a reality that, if I acknowledge it, annihilates me. There, abject and abjection are my safeguards. The primers of my culture.

THE IMPROPER/UNCLEAN

Loathing an item of food, a piece of filth, waste, or dung. The spasms and vomiting that protect me. The repugnance, the retching that thrusts me to the side and turns me away from defilement, sewage, and muck. The shame of compromise, of being in the middle of treachery. The fascinated start that leads me toward and separates me from them.

Food loathing is perhaps the most elementary and most archaic form of abjection. When the eyes see or the lips touch that skin on the surface of milk—harmless, thin as a sheet of cigarette paper, pitiful as a nail paring—I experience a gagging sensation and, still farther down, spasms in the stomach, the belly; and all the organs shrivel up the body, provoke tears and bile, increase heartbeat, cause forehead and hands to perspire. Along with sight-clouding dizziness, *nausea* makes me balk at that milk cream, separates me from the mother and father who proffer it. "I" want none of that element, sign of their desire; "I" do not want to listen, "I" do not assimilate it, "I" expel it. But since the food is not an "other" for "me," who am only in their desire, I expel *myself*, I spit *myself* out, I abject *myself* within the same motion through which "I" claim to establish *myself.* That detail, perhaps an insignificant one, but one that they ferret out, emphasize, evaluate, that trifle turns me inside out, guts sprawling; it is thus that *they* see that "I" am in the process of becoming an other at the expense of my own death. During that course in which "I" become, I give birth to myself amid the violence of sobs, of vomit. Mute protest of the symptom, shattering violence of a convulsion that, to be sure, is inscribed in a symbolic system, but in which, without either wanting or being able to become integrated in order to answer to it, it reacts, it abreacts. It abjects.

The corpse (or cadaver: *cadere*, to fall), that which has irremediably come a cropper, is cesspool, and death; it upsets even more violently the one who confronts it as fragile and fallacious chance. A wound with blood and pus, or the sickly, acrid smell of sweat, of decay, does not *signify* death. In the presence of signified death—a flat encephalograph, for instance—I would understand, react, or accept. No, as in true theater, without makeup or masks, refuse and corpses *show me* what I permanently thrust aside in order to live. These body fluids, this defilement, this shit are what life withstands, hardly and with difficulty, on the part of death. There, I am at the border of my condition as a living being. My body extricates itself, as being alive, from that border. Such wastes drop so that I might live, until, from loss to loss, nothing remains in me and my entire body falls beyond the limit—*cadere*, cadaver. If dung signifies the other side of the border, the place where I am not and which permits me to be, the corpse, the most sickening of wastes, is a border that has encroached upon everything. It is

no longer I who expel, "I" is expelled. The border has become
an object. How can I be without border? That elsewhere that
I imagine beyond the present, or that I hallucinate so that I
might, in a present time, speak to you, conceive of you—it is
now here, jetted, abjected, into "my" world. Deprived of
world, therefore, I *fall in a faint*. In that compelling, raw, in-
solent thing in the morgue's full sunlight, in that thing that no
longer matches and therefore no longer signifies anything, I
behold the breaking down of a world that has erased its borders:
fainting away. The corpse, seen without God and outside of
science, is the utmost of abjection. It is death infecting life.
Abject. It is something rejected from which one does not part,
from which one does not protect oneself as from an object.
Imaginary uncanniness and real threat, it beckons to us and
ends up engulfing us.

It is thus not lack of cleanliness or health that causes abjection
but what disturbs identity, system, order. What does not respect
borders, positions, rules. The in-between, the ambiguous, the
composite. The traitor, the liar, the criminal with a good conscience, the shameless rapist, the killer who claims he is a
savior. . . . Any crime, because it draws attention to the fragility of the law, is abject, but premeditated crime, cunning murder, hypocritical revenge are even more so because they
heighten the display of such fragility. He who denies morality
is not abject; there can be grandeur in amorality and even in
crime that flaunts its disrespect for the law—rebellious, liberating, and suicidal crime. Abjection, on the other hand, is im-
moral, sinister, scheming, and shady: a terror that dissembles,
a hatred that smiles, a passion that uses the body for barter
instead of inflaming it, a debtor who sells you up, a friend who
stabs you. . . .

In the dark halls of the museum that is now what remains
of Auschwitz, I see a heap of children's shoes, or something
like that, something I have already seen elsewhere, under a
Christmas tree, for instance, dolls I believe. The abjection of
Nazi crime reaches its apex when death, which, in any case,
kills me, interferes with what, in my living universe, is supposed to save me from death: childhood, science, among other
things.

THE ABJECTION OF SELF

If it be true that the abject simultaneously beseeches and pulverizes the subject, one can understand that it is experienced
at the peak of its strength when that subject, weary of fruitless
attempts to identify with something on the outside, finds the
impossible within; when it finds that the impossible constitutes
its very *being*, that it *is* none other than abject. The abjection
of self would be the culminating form of that experience of the
subject to which it is revealed that all its objects are based merely
on the inaugural *loss* that laid the foundations of its own being.
There is nothing like the abjection of self to show that all abjection is in fact recognition of the *want* on which any being,
meaning, language, or desire is founded. One always passes too
quickly over this word, "want," and today psychoanalysts are
finally taking into account only its more or less fetishized product, the "object of want." But if one imagines (and imagine
one must, for it is the working of imagination whose foundations are being laid here) the experience of *want* itself as logically preliminary to being and object—to the being of the
object—then one understands that abjection, and even more so
abjection of self, is its only signified. Its signifier, then, is none
but literature. Mystical Christendom turned this abjection of
self into the ultimate proof of humility before God, witness
Elizabeth of Hungary who "though a great princess, delighted
in nothing so much as in abasing herself."[1]

The question remains as to the ordeal, a secular one this time,
that abjection can constitute for someone who, in what is
termed knowledge of castration, turning away from perverse
dodges, presents himself with his own body and ego as the
most precious non-objects; they are no longer seen in their own
right but forfeited, abject. The termination of analysis can lead
us there, as we shall see. Such are the pangs and delights of
masochism.

Essentially different from "uncanniness," more violent, too,
abjection is elaborated through a failure to recognize its kin;
nothing is familiar, not even the shadow of a memory. I imagine
a child who has swallowed up his parents too soon, who frightens himself on that account, "all by himself," and, to save

himself, rejects and throws up everything that is given to him—all gifts, all objects. He has, he could have, a sense of the abject. Even before things for him *are*—hence before they are signifiable—he drives them out, dominated by drive as he is, and constitutes his own territory, edged by the abject. A sacred configuration. Fear cements his compound, conjoined to another world, thrown up, driven out, forfeited. What he has swallowed up instead of maternal love is an emptiness, or rather a maternal hatred without a word for the words of the father; that is what he tries to cleanse himself of, tirelessly. What solace does he come upon within such loathing? Perhaps a father, existing but unsettled, loving but unsteady, merely an apparition but an apparition that remains. Without him the holy brat would probably have no sense of the sacred; a blank subject, he would remain, discomfited, at the dump for non-objects that are always forfeited, from which, on the contrary, fortified by abjection, he tries to extricate himself. For he is not mad, he through whom the abject exists. Out of the daze that has petrified him before the untouchable, impossible, absent body of the mother, a daze that has cut off his impulses from their objects, that is, from their representations, out of such daze he causes, along with loathing, one word to crop up—fear. The phobic has no other object than the abject. But that word, "fear"—a fluid haze, an elusive clamminess—no sooner has it cropped up than it shades off like a mirage and permeates all words of the language with nonexistence, with a hallucinatory, ghostly glimmer. Thus, fear having been bracketed, discourse will seem tenable only if it ceaselessly confront that otherness, a burden both repellent and repelled, a deep well of memory that is unapproachable and intimate: the abject.

job of literature to define + confront the abject

BEYOND THE UNCONSCIOUS

Put another way, it means that there are lives not sustained by *desire*, as desire is always for objects. Such lives are based on *exclusion*. They are clearly distinguishable from those understood as neurotic or psychotic, articulated by *negation* and its modalities, *transgression, denial,* and *repudiation.* Their dynamics challenges the theory of the unconscious, seeing that the latter is dependent upon a dialectic of negativity.

The theory of the unconscious, as is well known, presupposes a repression of contents (affects and presentations) that, thereby, do not have access to consciousness but effect within the subject modifications, either of speech (parapraxes, etc.), or of the body (symptoms), or both (hallucinations, etc.). As correlative to the notion of *repression*, Freud put forward that of *denial* as a means of figuring out neurosis, that of *rejection* (*repudiation*) as a means of situating psychosis. The asymmetry of the two repressions becomes more marked owing to denial's bearing on the object whereas repudiation affects desire itself (Lacan, in perfect keeping with Freud's thought, interprets that as "repudiation of the Name of the Father").

Yet, facing the ab-ject and more specifically phobia and the splitting of the ego (a point I shall return to), one might ask if those articulations of negativity germane to the unconscious (inherited by Freud from philosophy and psychology) have not become inoperative. The "unconscious" contents remain here *excluded* but in strange fashion: not radically enough to allow for a secure differentiation between subject and object, and yet clearly enough for a defensive *position* to be established—one that implies a refusal but also a sublimating elaboration. As if the fundamental opposition were between I and Other or, in more archaic fashion, between Inside and Outside. As if such an opposition subsumed the one between Conscious and Unconscious, elaborated on the basis of neuroses.

Owing to the ambiguous opposition I/Other, Inside/Outside—an opposition that is vigorous but pervious, violent but uncertain—there are contents, "normally" unconscious in neurotics, that become explicit if not conscious in "borderline" patients' speeches and behavior. Such contents are often openly manifested through symbolic practices, without by the same token being integrated into the judging consciousness of those particular subjects. Since they make the conscious/unconscious distinction irrelevant, borderline subjects and their speech constitute propitious ground for a sublimating discourse ("aesthetic" or "mystical," etc.), rather than a scientific or rationalist one.

AN EXILE WHO ASKS, "WHERE?"

The one by whom the abject exists is thus a *deject* who places (himself), *separates* (himself), situates (himself), and therefore *strays* instead of getting his bearings, desiring, belonging, or refusing. Situationist in a sense, and not without laughter—since laughing is a way of placing or displacing abjection. Necessarily dichotomous, somewhat Manichaean, he divides, excludes, and without, properly speaking, wishing to know his abjections is not at all unaware of them. Often, moreover, he includes himself among them, thus casting within himself the scalpel that carries out his separations.

Instead of sounding himself as to his "being," he does so concerning his place: "*Where* am I?" instead of "*Who* am I?" For the space that engrosses the deject, the excluded, is never *one*, nor *homogeneous*, nor *totalizable*, but essentially divisible, foldable, and catastrophic. A deviser of territories, languages, works, the *deject* never stops demarcating his universe whose fluid confines—for they are constituted of a non-object, the abject—constantly question his solidity and impel him to start afresh. A tireless builder, the deject is in short a *stray*. He is on a journey, during the night, the end of which keeps receding. He has a sense of the danger, of the loss that the pseudo-object attracting him represents for him, but he cannot help taking the risk at the very moment he sets himself apart. And the more he strays, the more he is saved.

TIME: FORGETFULNESS AND THUNDER

For it is out of such straying on excluded ground that he draws his jouissance. The abject from which he does not cease separating is for him, in short, a *land of oblivion* that is constantly remembered. Once upon blotted-out time, the abject must have been a magnetized pole of covetousness. But the ashes of oblivion now serve as a screen and reflect aversion, repugnance. The clean and proper (in the sense of incorporated and incorporable) becomes filthy, the sought-after turns into the banished, fascination into shame. Then, forgotten time crops up suddenly and condenses into a flash of lightning an operation that, if it were thought out, would involve bringing together the two opposite terms but, on account of that flash, is discharged like thunder. The time of abjection is double: a time of oblivion and thunder, of veiled infinity and the moment when revelation bursts forth.

JOUISSANCE AND AFFECT

Jouissance, in short. For the stray considers himself as equivalent to a Third Party. He secures the latter's judgment, he acts on the strength of its power in order to condemn, he grounds himself on its law to tear the veil of oblivion but also to set up its object as inoperative. As jettisoned. Parachuted by the Other. A ternary structure, if you wish, held in keystone position by the Other, but a "structure" that is skewed, a topology of catastrophe. For, having provided itself with an *alter ego*, the Other no longer has a grip on the three apices of the triangle where subjective homogeneity resides; and so, it jettisons the object into an abominable real, inaccessible except through jouissance. It follows that jouissance alone causes the abject to exist as such. One does not know it, one does not desire it, one joys in it [*on en jouit*]. Violently and painfully. A passion. And, as in jouissance where the object of desire, known as object *a* [in Lacan's terminology], bursts with the shattered mirror where the ego gives up its image in order to contemplate itself in the Other, there is nothing either objective or objectal to the abject. It is simply a frontier, a repulsive gift that the Other, having become *alter ego*, drops so that "I" does not disappear in it but finds, in that sublime alienation, a forfeited existence. Hence a jouissance in which the subject is swallowed up but in which the Other, in return, keeps the subject from foundering by making it repugnant. One thus understands why so many victims of the abject are its fascinated victims—if not its submissive and willing ones.

We may call it a border; abjection is above all ambiguity. Because, while releasing a hold, it does not radically cut off the subject from what threatens it—on the contrary, abjection acknowledges it to be in perpetual danger. But also because abjection itself is a composite of judgment and affect, of condemnation and yearning, of signs and drives. Abjection preserves what existed in the archaism of pre-objectal relationship, in the immemorial violence with which a body becomes separated from another body in order to be—maintaining that night in which the outline of the signified thing vanishes and where only the imponderable affect is carried out. To be sure, if I am affected by what does not yet appear to me as a thing, it is because laws, connections, and even structures of meaning govern and condition me. That order, that glance, that voice, that gesture, which enact the law for my frightened body, constitute and bring about an effect and not yet a sign. I speak to it in vain in order to exclude it from what will no longer be, for myself, a world that can be assimilated. Obviously, I am only *like* someone else: mimetic logic of the advent of the ego, objects, and signs. But when I *seek* (myself), *lose* (myself), or experience *jouissance*—then "I" is *heterogeneous*. Discomfort, unease, dizziness stemming from an ambiguity that, through the violence of a revolt *agàinst*, demarcates a space out of which signs and objects arise. Thus braided, woven, ambivalent, a heterogeneous flux marks out a territory that I can call my own because the Other, having dwelt in me as *alter ego*, points it out to me through loathing.

This means once more that the heterogeneous flow, which portions the abject and sends back abjection, already dwells in a human animal that has been highly altered. I experience abjection only if an Other has settled in place and stead of what will be "me." Not at all an other with whom I identify and incorporate, but an Other who precedes and possesses me, and through such possession causes me to be. A possession previous to my advent: a being-there of the symbolic that a father might or might not embody. Significance is indeed inherent in the human body.

AT THE LIMIT OF PRIMAL REPRESSION

If, on account of that Other, a space becomes demarcated, separating the abject from what will be a subject and its objects, it is because a repression that one might call "primal" has been effected prior to the springing forth of the ego, of its objects and representations. The latter, in turn, as they depend on another repression, the "secondary" one, arrive only *a posteriori* on an enigmatic foundation that has already been marked off; its return, in a phobic, obsessional, psychotic guise, or more generally and in more imaginary fashion in the shape of *abjection*, notifies us of the limits of the human universe.

On such limits and at the limit one could say that there is no unconscious, which is elaborated when representations and affects (whether or not tied to representations) shape a logic. Here, on the contrary, consciousness has not assumed its rights and transformed into signifiers those fluid demarcations of yet unstable territories where an "I" that is taking shape is ceaselessly straying. We are no longer within the sphere of the unconscious but at the limit of primal repression that, nevertheless, has discovered an intrinsically corporeal and already signifying brand, symptom, and sign: repugnance, disgust, abjection. There is an effervescence of object and sign—not of desire but of intolerable significance; they tumble over into non-sense or the impossible real, but they appear even so in spite of "myself" (which is not) as abjection.

PREMISES OF THE SIGN, LININGS OF THE SUBLIME

Let us pause a while at this juncture. If the abject is already a wellspring of sign for a non-object, on the edges of primal repression, one can understand its skirting the somatic symptom on the one hand and sublimation on the other. The *symptom*: a language that gives up, a structure within the body, a non-assimilable alien, a monster, a tumor, a cancer that the listening devices of the unconscious do not hear, for its strayed subject is huddled outside the paths of desire. *Sublimation*, on the contrary, is nothing else than the possibility of naming the pre-nominal, the pre-objectal, which are in fact only a trans-nominal, a trans-objectal. In the symptom, the abject permeates me, I become abject. Through sublimation, I keep it under control. The abject is edged with the sublime. It is not the same moment on the journey, but the same subject and speech bring them into being.

For the sublime has no object either. When the starry sky, a vista of open seas or a stained glass window shedding purple beams fascinate me, there is a cluster of meaning, of colors, of words, of caresses, there are light touches, scents, sighs, cadences that arise, shroud me, carry me away, and sweep me beyond the things that I see, hear, or think. The "sublime" object dissolves in the raptures of a bottomless memory. It is such a memory, which, from stopping point to stopping point, remembrance to remembrance, love to love, transfers that object to the refulgent point of the dazzlement in which I stray in order to be. As soon as I perceive it, as soon as I name it, the sublime triggers—it has always already triggered—a spree of perceptions and words that expands memory boundlessly. I then forget the point of departure and find myself removed to a secondary universe, set off from the one where "I" am— delight and loss. Not at all short of but always with and through perception and words, the sublime is a *something added* that expands us, overstrains us, and causes us to be both *here*, as dejects, and *there*, as others and sparkling. A divergence, an impossible bounding. Everything missed, joy—fascination.

BEFORE THE BEGINNING: SEPARATION

The abject might then appear as the most *fragile* (from a synchronic point of view), the most *archaic* (from a diachronic one) sublimation of an "object" still inseparable from drives. The abject is that pseudo-object that is made up *before* but appears only *within* the gaps of secondary repression. *The abject would thus be the "object" of primal repression.*

But what is primal repression? Let us call it the ability of the speaking being, always already haunted by the Other, to divide, reject, repeat. Without *one* division, *one* separation, *one* subject/object having been constituted (not yet, or no longer yet). Why? Perhaps because of maternal anguish, unable to be satiated within the encompassing symbolic.

The abject confronts us, on the one hand, with those fragile states where man strays on the territories of *animal*. Thus, by way of abjection, primitive societies have marked out a precise area of their culture in order to remove it from the threatening world of animals or animalism, which were imagined as representatives of sex and murder.

The abject confronts us, on the other hand, and this time within our personal archeology, with our earliest attempts to release the hold of *maternal* entity even before ex-isting outside of her, thanks to the autonomy of language. It is a violent, clumsy breaking away, with the constant risk of falling back under the sway of a power as securing as it is stifling. The difficulty a mother has in acknowledging (or being acknowledged by) the symbolic realm—in other words, the problem she has with the phallus that her father or her husband stands for—is not such as to help the future subject leave the natural mansion. The child can serve its mother as token of her own authentication; there is, however, hardly any reason for her to serve as go-between for it to become autonomous and authentic in its turn. In such close combat, the symbolic light that a third party, eventually the father, can contribute helps the future subject, the more so if it happens to be endowed with a robust supply of drive energy, in pursuing a reluctant struggle against what, having been the mother, will turn into an abject. Repelling, rejecting; repelling itself, rejecting itself. Ab-jecting.

In this struggle, which fashions the human being, the *mimesis*, by means of which he becomes homologous to another in order to become himself, is in short logically and chronologically secondary. Even before being *like*, "I" am not but do *separate, reject, ab-ject*. Abjection, with a meaning broadened to take in subjective diachrony, *is a precondition of narcissism*. It is coexistent with it and causes it to be permanently brittle. The more or less beautiful image in which I behold or recognize myself rests upon an abjection that sunders it as soon as repression, the constant watchman, is relaxed.

THE "CHORA," RECEPTACLE OF NARCISSISM

Let us enter, for a moment, into that Freudian aporia called primal repression. Curious primacy, where what is repressed cannot really be held down, and where what represses always already borrows its strength and authority from what is apparently very secondary: language. Let us therefore not speak of primacy but of the instability of the symbolic function in its most significant aspect—the prohibition placed on the maternal body (as a defense against autoeroticism and incest taboo). Here, drives hold sway and constitute a strange space that I shall name, after Plato (*Timeus*, 48–53), a *chora*, a receptacle.

For the benefit of the ego or its detriment, drives, whether life drives or death drives, serve to correlate that "not yet" ego with an "object" in order to establish both of them. Such a process, while dichotomous (inside/outside, ego/not ego) and repetitive, has nevertheless something centripetal about it: it aims to settle the ego as center of a solar system of objects. If, by dint of coming back towards the center, the drive's motion should eventually become centrifugal, hence fasten on the Other and come into being as sign so as to produce meaning—that is, literally speaking, exorbitant.

But from that moment on, while I recognize my image as sign and change in order to signify, another economy is instituted. The sign represses the *chora* and its eternal return. Desire alone will henceforth be witness to that "primal" pulsation. But desire ex-patriates the *ego* toward an *other* subject and accepts the exactness of the ego only as narcissistic. Narcissism then appears as a regression to a position set back from the other, a return to a self-contemplative, conservative, self-sufficient haven. Actually, such narcissism never is the wrinkleless image of the Greek youth in a quiet fountain. The conflicts of drives muddle its bed, cloud its water, and bring forth everything that, by not becoming integrated with a given system of signs, is abjection for it.

Abjection is therefore a kind of *narcissistic crisis*: it is witness to the ephemeral aspect of the state called "narcissism" with reproachful jealousy, heaven knows why; what is more, abjection gives narcissism (the thing and the concept) its classification as "seeming."

Nevertheless, it is enough that a prohibition, which can be a superego, block the desire craving an other—or that this other, as its role demands, not fulfill it—for desire and its signifiers to turn back toward the "same," thus clouding the waters of Narcissus. It is precisely at the moment of narcissistic perturbation (all things considered, the permanent state of the speaking being, if he would only hear himself speak) that secondary repression, with its reserve of symbolic means, attempts to transfer to its own account, which has thus been overdrawn, the resources of primal repression. The archaic economy is brought into full light of day, signified, verbalized. Its strategies (rejecting, separating, repeating/abjecting) hence find a symbolic existence, and the very logic of the symbolic—arguments, demonstrations, proofs, etc.—must conform to it. It is then that the object ceases to be circumscribed, reasoned with, thrust aside: it appears as abject.

Two seemingly contradictory causes bring about the narcissistic crisis that provides, along with its truth, a view of the abject. *Too much strictness on the part of the Other*, confused with the One and the Law. The *lapse of the Other*, which shows through the breakdown of objects of desire. In both instances, the abject appears in order to uphold "I" within the Other. The abject is the violence of mourning for an "object" that has always already been lost. The abject shatters the wall of repression and its judgments. It takes the ego back to its source on the abominable limits from which, in order to be, the ego has broken away—it assigns it a source in the non-ego, drive, and death. Abjection is a resurrection that has gone through death (of the ego). It is an alchemy that transforms death drive into a start of life, of new significance.

PERVERSE OR ARTISTIC

The abject is related to perversion. The sense of abjection that I experience is anchored in the superego. The abject is perverse because it neither gives up nor assumes a prohibition, a rule, or a law; but turns them aside, misleads, corrupts; uses them, takes advantage of them, the better to deny them. It kills in the name of life—a progressive despot; it lives at the behest of death—an operator in genetic experimentations; it curbs the other's suffering for its own profit—a cynic (and a psychoanalyst); it establishes narcissistic power while pretending to reveal the abyss—an artist who practices his art as a "business." Corruption is its most common, most obvious appearance. That is the socialized appearance of the abject.

An unshakable adherence to Prohibition and Law is necessary if that perverse interspace of abjection is to be hemmed in and thrust aside. Religion, Morality, Law. Obviously always arbitrary, more or less; unfailingly oppressive, rather more than less; laboriously prevailing, more and more so.

Contemporary literature does not take their place. Rather, it seems to be written out of the untenable aspects of perverse or superego positions. It acknowledges the impossibility of Religion, Morality, and Law—their power play, their necessary and absurd seeming. Like perversion, it takes advantage of them, gets round them, and makes sport of them. Nevertheless, it maintains a distance where the abject is concerned. The writer, fascinated by the abject, imagines its logic, projects himself into it, introjects it, and as a consequence perverts language—style and content. But on the other hand, as the sense of abjection is both the abject's judge and accomplice, this is also true of the literature that confronts it. One might thus say that with such a literature there takes place a crossing over of the dichotomous categories of Pure and Impure, Prohibition and Sin, Morality and Immorality.

For the subject firmly settled in its superego, a writing of this sort is necessarily implicated in the interspace that characterizes perversion; and for that reason, it gives rises in turn to abjection. And yet, such texts call for a softening of the superego. Writing them implies an ability to imagine the abject, that is, to see oneself in its place and to thrust it aside only by means of the displacements of verbal play. It is only after his death, eventually, that the writer of abjection will escape his condition of waste, reject, abject. Then, he will either sink into oblivion or attain the rank of incommensurate ideal. Death would thus be the chief curator of our imaginary museum; it would protect us in the last resort from the abjection that contemporary literature claims to expend while uttering it. Such a protection, which gives its quietus to abjection, but also perhaps to the

bothersome, incandescent stake of the literary phenomenon itself, which, raised to the status of the sacred, is severed from
its specificity. Death thus keeps house in our contemporary
universe. By purifying (us from) literature, it establishes our
secular religion.

AS ABJECTION—SO THE SACRED

Abjection accompanies all religious structurings and reappears,
to be worked out in a new guise, at the time of their collapse.
Several structurations of abjection should be distinguished, each
one determining a specific form of the sacred.

Abjection appears as a rite of defilement and pollution in the
paganism that accompanies societies with a dominant or sur-
viving matrilinear character. It takes on the form of the *exclusion*
of a substance (nutritive or linked to sexuality), the execution
of which coincides with the sacred since it sets it up.

Abjection persists as *exclusion* or taboo (dietary or other) in
monotheistic religions, Judaism in particular, but drifts over to
more "secondary" forms such as *transgression* (of the Law)
within the same monotheistic economy. It finally encounters,
with Christian sin, a dialectic elaboration, as it becomes integrated in the Christian Word as a threatening otherness—but
always nameable, always totalizeable.

The various means of *purifying* the abject—the various ca-
tharses—make up the history of religions, and end up with that
catharsis par excellence called art, both on the far and near side
of religion. Seen from that standpoint, the artistic experience,
which is rooted in the abject it utters and by the same token
purifies, appears as the essential component of religiosity. That
is perhaps why it is destined to survive the collapse of the
historical forms of religions.

OUTSIDE OF THE SACRED, THE ABJECT IS WRITTEN

In the contemporary practice of the West and owing to the
crisis in Christianity, abjection elicits more archaic resonances
that are culturally prior to sin; through them it again assumes

its biblical status, and beyond it that of defilement in primitive societies. In a world in which the Other has collapsed, the aesthetic task—a descent into the foundations of the symbolic construct—amounts to retracing the fragile limits of the speaking being, closest to its dawn, to the bottomless "primacy" constituted by primal repression. Through that experience, which is nevertheless managed by the Other, "subject" and "object" push each other away, confront each other, collapse, and start again—inseparable, contaminated, condemned, at the boundary of what is assimilable, thinkable: abject. Great modern literature unfolds over that terrain: Dostoyevsky, Lautréamont, Proust, Artaud, Kafka, Céline.

DOSTOYEVSKY

The abject is, for Dostoyevsky, the "object" of *The Possessed*: it is the aim and motive of an existence whose meaning is lost in absolute degradation because it absolutely rejected the moral *limit* (a social, religious, familial, and individual one) as absolute—God. Abjection then wavers between the *fading away* of all meaning and all humanity, burnt as by the flames of a conflagration, and the *ecstasy* of an ego that, having lost its Other and its objects, reaches, at the precise moment of this suicide, the height of harmony with the promised land. Equally abject are Verkhovensky and Kirilov, murder and suicide.

A big fire at night always produces an exciting and exhilarating effect; this explains the attraction of fireworks; but in the case of fireworks, the graceful and regular shape of the flames and the complete immunity from danger produce a light and playful effect comparable to the effect of a glass of champagne. A real fire is quite another matter: there the horror and a certain sense of personal danger, combined with the well-known exhilarating effect of a fire at night, produce in the spectator (not, of course, in one whose house has burnt down) a certain shock to the brain and, as it were, a challenge to his own destructive instincts, which, alas, lie buried in the soul of even the meekest and most domesticated official of the lowest grade. This grim sensation is almost always delightful. "I really don't know if it is possible to watch a fire without some enjoyment."[2]

There are seconds—they come five or six at a time—when you suddenly feel the presence of eternal harmony in all its fullness. It is nothing earthly. I don't mean that it is heavenly, but a man in his earthly semblance can't endure it. He has to undergo a physical change or die. This feeling is clear and unmistakable. It is as though you suddenly apprehended all nature and suddenly said: "Yes, it is true—it is good." [. . .] What is so terrifying about it is that it is so terribly clear and such gladness. If it went on for more than five seconds, the soul could not endure it and must perish. In those five seconds I live through a lifetime, and I am ready to give my life for them, for it's worth it. To be able to endure it for ten seconds, you would have to undergo a physical change. I think man ought to stop begetting children. What do you want children for, what do you want mental development, if your goal has been attained? It is said in the gospel that in the resurrection they neither marry nor are given in marriage, but are the angels of God in heaven. It's a hint. Is your wife giving birth to a baby?[3]

Verkhovensky is abject because of his clammy, cunning appeal to ideals that no longer exist, from the moment when Prohibition (call it God) is lacking. Stavrogin is perhaps less so, for his immoralism admits of laughter and refusal, something artistic, a cynical and gratuitous expenditure that obviously becomes capitalized for the benefit of private narcissism but does not serve an arbitrary, exterminating power. It is possible to be cynical without being irremediably abject; abjection, on the other hand, is always brought about by that which attempts to get along with trampled-down law.

He's got everything perfect in his note-book, Verkhovensky went on. Spying. Every member of the society spies on the others, and he is obliged to inform against them. Everyone belongs to all the others, and all belong to everyone. All are slaves and equals in slavery. In extreme cases slander and murder, but, above all, equality. To begin with, the level of education, science, and accomplishment is lowered. A high level of scientific thought and accomplishment is open only to men of the highest abilities! Men of the highest ability have always seized the power and become autocrats. Such men cannot help being autocrats, and they've always done more harm than good; they are either banished or executed. A Cicero will have his tongue cut out, Copernicus will have his eyes gouged out, a Shakespeare will be stoned—there you have Shigalyov's doctrine! Slaves must be equal: without despotism there never has been any freedom or equality, but in a herd there is bound to be equality—there's the Shigalyov doctrine for you! Ha, ha, ha! You think it strange? I am for the Shigalyov doctrine![4]

Dostoyevsky has X-rayed sexual, moral, and religious abjection, displaying it as collapse of paternal laws. Is not the world of *The Possessed* a world of fathers, who are either repudiated, bogus, or dead, where matriarchs lusting for power hold sway—ferocious fetishes but nonetheless phantomlike? And by symbolizing the abject, through a masterful delivery of the jouissance produced by uttering it, Dostoyevsky delivered himself of that ruthless maternal burden.

But it is with Proust that we find the most immediately erotic, sexual, and desiring mainspring of abjection; and it is with Joyce that we shall discover that the feminine body, the maternal body, in its most un-signifiable, un-symbolizable aspect, shores up, in the individual, the fantasy of the loss in which he is engulfed or becomes inebriated, for want of the ability to name an object of desire.

PROUST

Abjection, recognized as inherent in the mellow and impossible alteration of the ego, hence recognized as welded to narcissism, has, in Proust, something domesticated about it; without belonging to the realm of "one's own clean and proper" or of the "self evident," it constitutes a scandal of which one has to acknowledge if not the banality at least the secrets of a telltale snob. Abjection, with Proust, is fashionable, if not social; it is the foul lining of society. That may be why he furnishes the only modern example, certified by dictionaries, of the use of the word "abject" with the weak meaning it has (in French) at the end of the eighteenth century:

In those regions that were almost slums, what a modest existence, abject, if you please, but delightful, nourished by tranquillity and happiness, he would have consented to lead indefinitely.[5]

Proust writes that if the object of desire is real it can only rest upon the abject, which is impossible to fulfill. The object of love then becomes unmentionable, a double of the subject, similar to it, but improper, because inseparable from an impossible identity. Loving desire is thus felt as an inner fold within that impossible identity, as an accident of narcissism, ob-ject, painful alteration, delightfully and dramatically condemned to find the other in the same sex only. As if one acceded to the truth, to the abject truth of sexuality, only through homosexuality—Sodom and Gomorrah, the *Cities of the Plain*.

I had not even cause to regret my not having arrived in the shop until several minutes had elapsed. For from what I heard first at Jupien's shop, which was only a series of inarticulate sounds, I imagine that few words had been exchanged. It is true that these sounds were so violent that, if one set had not always been taken up an octave higher by a parallel plaint, I might have thought that one person was strangling another within a few feet of me, and that subsequently the murderer and his resuscitated victim were taking a bath to wash away the traces of the crime. I concluded from this later on that there is another thing as vociferous as pain, namely pleasure, especially when there is added to it—failing the fear of an eventual parturition, which could not be present in this case, despite the hardly convincing example in the *Golden Legend*—an immediate afterthought of cleanliness.[6]

Compared to this one, the orgy in Sade, meshing with a gigantic philosophy, be it that of the boudoir, had nothing abject about it. Methodical, rhetorical, and, from that point of view, regular, it broadens Meaning, Body, and Universe but is not at all exorbitant: everything is nameable for it, the whole is nameable. Sade's scene integrates: it allows for no other, no unthinkable, nothing heterogeneous. Rational and optimistic, it does not exclude. That means that it does not recognize a sacred, and in that sense it is the anthropological and rhetorical acme of atheism. Proustian writing, to the contrary, never gives up a judging prerogative, perhaps a biblical one, which splits, banishes, shares out, or condemns; and it is in relation to it, with it and against it, that the web of Proust's sentence, memory, sexuality, and morality is elaborated—infinitely spinning together differences (sexes, classes, races) into a homogeneity that consists only in signs, a fragile net stretched out over an abyss of incompatibilities, rejections, and abjections. Desire and signs, with Proust, weave the infinite cloth that does not hide but causes the subdued foulness to appear. As lapse, discomfort, shame, or blunder. As permanent threat, in short, to the homogenizing rhetoric that the writer composes against and with the abject.

JOYCE

How dazzling, unending, eternal—and so weak, so insignificant, so sickly—is the rhetoric of Joycean language. Far from preserving us from the abject, Joyce causes it to break out in what he sees as prototype of literary utterance: Molly's monologue. If that monologue spreads out the abject, it is not because there is a woman speaking. But because, *from afar*, the writer approaches the hysterical body so that it might speak, so that he might speak, using it as springboard, of what eludes speech and turns out to be the hand to hand struggle of one woman with another, her mother of course, the absolute because primeval seat of the impossible—of the excluded, the outside-of-meaning, the abject. Atopia.

the woman hides it not to give all the trouble they do yes he came somewhere Im sure by his appetite anyway love its not or hed be off his feed thinking of her so either it was one of those night women if it was down there he was really and the hotel story he made up a pack of lies to hide it planning it Hynes kept me who did I meet ah yes I met do you remember Menton and who else who let me see that big babbyface I saw him and he not long married flirting with a young girl at Pooles Myriorama and turned my back on him when he slinked out looking quite conscious what harm but he had the impudence to make up to me one time well done to him mouth almighty and his boiled eyes of all the big stupoes I ever met and thats called a solicitor only for I hate having a long wrangle in bed or else if its not that its some little bitch or other he got in with somewhere or picked up on the sly if they only knew him as well as I do yes because the day before yesterday he was scribbling something a letter when I came into the front room for the matches to show him Dignam's death[6]

The abject here does not reside in the thematic of masculine sexuality as Molly might see it. Not even in the fascinated horror that the other women, sketched out in back of the men, imbue the speaker with. The abject lies, beyond the themes, and for Joyce generally, in the way one speaks; it is verbal communication, it is the Word that discloses the abject. But at the same time, the Word alone purifies from the abject, and that is what Joyce seems to say when he gives back to the masterly rhetoric that his *Work in progress* constitutes full powers against abjection. A single catharsis: the rhetoric of the pure signifier, of music in letters—*Finnegans Wake*.

Céline's journey, to the end of his night, will also encounter rhythm and music as being the only way out, the ultimate sublimation of the unsignifiable. Contrary to Joyce, however, Céline will not find salvation in it. Again carrying out a rejection, without redemption, himself forfeited, Céline will become, body and tongue, the apogee of that moral, political, and stylistic revulsion that brands our time. A time that seems to have, for a century now, gone into unending labor pains. The enchantment will have to wait for some other time, always and forever.

BORGES

According to Borges the "object" of literature is in any case vertiginous and hallucinatory. It is the Aleph, which appears, in its transfinite truth, at the time of a descent, worthy of Mallarmé's *Igitur*, into the cellar of the native house, condemned to destruction—by definition. A literature that dares to relate the dizzying pangs of such a descent is no more than mediocre mockery of an archaic memory that language lays out as much as it betrays it. The Aleph is exorbitant to the extent that, within the narrative, nothing could tap its power other than the narration of *infamy*. That is, of rampancy, boundlessness, the unthinkable, the untenable, the unsymbolizable. But what is it? Unless it be the untiring repetition of a drive, which, propelled by an initial loss, does not cease wandering, unsated, deceived, warped, until it finds its only stable object—death. Handling that repetition, staging it, cultivating it until it releases, beyond its eternal return, its sublime destiny of being a struggle with death—is it not that which characterizes writing? And yet, dealing with death in that manner, making sport of it, is that not infamy itself? The literary narrative that utters the workings of repetition must necessarily become, beyond fantastic tales, detective stories, and murder mysteries, a narrative of the infamous (*A Universal History of Infamy*). And the writer cannot but recognize himself, derisive and forfeited, in that abject character, Lazarus Morell, the frightful redeemer, who raises his slaves from the dead only to have them die more fully, but not until they have been circulated—and have brought in a return—like currency. Does that mean that literary objects, our fictional objects, like the slaves of Lazarus Morell, are merely ephemeral resurrections of that elusive Aleph? Does this Aleph, this impossible "object," this impossible imagination, sustain the work of writing, even though the latter is merely a temporary halt in the Borgesian race toward death, which is contained in the chasm of the maternal cave?

The stealing of horses in one state and selling them in another were barely more than a digression in Morell's criminal career, but they foreshadowed the method that now assures him his rightful place in a Universal History of Infamy. This method is unique not only for the popular circumstances that distinguished it but also for the sordidness it required, for its deadly manipulation of hope, and for its step by step development, so like the hideous unfolding of a nightmare. [. . .]

Flashing rings on their fingers to inspire respect, they traveled up and down the vast plantations of the South. They would pick out a wretched black and offer him freedom. They would tell him that if he ran away from his master and allowed them to sell him, he would receive a portion of the money paid for him, and they would then help him escape again, this second time sending him to a free state. Money and freedom, the jingle of silver dollars together with his liberty—what greater temptation could they offer him? The slave became emboldened for his first escape.

The river provided the natural route. A canoe; the hold of a steamboat; a scow; a great raft as big as the sky, with a cabin at the point or three or four wigwams—the means mattered little, what counted was feeling the movement and the safety of the unceasing river. The black would be sold on some other plantation, then run away again to the canebrakes or the morasses. There his terrible benefactors (about whom he now began to have serious misgivings) cited obscure expenses and told him they had to sell him one final time. On his return, they said, they would give him his part of both sales and his freedom. The man let himself be sold, worked for a while, and on his final escape defied the hounds and the whip. He then made his way back bloodied, sweaty, desperate, and sleepy. [. . .]

The runaway expected his freedom. Lazarus Morell's shadowy mulattoes would give out an order among themselves that was sometimes barely more than a nod of the head, and the slave would be freed from sight, hearing, touch, day, infamy, time, his benefactors, pity, the air, the hound packs, the world, hope, sweat, and himself. A bullet, a knife, or a blow, and the Mississippi turtles and catfish would receive the last evidence.

Just imagine that imaginary machine transformed into a social institution—and what you get is the infamy of fascism.

ARTAUD

An "I" overcome by the corpse—such is often the abject in Artaud's text. For it is death that most violently represents the strange state in which a non-subject, a stray, having lost its non-objects, imagines nothingness through the ordeal of abjection. The death that "I" am provokes horror, there is a choking sensation that does not separate inside from outside but draws them the one into the other, indefinitely. Artaud is the inescapable witness of that torture—of that truth.

The dead little girl says, I am the one who guffaws in horror inside the lungs of the live one. Get me out of there at once.[9]

Once dead, however, my corpse was thrown out on the dunghill, and I remember having been macerated I don't know now many days or how many hours while waiting to awaken. For I did not know at first that I was dead: I had to make up my mind to understand that before I could succeed in raising myself. A few friends, then, who had completely forsaken me at first, decided to come and embalm my corpse and were joylessly surprised at seeing me again, alive.[10]

I have no business going to bed with you, things, for I stink more than you do, god, and going to bed does not mean getting soiled but, to the contrary, clearing myself, from you.[11]

At that level of downfall in subject and object, the abject is the equivalent of death. And writing, which allows one to recover, is equal to a resurrection. The writer, then, finds himself marked out for identification with Christ, if only in order for him, too, to be rejected, ab-jected:

For, as ball-breaking as this may seem, I am that Artaud crucified on Golgotha, not as christ but as Artaud, in other words as complete atheist. I am that body persecuted by erotic golosity, the obscene sexual erotic golosity of mankind, for which pain is a humus, the liquid from a fertile mucus, a serum worth sipping by one who has never on his own gained by being a man while knowing that he was becoming one.[12]

These different literary texts name types of abjects that are answerable to, this goes without saying, different psychic structures. The types of articulation (narrative and syntactic structures, prosodic processes, etc. in the different texts) also vary. Thus the abject, depending on the writer, turns out to be named differently when it is not merely suggested by linguistic modifications that are always somewhat elliptic. In the final part of this essay I shall examine in detail a specific articulation of the abject—that of Céline. Let me just say at this point, as an introduction, that contemporary literature, in its multiple variants, and when it is written as the language, possible at last, of that impossible constituted either by a-subjectivity or by non-objectivity, propounds, as a matter of fact, a sublimation of abjection. Thus it becomes a substitute for the role formerly played by the sacred, at the limits of social and subjective identity. But we are dealing here with a sublimation without consecration. Forfeited.

CATHARSIS AND ANALYSIS

That *abjection*, which modernity has learned to repress, dodge, or fake, appears fundamental once the analytic point of view is assumed. Lacan says so when he links that word to the *saint-liness* of the analyst, a linkage in which the only aspect of humor that remains is blackness.[13]

One must keep open the wound where he or she who enters into the analytic adventure is located—a wound that the professional establishment, along with the cynicism of the times and of institutions, will soon manage to close up. There is nothing initiatory in that rite, if one understands by "initiation" the accession to a purity that the posture of *death* guaranteed (as in Plato's *Phaedo*) or the unadulterated treasure of the "pure signifier" (as is the gold of truth in *The Republic*, or the pure separatism of the statesman in the *Statesman*). It is rather a heterogeneous, corporeal, and verbal ordeal of fundamental incompleteness: a "gaping," "less One." For the unstabilized subject who comes out of that—like a crucified person opening up the stigmata of its desiring body to a speech that structures only on condition that it let go—any signifying or human phenomenon, insofar as it *is*, appears in its being as abjection. For what impossible *catharsis*? Freud, early in his career, used the same word to refer to a therapeutics, the rigor of which was to come out later.

WITH PLATO AND ARISTOTLE

The analyst is thus and forever sent back to the question that already haunted Plato when he wanted to take over where Apollonian or Dionysiac religion left off.[14] Purification is something only the Logos is capable of. But is that to be done in the manner of the *Phaedo*, stoically separating oneself from a body whose substance and passions are sources of impurity? Or rather, as in the *Sophist*, after having sorted out the worst from the best; or after the fashion of the *Philebus* by leaving the doors wide open to impurity, provided the eyes of the mind remain focused on truth? In such a case, pleasure, having become pure and true through the harmony of color and form as in the case of accurate and beautiful geometric form, has nothing in common, as the philosopher says, with "the pleasures of scratching" (*Philebus* 51).

Catharsis seems to be a concern that is intrinsic to philosophy, insofar as the latter is an ethics and unable to forget Plato. Even if the *mixture* seems inevitable towards the end of the Platonic course, it is the mind alone, as harmonious wisdom, that insures purity: catharsis has been transformed, where transcendental idealism is concerned, into philosophy. Of the cathartic incantation peculiar to mysteries, Plato has kept only, as we all know, the very uncertain role of poets whose frenzy would be useful to the state only after having been evaluated, sorted out, and purified in its turn by wise men.

Aristotelian catharsis is closer to sacred incantation. It is the one that has bequeathed its name to the common, esthetic concept of catharsis. Through the mimesis of passions—ranging from enthusiasm to suffering—in "language with pleasurable accessories," the most important of which being *rhythm* and *song* (see the *Poetics*), the soul reaches *orgy* and *purity* at the same time. What is involved is a purification of body and soul by means of a heterogeneous and complex circuit, going from "bile" to "fire," from "manly warmth" to the "enthusiasm" of the "mind." Rhythm and song hence arouse the impure, the other of mind, the passionate-corporeal-sexual-virile, but they harmonize it, arrange it differently than the wise man's knowledge does. They thus soothe frenzied outbursts (Plato, in the *Laws*, allowed such use of rhythm and meter only to the mother rocking her child), by contributing an *external* rule, a poetic one, which fills the gap, inherited from Plato, between body and soul. To Platonic *death*, which owned, so to speak, the state of purity, Aristotle opposed the act of *poetic purification*—in itself an impure process that protects from the abject only by dint of being immersed in it. The abject, mimed through sound and meaning, is *repeated*. Getting rid of it is out of the question—the final Platonic lesson has been understood, one does not get rid of the impure; one can, however, bring it into being a second time, and differently from the original impurity. It is a repetition through rhythm and song, therefore through what is not yet, or no longer is "meaning," but arranges, defers, differentiates and organizes, harmonizes pathos, bile, warmth, and enthusiasm. Benveniste translates "rhythm" by "trace" and "concatenation" [*enchaînement*]. Prometheus is "rhythmical," and we call him "bound" [*enchaîné*]. An attachment on the near and far side of language. Aristotle seems to say that there is a discourse of sex and that is not the discourse of knowledge—it is the only possible catharsis. That discourse is audible, and through the speech that it mimics it repeats on another register what the latter does not say.

PHILOSOPHICAL SADNESS AND THE SPOKEN DISASTER OF THE ANALYST

Poetic catharsis, which for more than two thousand years behaved as an underage sister of philosophy, face to face and incompatible with it, takes us away from purity, hence from Kantian ethics, which has long governed modern codes and remains more faithful to a certain Platonic stoicism. By means of the "universalizing of maxims," as is well known, the Kant of the *Foundations of the Metaphysics of Ethics* or of the *Metaphysical Principles of Virtue* advocated an "ethical gymnastics" in order to give us, by means of consciousness, control over our defilements and, through that very consciousness, making us free and joyous.

More skeptical and, from a certain point of view, more Aristotelian, Hegel, on the contrary, rejects a "calculation" that claims to eliminate defilement, for the latter seems *fundamental* to him. Probably echoing the Greek polis, he conceives of no other ethics than that of the *act*. Also distrustful, however, of those fine aestheticizing souls who find purity in the elaboration of empty forms, he obviously does not hold to the mimetic and orgiastic catharsis of Aristotle. It is in the *historical* act that Hegel sees fundamental impurity being expended; as a matter of fact, the latter is a sexual impurity whose historical achievement consists in marriage. But—and this is where transcendental idealism, too, sadly comes to an end—here it is that desire (*Lust*), thus normalized in order to escape abject concupiscence (*Begierde*), sinks into a banality that is sadness and silence. How come? Hegel does not condemn impurity because it is exterior to ideal consciousness; more profoundly—but also more craftily—he thinks that it can and should get rid of itself through the historico-social act, If he thereby differs from Kant, he nevertheless shares his condemnation of (sexual) impurity. He agrees with his aim to keep consciousness apart from defilement, which, nevertheless, dialectically constitutes it. Reabsorbed into the trajectory of the Idea, what can defilement become if not the negative side of consciousness—that is, lack of communication and speech? In other words, defilement as reabsorbed in marriage becomes sadness. In so doing, it has not strayed too far from its logic, according to which it is a border of discourse—a silence. [15]

It is obvious that the analyst, from the abyss of his silence, brushes against the ghost of the sadness Hegel saw in sexual normalization. Such sadness is the more obvious to him as his ethics is rigorous—founded, as it must be in the West, on the remains of transcendental idealism. But one can also argue that the Freudian stance, which is dualistic and dissolving, unsettles those foundations. In that sense, it causes the sad, analytic silence to hover above a strange, foreign discourse, which, strictly speaking, shatters verbal communication (made up of a knowledge and a truth that are nevertheless heard) by means of a device that mimics terror, enthusiasm, or orgy, and is more closely related to rhythm and song than it is to the World. There is mimesis (some say identification) in the analytic passage through castration. And yet it is necessary that the analyst's interpretative speech (and not only his literary or theoretical bilingualism) be affected by it in order to be analytical. As counterpoise to a purity that found its bearings in disillusioned sadness, it is the "poetic" unsettlement of analytic utterance that testifies to its closeness to, cohabitation with, and "knowledge" of abjection.

I am thinking, in short, of the completely mimetic *identification* (transference and countertransference) of the analyst with respect to analysands. That identification allows for securing in their place what, when parcelled out, makes them suffering and barren. It allows one to regress back to the affects that can be heard in the breaks in discourse, to provide rhythm, too, to concatenate (is that what "to become conscious" means?) the gaps of a speech saddened because it turned its back on its abject meaning. If there is analytic jouissance it is there, in the thoroughly poetic mimesis that runs through the architecture of speech and extends from coenesthetic image to logical and phantasmatic articulations. Without for that matter biologizing language, and while breaking away from identification by means of interpretation, analytic speech is one that becomes "incarnate" in the full sense of the term. On that condition only, it is "cathartic"—meaning thereby that it is the equivalent, for the analyst as well as for the analysand, not of purification but of rebirth with and against abjection.

This preliminary survey of abjection, phenomenological on the whole, will now lead me to a more straightforward consideration of analytic theory on the one hand, of the history of religions on the other, and finally of contemporary literary experience.

2

SOMETHING TO BE SCARED OF

A regal soul, inadvertently surrendering to the crab of lust, the octopus of weakmindedness, the shark of individual abjection, the boa of absent morality, and the monstrous snail of idiocracy!

Lautréamont, *Les Chants de Maldoror*

THE OBJECT AS TRIMMING OF ANGUISH

When psychoanalysts speak of an object they speak of the object of desire as it is elaborated within the Oedipian triangle. According to that trope, the father is the mainstay of the law and the mother the prototype of the object. Toward the mother there is convergence not only of survival needs but of the first mimetic yearnings. She is the other subject, an object that guarantees my being as subject. The mother is my first object—both desiring and signifiable.

No sooner sketched out, such a thesis is exploded by its contradictions and flimsiness.

Do we not find, *sooner* (chronologically and logically speaking), if not objects at least *pre*-objects, poles of attraction of a demand for air, food, and motion? Do we not also find, in the very process that constitutes the mother as other, a series of *semi*-objects that stake out the transition from a state of indifferentiation to one of discretion (subject/object)—semi-objects that are called precisely "transitional" by Winnicott?[1] Finally, do we not find a whole gradation within modalities of separation: a real *deprivation* of the breast, an imaginary *frustration* of the gift as maternal relation, and, to conclude, a symbolic *castration* inscribed in the Oedipus complex; a gradation constituting, in Lacan's brilliant formulation, the object relation insofar as it is always "a means of masking, of parrying the fundamental fund of anguish" (Seminar of 1956–1957)?

The matter of the object sets in motion, or implicates, the entire Freudian structure. *Narcissism*—beginning with what, or when, does it allow itself to be exceeded by sexual drive, which is drive toward the other? *Repression*—what type of repression yields symbolization, hence a signifiable object, and what other type, on the contrary, blocks the way toward symbolization and topples drive into the lack-of-object of asymbolia or the auto-object of somatization? The connection between the *unconscious and language*—what is the share of language learning or language activity in the constitution of object relation and its transformations?

It is with respect to the phobia of Little Hans that Freud tackles in the clearest fashion the matter of the relation to the object, which is crucial for the constitution of the subject.[2] From the start, fear and object are linked. Can that be by accident? The unending and uncertain identifications of *hysterics* did surely not throw light on Freud's work on this topic. This *obsessional* rumination—which ceaselessly elaborates signs so as better to protect, within the family vault, a sacred object that is missing—was probably of greater avail to him in dealing with the question. But why is it phobia that best allows one to tackle the matter of relation to the object? Why fear *and* object?

Confronted with states of distress that are evoked for us by the child who makes himself heard but is incapable of making himself understood, we, adults, use the word "fear." Birth trauma, according to Otto Rank, or the upsetting of the balance of drive integration elaborated by the maternal receptacle (Wilfred R. Bion) in the course of uterine life and by "good mothering," are theoretical artifacts: they rationalize a "zero state" of the subject, and also probably a zero state of theory as confronted with what the child has not uttered. *Fear*, therefore, in a first sense, could be the *upsetting* of a bio-drive balance. The constitution of object relation might then be a reiteration of fear, alternating with optimal but precarious states of balance. Fear and object proceed together until the one represses the other. But in which one of us is that fully successful?

HANS IS AFRAID OF THE UNNAMABLE

And yet, the fear of which one can speak, the one therefore that has a signifiable object, is a more belated and more logical product that assumes all earlier alarms of archaic, non-representable fear. Spoken fear, hence subsequent to language and necessarily caught in the Oedipus structure, is disclosed as the fear of an unlikely object that turns out to be the substitute for another. Another "object"? That is what Freud believes when he hears the story of little Hans who is afraid of horses. He detects the fear of castration—of his mother's "missing" sexual organ, of the loss of his own, of the guilty desire to reduce the father to the same unmanning or to the same death, and so forth.

This is astonishingly true, and not quite so. What is striking in the case of Hans, as little as he might be, what Freud does not cease to be astonished by, is his stupendous verbal skill: he assimilates and reproduces language with impressive eagerness and talent. So eager is he to name everything that he runs into the unnamable—street sounds, that ceaseless trade activity involving horses in front of the house, the intensity with which his father, a recent convert to psychoanalysis, is interested in his body, his love for small girls, the stories and fantasies that he (the father) sexualizes to the utmost; the somewhat elusive, somewhat frail presence of his mother. All of this, which has already considerable *sense* for Hans without having found its *significance*, is doubtless distributed, as Freud says, between narcissistic conversation drive and sexual drive. It all becomes necessarily crystallized in the epistemophilic experience of Hans who wants to know himself and to know everything; to know, in particular, what seems to be lacking in his mother or could be lacking in himself.

More generally, however, the phobia of horses becomes a *hieroglyph* that condenses *all fears*, from unnamable to namable.

From archaic fears to those that accompany language learning, at the same time as familiarization with the body, the street, animals, people. The statement, "to be afraid of horses," is a hieroglyph having the logic of metaphor and hallucination. By means of the signifier of the phobic object, the "horse," it calls attention to a *drive economy in want of an object*—that conglomerate of fear, deprivation, and nameless frustration, which, properly speaking, belongs to the unnamable. The phobic object shows up at the place of non-objectal states of drive[3] and assumes all the mishaps of drive as disappointed desires or as desires diverted from their objects.

The metaphor that is taxed with representing *want itself* (and not its consequences, such as transitional objects and their sequels, the "a" objects of the desiring quest) is constituted under the influence of a symbolizing agency. That symbolic law is not necessarily of the superego type, but it can also seep into the ego and the ideal of the ego.

PHOBIA AS ABORTIVE METAPHOR OF WANT

Metaphor of want as such, phobia bears the marks of the frailty of the subject's signifying system. It must be perceived that such a metaphor is inscribed not in verbal rhetoric but in the heterogeneity of the psychic system that is made up of drive presentations *and* thing presentations linked to word presentations. The infancy of little Hans does not entirely explain the frailty of the signifying system that forces metaphor to turn into drive and conversely. One must also conclude, and phobic adults confirm this, that within the symbolic law accruing to the function of the father, something remains blurred in the Oedipal triangle constituting the subject. Does Hans' father not play a bit too much the role of the mother whom he thrusts into the shadows? Does he not overly seek the surety of the professor? If phobia is a metaphor that has mistaken its place, forsaking language for drive and sight, it is because a father does not hold his own, be he the father of the subject or the father of its mother.

Freud understands this perfectly. After the first accounts by

Hans' father, he suggests to such a Hermes that he remember himself to his son and try, if only by means of his mustache and pince-nez, to take the horses' place.

The treatment obviously succeeded, up to a point at any rate, for Hans plays along and ventures to produce other metaphors of his fear of the unnamable in the framework of a rhetoric that on occasion clears itself of drive or, better, hysterizes it. *Fear*, as a matter of fact, retreats to the benefit of a *loathing* for raspberry syrup, the color of which alone evokes the edge of a gash.

But has phobia really disappeared? It does not seem to have. For at least two reasons.

First, the Freudian treatment, by referring to the apices of the family triangle what we have seen to be a fear of the unnamable—fear of want and of castration?—actually revives the phobia. The treatment *justifies* the phobic child. Freud tells Hans that he is right; you cannot not be afraid of castration, and upon your fear I found the truth of theory. In so doing, he rationalizes that fear and, even though such a rationalization is also, in effect, and because of transference, an elaboration, it remains in part an anticathexis of phobia. A certain handling of the analytic cure runs the risk of being nothing else but a *counter-phobic* treatment, if that cure remains at the level of fantasy and does not enter, after having traversed the latter, into the more subtle workings of the *metaphoric elaboration* constituted by the statement and the phobic "object," to the extent that this "object" is the representative of drive and not of an already present object. Indeed, as Freud is first to admit, the analytical apparatus is no match for that phobic condensation, for it cannot open it out:

In the process of the formation of a phobia from the unconscious thoughts underlying it, condensation takes place; and for that reason the course of the analysis can never follow that of the development of the neurosis.[4]

Obviously such an acknowledgment does no more than establish the difference between the analytic process and the neurotic condensation process. But one could also understand it as neglecting, through the linear, transferential approach of analysis (the more so as analysis is often undertaken on the level of the imaginary and even of the superego), the processes of condensation that oversee phobic work. In order to deal with such processes, it would be necessary to revive the work of introjection as well as to pay particular attention to displacements and condensations within the signifying chain.

On the other hand, taking that metaphoricalness into account • would amount to considering the phobic person as a subject in want of metaphoricalness. Incapable of producing metaphors by means of signs alone, he produces them in the very material of drives—and it turns out that the only rhetoric of which he is capable is that of affect, and it is projected, as often as not, by means of *images*. It will then fall upon analysis to give back a memory, hence a language, to the unnamable and namable states of fear, while emphasizing the former, which make up what is most unapproachable in the unconscious. It will also fall upon it, within the same temporality and the same logic, to make the analysand see the *void* upon which rests the play with the signifier and primary processes. Such a void and the arbitrariness of that play are the truest equivalents of fear. But does it not amount to diverting the analytic process towards literature, or even stylistics? Is this not asking the analyst to be rhetorical, to "write" instead of "interpreting"? Does this not also imply holding up a fetishist screen, that of the word, before a dissolving fear?

The fetishist episode peculiar to the unfolding of phobia is well known. It is perhaps unavoidable that, when a subject confronts the factitiousness of object relation, when he stands at the place of the want that founds it, the fetish becomes a life preserver, temporary and slippery, but nonetheless indispensable. But is not exactly language our ultimate and inseparable fetish? And language, precisely, is based on fetishist denial ("I know that, but just the same," "the sign is not the thing, but just the same," etc.) and defines us in our essence as speaking beings. Because of its founding status, the fetishism of "language" is perhaps the only one that is unanalyzable.

One might then view writing, or art in general, not as the only treatment but as the only "know-how" where phobia is concerned. Little Hans has become stage director for an opera house.

Finally, and this is the second reason why phobia does not disappear but slides beneath language, the phobic object is a proto-writing and, conversely, any practice of speech, inasmuch as it involves writing, is a language of fear. I mean a language of want as such, the want that positions sign, subject, and object. Not a language of the desiring exchange of messages or objects that are transmitted in a social contract of communication and desire beyond want, but a language of want, of the fear that edges up to it and runs along its edges. The one who tries to utter this "not yet a place," this no-grounds, can obviously only do so backwards, starting from an over-mastery of the linguistic and rhetorical code. But in the last analysis he refers to fear—a terrifying, abject referent. We encounter this discourse in our dreams, or when death brushes us by, depriving us of the assurance mechanical use of speech ordinarily gives us, the assurance of being ourselves, that is, untouchable, unchangeable, immortal. But the writer is permanently confronted with such a language. The writer is a phobic who succeeds in metaphorizing in order to keep from being frightened to death; instead he comes to life again in signs.

"I AM AFRAID OF BEING BITTEN" OR "I AM AFRAID OF BITING"?

Nevertheless, does not fear hide an aggression, a violence that returns to its source, its sign having been inverted? What was there in the beginning: want, deprivation, original fear, or the violence of rejection, aggressivity, the deadly death drive? Freud abandoned the vicious circle of cause and effect, of the chicken and the egg, by discovering a complex being completely alien to the angelism of the Rousseauistic child. At the same time as the Oedipus complex, he discovered infantile, perverse, polymorphic sexuality, always already a carrier of desire and death. But, and this is the master stroke, he accompanied that "given" with a completely symbolic causality that not only balances it but destroys it as fundamental determinism. I refer to the modeling and, in the final analysis, determining role of symbolic language relation. From the deprivation felt by the child because of the mother's absence to the paternal prohibitions that institute symbolism, that relation accompanies, forms, and elaborates the aggressivity of drives, which, consequently, never presents itself in a "pure" state. Let me say then that *want* and *aggressivity* are chronologically separable but logically coextensive. Aggressivity *appears* to us as a rejoinder to the original deprivation felt from the time of the mirage known as "primary narcissism"; it merely takes revenge on initial frustrations. But what can be *known* of their connection is that want and aggressivity are adapted to one another. To speak of want alone is to repudiate aggressivity in obsessional fashion; to speak of aggressivity alone, forgetting want, amounts to making transference paranoidal.

"I am afraid of horses, I am afraid of being bitten." Fear and the aggressivity intended to protect me from some not yet localizable cause are projected and come back to me from the outside: "I am threatened." The fantasy of incorporation by means of which I attempt to escape fear (I incorporate a portion of my mother's body, her breast, and thus I hold on to her) threatens me none the less, for a symbolic, paternal prohibition already dwells in me on account of my learning to speak at the same time. In the face of this second threat, a completely symbolic one, I attempt another procedure: I am not the one that devours, I am being devoured by him; a third person therefore (he, a third person) is devouring me.

PASSIVATION

Syntactical passivation, which heralds the subject's ability to put himself in the place of the object, is a radical stage in the constitution of subjectivity. What a fuss was made over "A Child Is Being Beaten," what efforts exerted to write passive sentences in those languages that have such a mood. I should point out here that the logic of the constitution of the phobic object also requires such a procedure of passivation. In parallel fashion to the setting up of the signifying function, phobia, which also functions under the aegis of censorship and repression, *displaces* by *inverting* the sign (the active becomes passive) before *metaphorizing*.

Only after such an inversion can the "horse" or the "dog" become the metaphor of my empty and incorporating mouth, which watches me, threatening, from the outside. Overdetermined like all metaphors, this "horse," this "dog" also contain speed, racing, flight, motion, the street, traffic, cars, walking—an entire world of others towards which they escape and where, in order to save myself, I try to escape. But rendered culpable, abashed, "I" come back, "I" withdraw, "I" meet with anguish again: "I" am afraid.

Of *what*?

This sort of question appears only at that moment, laden with all the meanings of object and pre-object relations, with all its weight for a correlative "ego," and not as an empty sign. This means that an *object* that is a *hallucination* is being made up. The phobic object is a complex elaboration, already comprising logical and linguistic workings that *are* attempts at drive introjection outlining the failure to introject that which is incorporated. If incorporation marks out the way toward the constitution of the object, phobia represents the failure of the concomitant drive introjection.

DEVOURING LANGUAGE

The phobia of a little girl, discussed during Anna Freud's seminar,[5] gives us the opportunity to measure the importance of orality in this matter. The fact that it is a *girl* who is afraid of being eaten up by a dog is perhaps not without importance in the emphasis on orality and passivation. Moreover, the phobia followed upon a separation from her mother and a reunion when the mother already belonged to another. Curiously, the more phobic Sandy got, the more she spoke: the observer noted, as a matter of fact, that she spoke with a rural accent, that she was talkative, that at the age of three and a half "she talks a lot, has an extensive vocabulary, expresses herself with ease and enjoys repeating strange and difficult words."

Through the mouth that I fill with words instead of my mother whom I miss from now on more than ever, I elaborate that want, and the aggressivity that accompanies it, by *saying*. It turns out that, under the circumstances, oral activity, which produces the linguistic signifier, coincides with the theme of devouring, which the "dog" metaphor has a first claim on. But one is rightfully led to suppose that *any* verbalizing activity, whether or not it names a phobic object related to orality, is an attempt to introject the incorporated items. In that sense, verbalization has always been confronted with the "ab-ject" that the phobic object is. Language learning takes place as an attempt to appropriate an oral "object" that slips away and whose hallucination, necessarily deformed, threatens us from the outside. Sandy's increasing interest in language, in proportion as her phobia grows, the verbal games in which she indulges, are on a par with the intense verbal activity of little Hans, which I discussed.

One might contrast with this relation between phobia and language in the child the commonplace observation on adult phobic discourse. The speech of the phobic adult is also characterized by extreme nimbleness. But that vertiginous skill is as if void of meaning, traveling at top speed over an untouched and untouchable abyss, of which, on occasion, only the affect shows up, giving not a sign but a signal. It happens because language has then become a counterphobic object; it no longer plays the role of an element of miscarried introjection, capable, in the child's phobia, of revealing the anguish of original want. In analyzing those structures one is led to thread one's way through the meshes of the non-spoken in order to get at the meaning of such a strongly barricaded discourse.

The child undergoing a phobic episode has not reached that point. His symptom, because he utters it, is already an elaboration of phobia. By means of the logical and linguistic work he undertakes at the same time, his symptom arrives at a complex and ambiguous elaboration. The phobic hallucination then stands halfway between the recognition of desire and counterphobic construction: not yet a defensive, over-coded discourse that knows too much and manipulates its objects wonderfully well; nor is it a recognition of the object of want as object of desire. The phobic object is precisely avoidance of choice, it tries as long as possible to maintain the subject far from a decision; this is not done through a superego blocking of symbolization or through asymbolia, but to the contrary through a *condensation* of intense *symbolic* activities that results in the heterogeneous agglomeration we call phobic hallucination.

HALLUCINATION OF NOTHING

It is, I said it earlier, a metaphor. And yet more than that. For to the activity of condensation and displacement that oversees its formation, there is added a *drive* dimension (heralded by fear) that has an anaphoric, *indexing* value, pointing to something else, to some non-thing, to something unknowable. The phobic object is in that sense the *hallucination of nothing*: a metaphor that is the anaphora of nothing.

What is "nothing"? The analyst wonders and answers, after "deprivation," "frustration," "want," etc.: "the maternal phallus." That, from his point of view, is not false. But such a position implies that, in order to bring fear to the surface, the confrontation with the impossible object (the maternal phallus, which *is not*) will be transformed into a fantasy of desire. On the trail of my fear I meet again with my desire, and I bind myself to it, thus leaving stranded the concatenation of discourse with which I have built my hallucination, my weakness and my strength, my investment and my ruin.

It is precisely at such a point that writing takes over, within the phobic child that we are, to the extent that we speak only of anguish. It is not into a fantasy of desire that writing transforms the confrontation with the ab-ject. It unfolds, on the contrary, the logical and psycho-drive strategies that make up the hallucination metaphor improperly called "the object of phobia." If we are all phobics in the sense that it is anguish that causes us to speak, provided that someone forbids it, we are not all scared of large horses or biting mouths. Hans has quite simply *written* earlier than others, or rather he has been stage director within a scription that encompassed his living space with all its extras, putting into flesh (a horse) those logical constructs that set us up as beings of abjection and/or as symbolic beings. He was a "writer," a precocious one, and also a failure. The mature writer, whether a failure or not (though perhaps never losing sight of those two alternatives), never stops harking back to symbolization mechanisms, within language itself, in order to find in a *process* of eternal return, and not in the *object* that it names or produces, the hollowing out of anguish in the face of nothing.

PHOBIC NARCISSISM

Phobia literally stages the instability of object relation. The lability of the "object" within the phobic "compromise"— which may also be seen in some psychotic structures—can lead us to consider the formation in question from the point of view not of object relation but of its opposite correlative, *narcissism*. There, too, we come up against difficulties of analytic theory that are linked, this time, to its postulating a primary narcissism following upon autoeroticism and to what amounts to a forcing of thought—the assignment of a *subject* to archaic, pre-linguistic narcissism, taking us back, in short, to the mother-child symbiosis. Freud accepted that difficulty: in postulating the existence of two kinds of drives, sexual drives directed toward others and ego drives aimed at self-preservation, he appears to have granted, in the phobic symptom, preponderance to the latter.

But however clear may have been *the victory* in Hans's phobia *of the forces that were opposed to sexuality*, nevertheless, since such an illness is in its very nature a compromise, this cannot have been all that the repressed drives obtained.[6]

Thus, even if sexual drives gain the upper hand again with Hans, and this with the obsessed and obsessive help of the father and the psychoanalyst, we are witnessing a victory of "the forces that were opposed to sexuality." Such a narcissism presents us with at least two problems. How can one account for its strength, which hands over the object drive? How does it happen that, dominating as it may be, it does not lead to autism?

A particular biological makeup, imaginable although enigmatic, could provide a partial answer to the first question. And yet it is the failure of the triangular relationship, which alone posits the existence of an object, that seems to be implicated here. In the final analysis, the so-called narcissistic drive dominates only if instability of the paternal metaphor prevents the subject from finding its place within a triadic structure giving an object to its drives. That means that the object relationship of drives is a belated and even nonessential phenomenon. And it is not by accident that Freud subordinates the question of the drive object to the smoothing, if not the quenching, of the drive.

The *object* of a drive is the thing in regard to which or through which the drive is able to achieve its aim. It is what is most variable about a drive and *is not originally connected with it*, but becomes assigned to it only in consequence of being particularly fitted to make satisfaction possible.[7]

This is easy enough to understand if one takes the word object in its strongest acceptation—as the correlative of a subject in a symbolic chain. The paternal agency alone, to the extent that it introduces the symbolic dimension between "subject" (child) and "object" (mother), can generate such a strict object relation. Otherwise, what is called "narcissism," without always or necessarily being conservative, becomes the unleashing of drive as such, without object, threatening all identity, including that of the subject itself. We are then in the presence of psychosis.

THE "OBJECT" OF PHOBIC DESIRE: SIGNS

The point, however, of the hallucinatory metaphor of the phobic is precisely that, while displaying the victory of "the forces that were opposed to sexuality," it finds a certain "object." Which one? Not the object of sexual drive; the mother, or her parts, or her representatives; no more than some neutral referent or other, but *symbolic activity itself.* If the latter is often eroticized, and if the phobic, in that case, cumulates with the obsessive, this does not detract from the originality of the structure, which consists in the following: symbolicity itself is cathected by a drive that is not object-oriented in the classic sense of the term (we are not dealing with an object of *need* or *desire*), nor is it narcissistic (it does not return to collapse upon the subject or to cause its collapse). Since it is not sex-oriented, it denies the question of sexual difference; the subject that houses it can produce homosexual symptoms while being strictly speaking indifferent to them: that is not where the subject is. If it is true that such cathexis of symbolicity as sole site of drive and desire is a means of preservation, it is obviously not the specular *ego*— the reflection of the maternal phallus—that sees itself thus preserved; on the contrary, the ego, here, is rather in abeyance. Strangely enough, however, it is the *subject* that is built up, to the extent that it is the correlative of the paternal metaphor, disregarding the failure of its support—the subject, that is, as correlative of the Other.

A representative of the paternal function takes the place of the good maternal object that is wanting. There is language instead of the good breast. Discourse is being substituted for maternal care, and with it a fatherhood belonging more to the realm of the ideal than of the superego. One can vary the patterns within which such an ascendency of the Other, replacing the object and taking over where narcissism left off, produces a hallucinatory metaphor. There is fear and fascination. The body (of the ego) and the (sexual) object are completely absorbed in it.

Abjection—at the crossroads of phobia, obsession, and perversion—shares in the same arrangement. The loathing that is implied in it does not take on the aspect of hysteric conversion; the latter is the symptom of an ego that, overtaxed by a "bad object," turns away from it, cleanses itself of it, and vomits it. In abjection, revolt is completely within being. Within the being of language. Contrary to hysteria, which brings about, ignores, or seduces the symbolic but does not produce it, the subject of abjection is eminently productive of culture. Its symptom is the rejection and reconstruction of languages.

AIMING AT THE APOCALYPSE: SIGHT

To speak of hallucination in connection with such an unstable "object" suggests at once that there is a visual cathexis in the phobic mirage—and at least a speculative cathexis in the abject. Elusive, fleeting, and baffling as it is, that non-object can be grasped only as a sign. It is through the intermediary of a *representation*, hence a *seeing*, that it holds together. A visual hallucination that, in the final analysis, gathers up the others (those that are auditory, tactile, etc.) and, as it bursts into a symbolicity that is normally calm and neutral, represents the subject's desire. For the absent object, there is a sign. For the desire of that want, there is a visual hallucination. More than that, a cathexis of looking, in parallel with the symbolic domination taking the place of narcissism, often leads to voyeuristic "side effects" of phobia. Voyeurism is a structural necessity in the constitution of object relation, showing up every time the object shifts towards the abject; it becomes true perversion only if there is a failure to symbolize the subject/object instability. Voyeurism accompanies the writing of abjection. When that writing stops, voyeurism becomes a perversion.[8]

A FORTIFIED CASTLE

Whether it be projected metaphor or hallucination, the phobic object has led us, on the one hand, to the borders of psychosis and, on the other, to the strongly structuring power of symbolicity. In either case, we are confronted with a limit that turns the speaking being into a separate being who utters only by separating—from within the discreteness of the phonemic chain up to and including logical and ideological constructs.

How does such a limit become established without changing into a prison? If the radical effect of the founding division is the establishment of the subject/object division, how can one prevent its misfires from leading either to the secret confinement of archaic narcissism, or to the indifferent scattering of objects that are experienced as false? The glance cast on phobic symptom has allowed us to witness the painful dawning, splendid in its symbolic complexity, of the (verbal) *sign* in the grip of *drive* (fear, aggressivity) and *sight* (projection of the ego onto the other). But analytic reality, mindful of what is called the "unanalyzable," seems to cause experience to arise from another symptom, one that emerges from the same very problematic separation subject/object—but now seemingly at the opposite end of phobic hallucination.

The constituting barrier between subject and object has here become an unsurmountable wall. An ego, wounded to the point of annulment, barricaded and untouchable, cowers somewhere, nowhere, at no other place than the one that cannot be found. Where objects are concerned he delegates phantoms, ghosts, "false cards": a stream of spurious egos and for that very reason spurious objects, seeming egos that confront undesirable objects. Separation exists, and so does language, even brilliantly at times, with apparently remarkable intellectual realizations. But no current flows—it is a pure and simple splitting, an abyss without any possible means of conveyance between its two edges. No subject, no object: petrification on one side, falsehood on the other.

Letting current flow into such a "fortified castle" amounts to causing desire to rise. But one soon realizes, during transference, that desire, if it dawns, is only a substitute for adaptation to a social norm (is desire ever anything else but desire for an idealized norm, the norm of the Other?). On the way, as if hatched by what, for others, will be desire, the patient encounters abjection. It seems to be the first authentic feeling of a subject in the process of constituting itself as such, as it emerges out of its jail and goes to meet what will become, but only later, objects. Abjection of self: the first approach to a self that would otherwise be walled in. Abjection of others, of the other ("I feel like vomiting the mother"), of the analyst, the only violent link to the world. A rape of anality, a stifled aspiration towards an other as prohibited as it is desired—abject.

The outburst of abjection is doubtless only a moment in the treatment of borderline cases. I call attention to it here because of the key position it assumes in the dynamics of the subject's constitution, which is nothing other than a slow, laborious production of object relation. When the fortified castle of the borderline patient begins to see its walls crumble, and its indifferent pseudo-objects start losing their obsessive mask, the subject-effect—fleeting, fragile, but authentic—allows itself to be heard in the advent of that interspace, which is abjection.

It is not within the scheme of the analytic setup, probably because it does not have the power to do so, to linger over that blossoming. Emphasizing it would lead the patient into paranoia or, at best, into morality; now, the psychoanalyst does not believe he exists for that purpose. He follows or diverts the path, leading the patient towards the "good" object—the object of desire, which is, whatever may be said, fantasized according to the normal criteria of the Oedipus complex: a desire for the other sex.

That, however, is not where we stand with respect to abjection in the case of the borderline patient. It had barely begun to slide the bolt of narcissism and had changed the walls behind which he protected himself into a barely pervious limit—and for that very reason, a threatening, abominable one. Hence there was not yet an other, an ob-ject: merely an ab-ject. What is to be done with this ab-ject? Allow it to drift towards the libido so as to constitute an object of desire? Or towards symbolicity, to change it into a sign of love, hatred, enthusiasm, or damnation? The question might well remain undecided, undecidable.

It is within that undecidable space, logically coming before the choice of the sexual object, that the religious answer to abjection breaks in: *defilement, taboo,* or *sin.* In dealing with such notions, rehabilitating them will not be the point. My aim will be to bring to light the variants of the subject/object relation that religions implied, avoiding the nonexistence of separation just as much as the rigidity of the splitting. In other words, I shall need to look into the solutions given for phobia and psychosis by religious codes.

POWERLESS OUTSIDE, IMPOSSIBLE INSIDE

Constructed on the one hand by the incestuous desire of (for) his mother and on the other by an overly brutal separation from her, the borderline patient, even though he may be a fortified castle, is nevertheless an empty castle. The absence, or the failure, of paternal function to establish a unitary bent between subject and object, produces this strange configuration: an encompassment that is stifling (the container compressing the ego) and, at the same time, draining (the want of an other, qua object, produces nullity in the place of the subject). The ego then plunges into a pursuit of identifications that could repair narcissism—identifications that the subject will experience as in-significant, "empty," "null," "devitalized," "puppet-like." An empty castle, haunted by unappealing ghosts—"powerless" outside, "impossible" inside.

It is worth noting what repercussions such a foreclosure of the Name of the Father have on language. That of the borderline patient is often abstract, made up of stereotypes that are bound to seem cultured; he aims at precision, indulges in self-examination, in meticulous comprehension, which easily brings to mind obsessional discourse. But there is more to it than that. That shell of ultra-protected signifier keeps breaking up to the point of desemantization, to the point of reverberating only as notes, music, "pure signifier" to be reparcelled out and re-semanticized anew. It is a breaking up that puts a check on free association and pulverizes fantasy before it can take shape. It is, in short, a reduction of discourse to the state of "pure" signifier, which insures the disconnection between verbal signs on the one hand and drive representations on the other. And it is precisely at such a boundary of language splitting that the *affect* makes an imprint. Within the blanks that separate dislocated themes (like the limbs of a fragmented body), or through the shimmering of a signifier that, terrified, flees its signified, the analyst can perceive the imprint of that affect, participating in the language cluster that everyday usage of speech absorbs but, with the borderline patient, becomes dissociated and collapses. The affect is first enunciated as a coenesthetic image of painful fixation; the borderline patient speaks of a numbed body, of hands that hurt, of paralyzed legs. But also, as a motion metaphor binding significance: rotation, vertigo, or infinite quest. The problem then, starting with transference, is to tap these remainders of signifying *vectorization* (which the paternal metaphor makes fast and stabilizes into "normal discourse" in the case of the normative Oedipus triangle, which is here absent) by giving them a desiring and/or deathly signification. In short, one unfailingly orients them toward the other: another object, perhaps another sex, and, why not, another discourse—a text, a life to relive.

WHY DOES LANGUAGE APPEAR TO BE "ALIEN"?

Finally, foreclosure of paternal function affects what, in the sign, stems from condensation (or metaphor), that is, the ability of the sound-trace to maintain and go beyond (in the sense of an *Aufhebung*) the signified, which always involves a relation to the addressee as a perception, as well as *coenesthetic* representation of object relation and of the relation to the discourse of the other subject. With the borderline patient there is a collapse of the nexus constituted by the verbal signifier effecting the simultaneous *Aufhebung* of both *signified* and *affect*. A consequence of that disconnection, involving the very function of language in its psychic economy, is that verbalization, as he says, is alien to him. More so than with the neurotic, it is by means of the signifier alone that the unconscious meaning of the borderline patient is delivered. Only seldom is metaphor included in his speech; when it is, more than with anyone else, it is a literal one—to be understood as metonymy for unnamable desire. "I displace, therefore you must associate and condense for me," says such an analysand, who, in short, is asking the analyst to build up an imagination for him. He is asking to be saved like Moses, to be born like Christ. He is asking for a rebirth that—the analysand knows it, he tells it to us—will result from a speech that is recovered, rediscovered as belonging to him. Lacan had perceived this: the metaphor retraces within the unconscious the path of paternal myth, and it is quite deliberately that Victor Hugo's metaphor in *Booz endormi* is chosen, in *Ecrits*, as illustration of all metaphoricity.[9] But with the borderline patient, sense does not emerge out of non-sense, metaphorical or witty though it might be. On the contrary, non-sense runs through signs and sense, and the resulting ma-

nipulation of words is not an intellectual play but, without any
laughter, a desperate attempt to hold on to the ultimate obstacles
of a pure signifier that has been abandoned by the paternal
metaphor. It is a frantic attempt made by a subject threatened
with sinking into the void. A void that is not nothing but •
indicates, within its discourse, a challenge to symbolization.
Whether we call it an *affect*[10] or link it with infantile semioti-
zation—for which pre-signifying articulations are merely *equa-
tions* rather than symbolic *equivalents* for objects,[11] we must
point to a necessity within analysis. This necessity, emphasized
by that type of structure, consists in not reducing analytic attention to language to that of philosophical idealism and, in its
wake, to linguistics; the point is, quite to the contrary, to posit
a *heterogeneity of signifiance*. It stands to reason that one can say
nothing of such (effective or semiotic) heterogeneity without
making it homologous with the linguistic signifier. But it is
precisely that *powerlessness* that the "empty" signifier, the dis-
sociation of discourse, and the fully physical suffering of these
patients within the faults of the Word come to indicate.

THE "SIGN" ACCORDING TO FREUD

It is necessary, therefore, to go back to the Freudian theory of
language. And, returning to the moment when it starts off from
neurophysiology,[12] one notes the heterogeneity of the Freudian
sign. This sign is articulated as establishing a relation between
word Presentation and object Presentation (which becomes
thing Presentation as early as 1915). The former is already a
closed heterogeneous set (sound image, reading image, written
image, spoken motor image), as is the latter, but this one is
open (acoustic image, tactile image, visual image). Obviously
privileged here, the *sound* image of word presentation and the
visual image of object presentation become linked, calling to
mind very precisely the matrix of the sign belonging to philosophical tradition and to which Saussurian semiology gave
new currency. But it is easy to forget the other elements belonging to the sets thus tied together. They are what constitutes
all the originality of Freudian "semiology" and guarantee its

hold on the heterogeneous economy (body and discourse) of the speaking being (and particularly on the psychosomatic "disturbances" of speech).

One might think that Freud's later concern with neurotic discourse had centered his thought solely on the relation between sound image and visual image.[13] But there are two things that allow me to say that Freud's research constantly left open the hypothetical suture of the "pure signifier" that an overly philosophical reading, in a word a Kantian one, might compel; these are, on the one hand, the discovery of the Oedipus complex and, on the other, that of the splitting of the Ego and the second topography, together with, precisely, the very heterogeneous (involving both drive and thought) importance of the symbol of negation.[14] Although a reductiveness of this sort amounts to a true castration of the Freudian discovery, one should not forget the advantages that centering the heterogeneous Freudian sign in the Saussurian one afforded. Essentially, they can be summed up in the explicit statement of a question that has haunted Freud ever since the discovery of the Oedipus complex.

THE SIGN—A CONDENSATION

What is it that insures the existence of the sign, that is, of the *relation* that is a *condensation* between sound image (on the side of word presentation) and visual image (on the side of thing presentation)? Condensation is indeed what we are dealing with, and the logic of dreams testifies to it when it brings together elements from different perception registers or when it engages in ellipses. The figure of speech known as metaphor merely actuates, within the synchronic handling of discourse, the process that, genetically and diachronically, makes up one signifying unit out of at least two (sound and sight) components. But the speaking subject enjoys the possibility of condensation because it is inscribed in the Oedipal triangle. By means of that inscription, not only beginning with the so-called Oedipal stage but from the time of its advent into the world, which is always already a world of discourse, it finds itself subjected to paternal function. Thus, when Lacan posits the Name of the Father as the keystone to all sign, meaning, and discourse, he points to the *necessary condition* of one and only one process of the signifying unit, albeit a constitutive one: the process of condensing one heterogeneous set (that of word presentation) with another (that of thing presentation), releasing the one into the other, and insuring its "unitary bent." Such a statement of the problem enables one to avoid all the metaphysics, not to mention the arbitrariness, that underlies, in the wake of John Stuart Mill, to whom Freud alludes, the Freudian notions of "presentation." The stress shifts from the terms (images) to the functions that tie them together (condensation, metaphoricalness, and more strongly yet, paternal function), and ultimately to the space, the topology that emerges out of them (unitary bent).

Nevertheless, when the condensation function that constitutes the sign collapses (and in that case one always discovers a collapse of the Oedipal triangulation that supports it), once the sound image/sight image solidarity is undone, such a splitting allows one to detect an attempt at *direct semantization* of acoustic, tactile, motor, visual, etc., coenesthesia. A language now manifests itself whose *complaint* repudiates the common code, then builds itself into an *idiolect*, and finally resolves itself through the sudden irruption of *affect*.

THE HORROR WITHIN

The body's inside, in that case, shows up in order to compensate for the collapse of the border between inside and outside. It is as if the skin, a fragile container, no longer guaranteed the integrity of one's "own and clean self" but, scraped or transparent, invisible or taut, gave way before the dejection of its contents. Urine, blood, sperm, excrement then show up in order to reassure a subject that is lacking its "own and clean self." The abjection of those flows from within suddenly become the sole "object" of sexual desire—a true "ab-ject" where man, frightened, crosses over the horrors of maternal bowels and, in an immersion that enables him to avoid coming face to face with an other, spares himself the risk of castration. But at the same time that immersion gives him the full power of possessing, if not being, the bad object that inhabits the maternal body. Abjection then takes the place of the other, to the extent of affording him jouissance, often the only one for the borderline patient who, on that account, transforms the abject into the site of the Other.[15] Such a frontiersman is a metaphysician who carries the experience of the impossible to the point of scatology. When a woman ventures out in those regions it is usually to gratify, in very maternal fashion, the desire for the abject that insures the life (that is, the sexual life) of the man whose symbolic authority she accepts. Very logically, this is an abjection from which she is frequently absent; she does not think about it, preoccupied as she is with settling accounts (obviously anal) with her own mother. Rarely does a woman tie her desire and her sexual life to that abjection, which, coming to her from the other, anchors her interiorly in the Other. When that happens, one notes that it is through the expedient of writing that she gets there, and on that account she still has quite a way to go within the Oedipal mosaic before identifying with the owner of the penis.

CONFRONTING THE MATERNAL

But devotees of the abject, she as well as he, do not cease looking, within what flows from the other's "innermost being," for the desirable and terrifying, nourishing and murderous, fascinating and abject inside of the maternal body. For in the misfire of identification with the mother as well as with the father, how else are they to be maintained in the Other? How, if not by incorporating a devouring mother, for want of having been able to introject her and joy in what manifests her, for want of being able to signify her: urine, blood, sperm, excrement. Harebrained staging of an abortion, of a self-giving birth ever miscarried, endlessly to be renewed, the hope for rebirth is short-circuited by the very splitting: the advent of one's own identity demands a law that mutilates, whereas jouissance demands an *abjection* from which identity becomes absent.

This erotic cult of the abject makes one think of a perversion, but it must be distinguished at once from what simply dodges castration. For even if our borderlander is, like any speaking being, subject to castration to the extent that he must deal with the symbolic, he in fact runs a far greater risk than others do. It is not a part of himself, vital though it may be, that he is threatened with losing, but his whole life. To preserve himself from severance, he is ready for more—flow, discharge, hemorrhage. All mortal. Freud had, in enigmatic fashion, noted in connection with melancholy: "wound," "internal hemorrhage," "a hole in the psyche."[16] The erotization of abjection, and perhaps any abjection to the extent that it is already eroticized, is an attempt at stopping the hemorrhage: a threshold before death, a halt or a respite?

3

FROM FILTH TO DEFILEMENT

Abjection [. . .] is merely the inability to assume with sufficient strength the imperative act of excluding abject things (and that act establishes the foundations of collective existence).

[. . .] The act of exclusion has the same meaning as social or divine sovereignty, but it is not located on the same level; it is precisely located in the domain of things and not, like sovereignty, in the domain of persons. It differs from the latter in the same way that anal eroticism differs from sadism.

Georges Bataille, *Essais de sociologie*

× read this

MOTHER-PHOBIA AND THE MURDER OF THE FATHER

In psychoanalysis as in anthropology one commonly links the sacred and the establishment of the religious bond that it presupposes with *sacrifice*. Freud tied the sacred to taboo and totemism,[1] and concluded that, "we consider ourselves justified in substituting the father for the totem animal in the male's formula of totemism."[2] We are all familiar with that Freudian thesis as to the murder of the father and, more specifically, with the one he develops in *Moses and Monotheism*: in connection with Judaic religion the archaic father and master of the primeval horde is killed by the conspiring sons who, later seized with a sense of guilt for an act that was upon the whole inspired by ambivalent feelings, end up restoring paternal authority, no longer as an arbitrary power but as a right; thus renouncing the possession of all women in their turn, they establish at one stroke the sacred, exogamy, and society.

There is nevertheless a strange slippage in the Freudian argument, one that has not been sufficiently noticed. Relying on numerous readings in ethnology and the history of religions, more specifically on Frazer and Robertson Smith, Freud notes that the morality of man starts with "the two taboos of totemism"—*murder* and *incest*.[3] *Totem and Taboo* begins with an evocation of the "dread of incest," and Freud discusses it at length in connection with taboo, totemism, and more specifically with food and sex prohibitions. The woman- or mother-image haunts a large part of that book and keeps shaping its background even when, relying on the testimony of obsessional neurotics, Freud slips from dread (p. 23: "His incest dread"; p. 24: "the incest dread of savages"; p. 161: "The interpretation of incest dread," "This dread of incest") to the inclusion of dread symptom in obsessional neurosis. At the same time he leaves off speculating on incest ("we do not know the origin of incest dread and do not even know how to guess at it," p. 162) in order to center his conclusion in the second taboo, the one against murder, which he reveals to be the murder of the father.

That such a murderous event could be as much mythical as endowed with founding properties, that it should be both the keystone to the desire henceforth known as Oedipal and a severance that sets up a signifier admitting of logical concatenation, analytic attention now knows only too well. Divergences from and even contradictions with this Freudian thesis[4] are finally no more than variants and confirmations. What will concern me here is not that aspect of the Freudian position, which I shall consider to have been logically established. I shall attempt to question the other side of the religious phenomenon, the one that Freud points to when he brings up dread, incest, and the mother; one that, even though it is presented as the second taboo founding religion, nevertheless disappears during the final elucidation of the problem.

THE TWO-SIDED SACRED

Could the sacred be, whatever its variants, a two-sided formation? One aspect founded by murder and the social bond made up of murder's guilt-ridden atonement, with all the projective mechanisms and obsessive rituals that accompany it; and another aspect, like a lining, more secret still and invisible, non-representable, oriented toward those uncertain spaces of unstable identity, toward the fragility—both threatening and fusional—of the archaic dyad, toward the non-separation of subject/object, on which language has no hold but one woven of fright and repulsion? One aspect is defensive and socializing, the other shows fear and indifferentiation. The similarities that Freud delineates between religion and obsessional neurosis would then involve the defensive side of the sacred. Now, to throw light on the subjective economy of its other side, it is phobia as such, and its drifting toward psychosis, that one would need to tackle head on.

That, at any rate, will be my point of departure. For we shall see, in a large number of rituals and discourses involved in making up the sacred—notably those dealing with *defilement* and its derivations in different religions—an attempt at *coding* the other taboo that the earliest ethnologists and psychoanalysts viewed as presiding over social formations: beside death, *incest*. Lévi-Strauss' structural anthropology has shown how all systems of knowledge in so-called primitive societies, and myths in particular, are a later elaboration, within stages of symbolicity, of the prohibition that weighs on incest and founds the signifying function as well as the social aggregate. What will concern me here is not the socially productive value of the son-mother incest *prohibition* but the alterations, within subjectivity and within the very symbolic competence, implied by the *confrontation with the feminine* and the way in which societies code themselves in order to accompany as far as possible the speaking subject on that journey. Abjection, or the journey to the end of the night.

PROHIBITED INCEST VS. COMING FACE TO FACE WITH THE UNNAMABLE

What we designate as "feminine," far from being a primeval essence, will be seen as an "other" without a name, which subjective experience confronts when it does not stop at the appearance of its identity. Assuming that any Other is appended to the triangulating function of the paternal prohibition, what will be dealt with here, beyond and through the paternal function, is a coming face to face with an unnamable otherness—the solid rock of jouissance and writing as well.

I shall set aside in this essay a different version of the confrontation with the feminine, one that, going beyond abjection and fright, is enunciated as ecstatic. "The light-suffused face of the young Persian god" Freud refers to, and similarly, in a more secular fashion, Mallarmé's claim to be that "startled hero," "merry" for having overcome the "dishevelled tuft"—both point to another manner of coming to terms with the unnamable. That kind of confrontation appears, where our civilization is concerned, only in a few rare flashes of writing. Céline's laughter, beyond horror, also comes close to it, perhaps.

NARCISSUS AND MURKY WATERS

Freud had strongly emphasized, at the outset of *Totem and Taboo*, "man's deep aversion to his former incest wishes" (p. 24). He had reminded us of the properties of the taboo: it is "sacred, consecrated; but on the other hand it means uncanny, dangerous, forbidden and unclean" (p. 26); as to the object of taboos, "The prohibition mostly concerns matters that are capable of enjoyment" [*Genussgefähig*] (p. 31), they include the "unclean" (p. 32). The contact avoidance that he observes in it nevertheless makes him think only of compulsion and its rituals, while the ambivalent hostility it harbors suggests to him paranoid projection. The two structures cause the threat that would be hovering over the subject to converge on the paternal apex—the one that prohibits, separates, prevents contact (between son and mother?). This hypothesis would suggest an idyllic dual relationship (mother-child), which, to the extent that the father prevents it, changes into an ulterior aversion to incest. The idea of such a soothing dual relationship crops up again when Freud draws up the hypothesis of a transition between the primeval horde and civilized society, transition in which the sons, out of "maternal love,"[5] and/or supported by "homosexual feelings and activities" (p. 186), would renounce mothers and sisters and set up an organization based at first on matriarchal law, and ultimately on patriarchal law.

Nevertheless there are other thoughts of Freud, from which he will not draw any conclusions, that allow one to progress in another direction. He first appears to refer states of fear and impurity to primary narcissism, a narcissism laden with hostility and which does not yet know its limits. For we are dealing with imprecise boundaries in that place, at that moment, where pain is born out of an excess of fondness and a hate that, refusing to admit the satisfaction it also provides, is projected toward an other. Inside and outside are not precisely differentiated here, nor is language an active practice or the subject separated from the other. Melanie Klein will make of this area her privileged field of observation; it is well known that Winnicot found in it a fruitful terrain for the etiology of psychoses and "false selves" as well as for creation and play. But it is Freud indeed who blazes the trail. Let us read more carefully the following passages, which can be understood in another way than as preludes to the obsessional or paranoid structure.

Under conditions whose nature has not yet been sufficiently established, internal perceptions of emotional and thought processes can be projected outwards in the same way as sense perceptions; they are thus employed for building up the external world, though they should by rights remain part of the internal world. This may have some genetic connection with the fact that the function of attention was originally directed not towards the internal world but towards the stimuli that stream in from the external world, and that that function's only information upon endopsychic processes was received from feelings of pleasure and unpleasure. It was not until a language of abstract thought had been developed, that is to say, not until the sensory residues of verbal presentations had been linked to the internal processes, that the latter themselves gradually became capable of being perceived. Before that, owing to the projection outwards of internal perceptions, primitive men arrived at a picture of the external world which we, with our intensified conscious perception, have now to translate back into psychology.[6]

And further along, in a footnote:

The projected creations of primitive men resemble the personifications constructed by creative writers; for the latter externalize in the form of separate individuals the opposing instinctual impulses struggling within them.[7]

INCEST AND THE PRE-VERBAL

Let me sum up. There would be a "beginning" preceding the word. Freud, echoing Goethe, says so at the end of *Totem and Taboo*: "In the beginning was the deed."[8] In that anteriority to language, the outside is elaborated by means of a projection from within, of which the only experience we have is one of pleasure and pain. An outside in the image of the inside, made of pleasure and pain. The non-distinctiveness of inside and outside would thus be unnamable, a border passable in both directions by pleasure and pain. Naming the latter, hence differentiating them, amounts to introducing language, which, just as it distinguishes pleasure from pain as it does all other oppositions, founds the separation inside/outside. And yet, there would be witnesses to the perviousness of the limit, artisans after a fashion who would try to tap that pre-verbal "beginning" within a word that is flush with pleasure and pain. They are *primitive man* through his ambivalences and the *poet* through the personification of his opposing states of feeling—but also perhaps through the rhetorical recasting of language that he effects and over which Freud, who says he is heedful and fascinated, never tarries. If the *murder* of the father is that historical event constituting the social code as such, that is, symbolic exchange and the exchange of women, its equivalent on the level of the subjective history of each individual is therefore the *advent of language*, which breaks with perviousness if not with the chaos that precedes it and sets up denomination as an exchange of linguistic signs. Poetic language would then be, contrary to murder and the univocity of verbal message, a reconciliation with what murder as well as names were separated from. It would be an attempt to symbolize the "beginning," an attempt to name the other facet of taboo: pleasure, pain. Are we finally dealing with incest?

Not quite, or not directly. When Freud again speaks, still in *Totem and Taboo*, "of the first beginnings in childhood" of libidinal trends, he asserts that "from the very first" "they are not yet directed toward any external object." As he did in *Three Essays on the Theory of Sexuality*, he calls autoeroticism the phase which gives way to object-choice. Nevertheless he inserts between the two stages a third one that will hold our attention.

In this intermediary stage [. . .] the sexual impulses which formerly were separate have already formed into a unit and have also found an object; but this object is not external and foreign to the individual, but is his own ego, which is formed at this period.[9]

Fixation at this stage will be called *narcissism*. Let me try to point out the latent meanings of the definition. Narcissism is predicated on the existence of the *ego* but not of an *external object*; we are faced with the strange correlation between an entity (the ego) and its converse (the object), which is nevertheless not yet constituted; with an "ego" in relation to a non-object.

Two consequences seem necessarily to follow from such a structure. On the one hand, the non-constitution of the (outside) object as such renders unstable the ego's identity, which could not be precisely established without having been differentiated from an other, from its object. The ego of primary narcissism is thus uncertain, fragile, threatened, subjected just as much as its non-object to spatial ambivalence (inside/outside uncertainty) and to ambiguity of perception (pleasure/pain). On the other hand, one has to admit that such a narcissistic topology has no other underpinning in psychosomatic reality than the mother-child dyad. Now, though that relation has always been immersed in language, it allows the latter's inscription in the future subject only when biophysiological preconditions and the conditions of the Oedipus complex permit the setting up of a triadic relationship. The subject's *active* use of the signifier truly dates only from this moment. By stressing the inherence of language in the human state, by overestimating the subject's having been the slave of language since before his birth, one avoids noting the two moods, active and passive, according to which the subject is constituted in the signifier; by the same token one neglects the economy of narcissism in the elaboration and practice of the symbolic function.

That having been said, the archaic relation to the mother, narcissistic though it may be, is from my point of view of no solace to the protagonists and even less so to Narcissus. For the subject will always be marked by the uncertainty of his borders and of his affective valency as well; these are all the more determining as the paternal function was weak or even nonexistent, opening the door to perversion or psychosis. The edenic image of primary narcissism is perhaps a defensive negation elaborated by the neurotic subject when he sets himself under the aegis of the father. On the other hand, patients who have recently come to the couch (borderline cases, false selves, etc.) reveal the horror of that dual war, its terror, and the ensuing fear of being rotten, drained, or blocked.

DEFILEMENT AS RITUAL RESCUE FROM PHOBIA AND PSYCHOSIS

This abjection, which threatens the ego and results from the dual confrontation in which the uncertainties of primary narcissism reside—is it such as to motivate, if not explain, the incest dread of which Freud speaks? I believe so. If it be true, as Claude Lévi-Strauss has demonstrated, that the prohibition of incest has the logical import of founding, by means of that very prohibition, the discreteness of interchangeable units, thus establishing social order and the symbolic, I shall maintain that such a logical operation is carried out owing to a subjective benefit derived from it on the level of libidinal economy. Incest prohibition throws a veil over primary narcissism and the always ambivalent threats with which it menaces subjective identity. It cuts short the temptation to return, with abjection and jouissance, to that passivity status within the symbolic function, where the subject, fluctuating between inside and outside, pleasure and pain, word and deed, would find death, along with nirvana. Phobia alone, crossroad of neurosis and psychosis, and of course conditions verging on psychosis, testify to the appeal of such a risk; as if, with regard to it, the taboo barring contact with the mother and/or primary narcissism suddenly disintegrated.

A whole facet of the sacred, true lining of the sacrificial, compulsive, and paranoid side of religions, assumes the task of warding off that danger. This is precisely where we encounter the rituals of defilement and their derivatives, which, based on the feeling of abjection and all converging on the maternal, attempt to symbolize the other threat to the subject: that of being swamped by the dual relationship, thereby risking the loss not of a part (castration) but of the totality of his living being. The function of these religious rituals is to ward off the subject's fear of his very own identity sinking irretrievably into the mother.

THE POVERTY OF PROHIBITION: GEORGES BATAILLE

The logic of prohibition, which founds the abject, has been outlined and made explicit by a number of anthropologists concerned with defilement and its sacred function in so-called primitive societies. And yet Georges Bataille remains the only one, to my knowledge, who has linked the production of the abject to *the weakness of that prohibition*, which, in other respects, necessarily constitutes each social order. He links abjection to "the inability to assume with sufficient strength the imperative act of excluding." Bataille is also the first to have specified that the plane of abjection is that of the *subject/object relationsip* (and not subject/other subject) and that this archaism is rooted in anal eroticism rather than sadism.[10]

In the following, my point will be to suggest that such an archaic relationship to the *object* interprets, as it were, the relationship to the *mother*. Her being coded as "abject" points to the considerable importance some societies attribute to women (matrilineal or related filiation, endogamy, decisive role of procreation for the survival of the social group, etc.). The symbolic "exclusory prohibition" that, as a matter of fact, constitutes collective existence does not seem to have, in such cases, sufficient strength to dam up the abject or demoniacal potential of the feminine. The latter, precisely on account of its power, does not succeed in differentiating itself as *other* but threatens one's *own and clean self*, which is the underpinning of any organization constituted by exclusions and hierarchies.

But before outlining the *weakness of prohibition* and finally the *matrilineal order* that can be perceived in those communities, let us return to the anthropological delineation of the logic of *exclusion* that causes the abject to exist.

THE FUNDAMENTAL WORK OF MARY DOUGLAS

Anthropologists, since Sir James George Frazer, W. Robertson Smith, Arnold van Gennep, and Alfred Reginald Radcliff-Brown, or Rudolf Steiner, have noted that secular "filth," which has become sacred "defilement," is the *excluded* on the basis of which religious prohibition is made up. In a number of primitive societies religious rites are purification rites whose function is to separate this or that social, sexual, or age group from another one, by means of prohibiting a filthy, defiling element. It is as if dividing lines were built up between society and a certain nature, as well as within the social aggregate, on the basis of the simple logic of *excluding filth*, which, promoted to the ritual level of *defilement*, founded the "self and clean" of each social group if not of each subject.

The purification rite appears then as that essential ridge, which, prohibiting the filthy object, extracts it from the secular order and lines it at once with a sacred facet. Because it is excluded as a possible object, asserted to be a non-object of desire, abominated as ab-ject, as abjection, filth becomes defilement and founds on the henceforth released side of the "self and clean" the order that is thus only (and therefore, always already) sacred.

Defilement is what is jettisoned from the *"symbolic system."* It is what escapes that social rationality, that logical order on which a social aggregate is based, which then becomes differentiated from a temporary agglomeration of individuals and, in short, constitutes a *classification system* or a *structure*.

The British anthropologist Mary Douglas begins by construing the "symbolic system" of religious prohibitions as a reflection of social divisions or even contradictions. As if the social being, coextensive with a "symbolic system," were always present to itself through its religious structures, which transfer its contradictions to the level of rituals. And yet, at a second stage of her thinking, Mary Douglas seems to find in the human body the prototype of that translucid being constituted by society as symbolic system. As a matter of fact, the explanation she gives of defilement assigns in turn different statuses to the human body: as ultimate cause of the socio-economic causality, or simply as metaphor of that socio-symbolic being constituted by the human universe always present to itself. In so doing, however, Mary Douglas introduces willy-nilly the possibility of a subjective dimension within anthropological thought on religions. Where then lies the subjective value of those demarcations, exclusions, and prohibitions that establish the social organism as a "symbolic system"? The anthropological analysis of these phenomena was for Mary Douglas essentially *syntactic* at first: defilement is an element connected with the boundary, the margin, etc., of an order. Henceforth she finds herself led to *semantic* problems: what is the *meaning* that such a border-element assumes in other psychological, economic, etc., systems? At this moment of her thinking there emerges a concern to integrate Freudian data as semantic values connected with the psychosomatic functioning of the speaking subject. But a hasty assimilation of such data leads Mary Douglas naively to *reject* Freudian premises.

Finally, such a conception disregards both *subjective dynamics* (if one wishes to consider the social set in its utmost particularization) and *language as common and universal code* (if one wishes to consider the aggregate and the social aggregates in their greatest generality). Lévi-Strauss' structural anthropology had one advantage among others; it linked a classification system, that is, a symbolic system, within a given society, to the order of language in its universality (binary aspects of phonology, signifier-signified dependencies and autonomies, etc.). In thus attaining universal truth, it nevertheless neglected the subjective dimension and/or the diachronic and synchronic implication of the speaking subject in the universal order of language.

Consequently, when I speak of *symbolic order*, I shall imply the dependence and articulation of the speaking subject in the order of language, such as they appear diachronically in the advent of each speaking being, and as analytic listening discovers them synchronically in the speech of analysands. I shall consider as an established fact the analytic finding that different subjective structures are possible within that symbolic order, even if the different types presently recorded seem subject to discussion and refinement, if not reevaluation.

One might advance the hypothesis that a (social) symbolic system *corresponds* to a specific structuration of the speaking subject in the *symbolic order*. To say that it "corresponds" leaves out questions of cause and effect; is the social determined by the subjective, or is it the other way around? The subjective-symbolic dimension that I am introducing does not therefore reinstate some deep or primary causality in the social *symbolic system*. It merely presents the *effects* and especially the *benefits* that accrue to the speaking subject from a precise symbolic organization; perhaps it explains what desiring motives are required in order to maintain a given social symbolics. Furthermore, it seems to me that such a statement of the problem has the advantage of not turning the "symbolic system" into a secular replica of the "preestablished harmony" or the "divine order"; rather, it roots it, as a *possible variant*, within the only concrete universality that defines the speaking being—the signifying process.

IN THE SAME FASHION AS INCEST PROHIBITION

We are now in a position to recall what was suggested earlier concerning that border of subjectivity where the object no longer has, or does not yet have a correlative function bonding the subject. On that location, to the contrary, the vacillating, fascinating, threatening, and dangerous object is silhouetted as non-being—as the abjection into which the speaking being is permanently engulfed.

Defilement, by means of the rituals that consecrate it, is perhaps, for a social aggregate, only one of the possible foundings of abjection bordering the frail identity of the speaking being.

In this sense, abjection is coextensive with social and symbolic order, on the individual as well as on the collective level. By virtue of this, abjection, just like *prohibition of incest*, is a universal phenomenon; one encounters it as soon as the symbolic and/or social dimension of man is constituted, and this throughout the course of civilization. But abjection assumes specific shapes and different codings according to the various "symbolic systems." I shall attempt to examine some of its variants: *defilement, food taboo*, and *sin*.

Socio-historical considerations can be brought in at a second stage. They will allow us to understand why that demarcating imperative, which is subjectively experienced as abjection, varies according to time and space, even though it is universal. I shall nevertheless stick to a typological argument. Prohibitions and conflicts that are specific to a given subject and ritualized by religion for a given type of body will appear as isomorphic with the prohibitions and conflicts of the social group within which they happen. Leaving aside the question of the priority of one over the other (the social does not represent the subjective any more than the subjective represents the social), I shall posit that they both follow the same logic, with no other goal than the survival of both group and subject.

My reflections will make their way through anthropological domains and analyses in order to aim at a deep psycho-symbolic economy: the general, logical determination that underlies anthropological variants (social structures, marriage rules, religious rites) and evinces a specific economy of the speaking subject, no matter what its historical manifestations may be. In short, an economy that analytic listening and semanalytic deciphering discover in our contemporaries. Such a procedure seems to me to be directly in keeping with Freudian utilization of anthropological data. It inevitably entails a share of *disappointment* for the empirically minded ethnologist. It does not unfold without a share of *fiction*, the nucleus of which, drawn from actuality and the subjective experience of the one who writes, is projected upon data collected from the life of other cultures, less to justify itself than to throw light on them by means of an interpretation to which they obviously offer resistance.

THE MARGIN OF A FLOATING STRUCTURE

Taking a closer look at defilement, as Mary Douglas has done, one ascertains the following. In the first place, filth is not a quality in itself, but it applies only to what relates to a *boundary* and, more particularly, represents the object jettisoned out of that boundary, its other side, a margin. *margin is not liminal?*

> Matter issuing from them [the orifices of the body] is marginal stuff of the most obvious kind. Spittle, blood, milk, urine, faeces or tears by simply issuing forth have traversed the boundary of the body. [. . .] The mistake is to treat bodily margins in isolation from all other margins.[11]

The potency of pollution is therefore not an inherent one; it is proportional to the potency of the prohibition that founds it.

> It follows from this that pollution is a type of danger which is not likely to occur except where the lines of structure, cosmic or social, are clearly defined.[12]

Finally, even if human beings are involved with it, the dangers entailed by defilement are not within their power to deal with but depend on a power "inhering in the structure of ideas."[13] Let us posit that defilement is an objective evil undergone by the subject. Or, to put it another way, the danger of filth represents for the subject the risk to which the very symbolic order is permanently exposed, to the extent that it is a device of discriminations, of differences. But from where and from what does the threat issue? From nothing else but an equally objective reason, even if individuals can contribute to it, and which would be, in a way, the frailty of the symbolic order itself. A threat issued from the prohibitions that found the inner and outer borders in which and through which the speaking subject is constituted—borders also determined by the phonological and semantic differences that articulate the syntax of language.

And yet, in the light of this structural-functional X-ray of defilement, which draws on the major anthropological works of modern times, from Robertson Smith to Marcel Mauss, from Emile Durkheim to Lévi-Strauss, one question remains unanswered. Why does *corporeal waste*, menstrual blood and excrement, or everything that is assimilated to them, from nail-parings to decay, represent—like a metaphor that would have become incarnate—the objective frailty of symbolic order?

One might be tempted at first to seek the answer in a type of society where defilement takes the place of supreme danger or absolute evil.

BETWEEN TWO POWERS

Nevertheless, no matter what differences there may be among societies where religious prohibitions, which are above all behavior prohibitions, are supposed to afford protection from defilement, one sees everywhere the importance, both social and symbolic, of women and particularly the mother. In societies where it occurs, ritualization of defilement is accompanied by a strong concern for separating the sexes, and this means giving men rights over women. The latter, apparently put in the position of passive objects, are none the less felt to be wily powers, "baleful schemers" from whom rightful beneficiaries must protect themselves. It is as if, lacking a central authoritarian power that would settle the definitive supremacy of one sex—or lacking a legal establishment that would balance the prerogatives of both sexes—two powers attempted to share out society. One of them, the masculine, apparently victorious, confesses through its very relentlessness against the other, the feminine, that it is threatened by an asymmetrical, irrational, wily, uncontrollable power. Is this a survival of a matrilineal society or the specific particularity of a structure (without the incidence of diachrony)? The question of the origins of such a handling of sexual difference remains moot. But whether it be within the highly hierarchical society of India or the Lele in Africa[14] it is always to be noticed that the attempt to establish a male, phallic power is vigorously threatened by the no less virulent power of the other sex, which is oppressed (recently? or not sufficiently for the survival needs of society?). That other sex, the feminine, becomes synonymous with a radical evil that is to be suppressed.[15]

Let us keep that fact in mind; I shall return to it later on for the interpretation of defilement and its rites. In the meantime I turn to the particulars—the prohibited objects and the symbolic devices that accompany those prohibitions.

EXCREMENTS AND MENSTRUAL BLOOD

While they always relate to corporeal orifices as to so many landmarks parceling-constituting the body's territory, polluting objects fall, schematically, into two types: excremental and menstrual. Neither tears nor sperm, for instance, although they belong to borders of the body, have any polluting value.

Excrement and its equivalents (decay, infection, disease, corpse, etc.) stand for the danger to identity that comes from without: the ego threatened by the non-ego, society threatened by its outside, life by death. Menstrual blood, on the contrary, stands for the danger issuing from within the identity (social or sexual); it threatens the relationship between the sexes within a social aggregate and, through internalization, the identity of each sex in the face of sexual difference.

MATERNAL AUTHORITY AS TRUSTEE OF THE SELF'S CLEAN AND PROPER BODY

What can the two types of defilement have in common? Without having recourse to anal eroticism or the fear of castration—one cannot help *hearing* the reticence of anthropologists when confronted with that explanation—it might be suggested, by means of another psychoanalytic approach, that those *two* defilements stem from the *maternal* and/or the feminine, of which the maternal is the real support. That goes without saying where menstrual blood signifies sexual difference. But what about excrement? It will be remembered that the anal penis is also the phallus with which infantile imagination provides the feminine sex and that, on the other hand, maternal authority is experienced first and above all, after the first essentially oral frustrations, as sphincteral training. It is as if, while having been forever immersed in the symbolics of language, the human being

experienced, in addition, an *authority* that was a—chronologically and logically immediate—repetition of the *laws* of language. Through frustrations and prohibitions, this authority
shapes the body into a *territory* having areas, orifices, points and
lines, surfaces and hollows, where the archaic power of mastery
and neglect, of the differentiation of proper-clean and improper-
dirty, possible and impossible, is impressed and exerted. It is
a "binary logic," a primal mapping of the body that I call
semiotic to say that, while being the precondition of language,
it is dependent upon meaning, but in a way that is not that of
linguistic signs nor of the *symbolic* order they found. Maternal
authority is the trustee of that mapping of the self's clean and
proper body; it is distinguished from paternal laws within
which, with the phallic phase and acquisition of language, the
destiny of man will take shape.

If language, like culture, sets up a separation and, starting
with discrete elements, concatenates an order, it does so precisely by repressing maternal authority and the corporeal mapping that abuts against them. It is then appropriate to ask what
happens to such a repressed item when the legal, phallic, linguistic symbolic establishment does not carry out the separation
in radical fashion—or else, more basically, when the speaking
being attempts to think through its advent in order better to
establish its effectiveness.

DEFILEMENT RITE—A SOCIAL ELABORATION OF THE BORDERLINE PATIENT?

The structuralist hypothesis is well known. Basic symbolic institutions, such as *sacrifice* or *myths*, expand on logical processes
inherent in the economy of language itself; in doing so they
realize for the community what makes up in depth, historically
and logically, the speaking being as such. Thus *myth* projects
on contents that are vitally important for a given community
those binary oppositions discovered at the level of phonematic
concatenation of language. As for *sacrifice*, it solemnizes the
vertical dimension of the sign: the one that leads from the thing

that is left behind, or killed, to the meaning of the word and transcendence.

Following that line, one could suggest that the rites surrounding defilement, particularly those involving excremential and menstrual variants, shift the *border* (in the psychoanalytic meaning relating to borderline patients) that separates the body's territory from the signifying chain; they illustrate the boundary between semiotic authority and symbolic law. Through language and within highly hierarchical religious institutions, man hallucinates partial "objects"—witnesses to an archaic differentiation of the body on its way toward ego identity, which is also sexual identity. The *defilement* from which ritual protects us is neither sign nor matter. Within the rite that extracts it from repression and depraved desire, defilement is the translinguistic spoor of the most archaic boundaries of the self's clean and proper body. In that sense, if it is a jettisoned object, it is so from the mother. It absorbs within itself all the experiences of the non-objectal that accompany the differentiation mother-speaking being, hence all ab-jects (from those the phobic shuns to those that hem in split subjects). As if purification rites, through a language that is already there, looked back toward an archaic experience and obtained from it a partial-object, not as such but only as a *spoor* of a pre-object, an archaic parceling. By means of the symbolic institution of ritual, that is to say, by means of a system of ritual exclusions, the partial-object consequently becomes *scription*—an inscription of limits, an emphasis placed not on the (paternal) Law but on (maternal) Authority through the very signifying order.

There follows something quite particular for the ritual device itself.

A SCRIPTION WITHOUT SIGNS

First, those rites concerning defilement (but perhaps also any rite, defilement rite being prototypical) effect an abreaction of the pre-sign impact, the semiotic impact of language. In any event it is thus that one can underpin anthropologists' definitions, according to which rites are *acts* rather than *symbols*. In other words, rites would not be limited to their signifying dimension, they would also have a material, active, translinguistic, magical impact.

In the second place, the strong ritualization of defilement, which may be observed, for instance, within the castes of India, appears to be accompanied by one's being totally blind to filth itself, even though it is the object of those rites. It is as if one had maintained, so to speak, only the sacred, prohibited facet of defilement, allowing the anal object that such a sacralization had in view to become lost within the dazzling light of unconsciousness if not of the unconscious. V. S. Naipaul points out that Hindus defecate everywhere without anyone ever mentioning, either in speech or in books, those squatting figures, because, quite simply, no one sees them.[16] It is not a form of censorship due to modesty that would demand the omission in discourse of a function that has, in other respects, been ritualized. It is blunt foreclosure that voids those acts and objects from conscious representation. A split seems to have set in between, on the one hand, the body's territory where an authority without guilt prevails, a kind of fusion between mother and nature, and on the other hand, a totally different universe of socially signifying performances where embarrassment, shame, guilt, desire, etc. come into play—the order of the phallus. Such a split, which in another cultural universe would produce psychosis, thus finds in this context a perfect socialization. That may be because setting up the rite of defilement takes on the function of the hyphen, the virgule, allowing the two universes of *filth* and of *prohibition* to brush lightly against each other without necessarily being identified as such, as *object* and as *law*. On account of the flexibility at work in rites of defilement, the subjective economy of the speaking being who is involved abuts on both edges of the unnamable (the non-object, the off-limits) and the absolute (the relentless coherence of Prohibition, sole donor of Meaning).

Finally, the frequency of defilement rites in societies *without writing* leads one to think that such cathartic rites function like a "writing of the real." They parcel out, demarcate, delineate an order, a framework, a sociality, without having any other signification than the one inhering in that very parceling and the order thus concatenated. One might ask, proceeding in reverse, if all writing is not a second level rite, at the level of language, that is, which causes one to be reminded, through the linguistic signs themselves, of the demarcations that precondition them and go beyond them. Indeed, writing causes the subject who ventures in it to confront an archaic authority, on the nether side of the proper Name. The maternal connotations of this authority never escaped great writers, no more than the coming face to face with what we have called abjection. From "I am Madame Bovary" to Molly's monologue and to Céline's emotion, which does injury to syntax before opening on to music, the ballerina, or nothing.

POLLUTION BY FOOD—A COMPOUND

When food appears as a polluting object, it does so as oral object only to the extent that orality signifies a boundary of the self's clean and proper body. Food becomes abject only if it is a border between two distinct entities or territories. A boundary between nature and culture, between the human and the non-human. This may be noticed in India and Polynesia, for instance, in the case of cooked foods whose vulnerability to impurity is characteristic.[17] In contrast to a ripe fruit that may be eaten without danger, food that is treated with fire is polluting and must be surrounded with a series of taboos. It is as if fire, contrary to what hygienist conceptions posit, far from purifying, pointed to a contact, to organic food's meddling with the familial and the social. The virtual impurity of such food comes close to excremental abjection, which is the most striking example of the interference of the organic within the social.

The fact remains nevertheless that all food is liable to defile. Thus the Brahmin who surrounds his meal and his food with very strict regulations is less pure after eating than before. Food in this instance designates the other (the natural) that is opposed to the social condition of man and penetrates the self's clean and proper body. In other respects, food is the oral object (the abject) that sets up archaic relationships between the human being and the other, its mother, who wields a power that is as vital as it is fierce.

THE REMAINDER: DEFILEMENT AND REBIRTH

The nature of the repulsion aroused by *food remainders* in Brahmanism is very significant from that point of view. More defiling still than any other food, they do not seem to be so on account of that ambivalence, duplicity, or permanent or potential compound between same and other that all nourishment signifies, as I have just shown. Remainders are residues of something but especially of someone. They pollute on account of incompleteness. Under certain conditions, however, the Brahmin can eat remainders, which, instead of polluting him, make him qualified to undertake a journey or even accomplish his specific office, the priestly act.

That ambivalence of residues (pollution *and* potential for renewal, remainder and fresh start) can also be seen in domains unrelated to food. Some cosmogonies represent the remainder, after the flood, in the shape of a serpent that becomes the supporter of Vishnu and thus insures the rebirth of the universe. In similar fashion, if what remains of a sacrifice can be called abject, in another connection consuming the leavings of a sacrifice can also be the cause of a series of good rebirths and can even lead to finding salvation. The remainder is thus a strongly ambivalent notion in Brahmanism—defilement as well as rebirth, abjection as much as high purity, obstacle at the same time as incentive toward holiness. But here is perhaps the essential point: the remainder appears to be coextensive with the entire architecture of non-totalizing thought. In its view there is nothing that is everything; nothing is exhaustive, there is a residue in every system—in cosmogony, food ritual, and even sacrifice, which deposits, through ashes for instance, ambivalent remains. A challenge to our mono-theistic and mono-logical universes such a mode of thinking apparently needs the ambivalence of remainder if it is not to become enclosed within *One* single-level symbolics, and thus always posit a non-object as polluting as it is reviving—defilement and genesis. That is

why the poet of the *Atharva Veda* extols the defiling and re-
generating remainder (*uchista*) as precondition for all form.
"Upon remainder the name and the form are founded, upon
remainder the world is founded . . . Being and non-being, both
are in the remainder, death, vigor."[18]

FEAR OF WOMEN—FEAR OF PROCREATION

Fear of the archaic mother turns out to be essentially fear of
her generative power. It is this power, a dreaded one, that
patrilineal filiation has the burden of subduing. It is thus not
surprising to see pollution rituals proliferating in societies where
patrilineal power is poorly secured, as if the latter sought, by
means of purification, a support against excessive matrilineality.

Thus, in a society where religious prohibitions correspond
to the sexual prohibitions intended to separate men from
women and insure the power of the former over the latter, it
has been possible to note—as with the Gidjingali in Australia—
the considerable sway of maternal authority over the sons. On
the other hand, with the neighboring Aranda, where paternal
control is much more important than with the Gidjingali, there
is no connection between sexual and religious prohibitions.[19]

The instance of the Nuer, analyzed by Evans Pritchard and
again by Mary Douglas, is very significant in that respect. It
involves a society that is dominated, at least among the aris-
tocrats, by the agnatic principle and in which women are a
divisive factor; essential for reproduction, they nevertheless
endanger the ideal norms of the agnatic group, the more so as
cohabitation with maternal relatives seems common. Menstrual
pollution, as well as prohibition of incest with the mother,
considered the most dangerous of all, can be interpreted as the
symbolic equivalent of that conflict.[20]

A loathing of defilement as protection against the poorly
controlled power of mothers seems even clearer with the
Bemba. Ritually impure and contaminating, menstrual defilement wields with them, in addition, a cataclysmic power such
that one is led to speak, under the circumstances, not only of
ritual impurity but also of the *power of pollution*. Thus, if a woman

undergoing her period touches fire (a masculine and patrilineal symbol), food cooked on that fire makes her ill and threatens her with death. Now, among the Bemba, power is in the hands of men, but filiation is matrilineal and residence, after marriage, is matrilocal. There is a great contradiction between male rule and matrilocal residence; the young bridegroom is subjected to the authority of the bride's family, and he must override it through personal excellence during his maturity. He remains nevertheless, because of matrilineality, in conflict with the maternal uncle who is the legal guardian of the children especially when they are growing up.[21] The power of pollution (the threat of illness or death through the conjunction blood-fire) thus transposes, on the symbolic level, the permanent conflict resulting from an unsettled separation between masculine and feminine power at the level of social institutions. Non-separation would threaten the whole society with disintegration.

Here is a significant fact. Again as protection against the generative power of women, pollution rites arise within societies that are afraid of overpopulation (in barren regions, for instance). One thus finds them, as part of a whole system of restraining procreation, along with incest taboo, etc., among the Enga of New Guinea. On the other hand, with their Fore neighbors, the desire to procreate, encouraged for opposite ecological reasons, entails, one might say symmetrically, the disappearance of incest taboo and pollution rites. Such a relaxation of prohibitions among the Fore, for the sake of a single objective—reproduction at any cost—is accompanied by such a lack of the "clean and proper" and hence of the "abject" that cannibalism of the dead seems to be current practice. Contrariwise the Enga, heedful of pollution and subjected to fear of procreation, are not acquainted with cannibalism.[22]

Is that parallel sufficient to suggest that defilement reveals, at the same time as an attempt to throttle matrilineality, an attempt at separating the speaking being from his body in order that the latter accede to the status of clean and proper body, that is to say, non-assimilable, uneatable, abject? It is only at such a cost that the body is capable of being defended, protected—and also, eventually, sublimated. Fear of the uncontrollable generative mother repels me from the body; I give up cannibalism because abjection (of the mother) leads me toward respect for the body of the other, my fellow man, my brother.

DEFILEMENT AND ENDOGAMY IN INDIA

It is of course the hierarchic caste system in India that provides the most complex and striking instance of a social, moral, and religious system based on pollution and purification, on the pure and the impure. It is worth confronting, as Louis Dumont has done, this hierarchic system with the regulation of marriage.[23] Dumont concludes that the endogamy in castes is only a consequence of the initial hierarchic principle based on the opposition pure/impure. Without going into the details of his demonstration or into the numerous infractions to endogamy— which are moreover inscribed naturally within the hierarchic order, complicating it and strengthening it—I shall, for my purpose, note the following.

The endogamic principle inherent in caste system amounts, as everywhere else, to having the individual marry within his group, or rather to his being prohibited from marrying outside of it. Endogamy, in Indian castes, implies in addition a specific filiation: the passing on of membership in the group by *both parents at the same time.* The result of such a regulation is in fact a balancing, symbolic and real, of the role of both sexes within that socio-symbolic unit constituted by caste. The highly hierarchical nature of Indian society does not come into play between the sexes, at least not where filiation is concerned—a major criterion of power in those societies. One could say that caste is a hierarchic device that, in addition to professional specializations, insures, in the passing on of group membership, an *equal share to the father and to the mother.*

Starting from there, the question as to whether the pure/ impure opposition determines the hierarchic order, or whether caste endogamy is the initial principle, appears in a different light. Let us put aside the debate over cause and effect, the chicken and the egg. Let me note only that in an organization like this one, without classic exogamy, social order is not elaborated on the basis of clear-cut oppositions represented by *men* and *women* as tokens of "one's own" and the "foreign," the "same" and the "different" (sex, group, clan, etc.). Nevertheless, as though making up for that lack of differentiation, meticulous rules of separation, rejection, and repulsion are introduced. Subjects and objects have only, on that basis, the status of ab-jects for one another. In short, when one avoids the binarism of the exogamic system, that is, the father/mother, man/woman strangeness at the level of the *matrimonial* institution, then, at the *ritual* level, one multiplies abjections between the sexes, between subjects and objects (essentially borderlanders, a point to which I shall return), and between castes.

Beside that general rule, there are specific situations that confirm the impression that the strong caste hierarchy compensates for the man/woman balance introduced by Indian endogamy. Let me take note, among other matters, of the various forms of marriage, often challenged and contradicted, that some have been able to interpret as dual filiation, paternal and maternal. Thus, for M. B. Emenau,[24] there is in southern India a dual unilineal descent, while for Louis Dumont the two unilineal principles are found separately, even if paternal and maternal traits can interfere in several ways within the same group.[25] In another connection, certain cases of hypergamy (the possibility for the daughter to marry into a family superior to her own without affecting the status of her children or excluding endogamy), while they may amount to a promotion for the woman, are valid only for her, since the marriage is of no account for the husband. That very particular search for a father having a higher status is interpreted as maintaining "matrilineal filiation in a patrilineal environment."[26]

Ethnologists could multiply and specify examples. The conclusion that I shall draw is as follows. If any organization is necessarily made up of differences, separations, and oppositions, the caste system, by reason of the endogamy that goes with it and the balance between the two sexes that the latter institutionalizes, seems to translate a difference *elsewhere* by *multiplying* it; that difference, in exogamic societies, is *one* and acts fundamentally between the *two sexes* as representatives and the two entities that are territorial, economic, political, ethnic, etc.

It is as if the more the balance between the two sexual powers was maintained by endogamy, the greater was the need to have *other* differences come into play. That inseparability, one might even say that immanence to endogamy, of the hierarchic principle, like the cloth and lining of a single organization, perhaps explains why marriage (the rite of joining, of maintaining the identity and balance of the two) is the only rite of passage that "is not accompanied by any impurity."[27] It gives the Hindu the impression that he is "symbolically and temporarily raised from his condition (which is hierarchical, governed by the pure/impure) and assimilated to the highest, that of prince or Brahman for a non-Brahman, god for a Brahman."[28] Everywhere else the principle of separation holds sway, one that Bouglé likens to a repulsion.

MARRIAGE OR LOATHING?

Dumont's distrust for Bouglé's term and the logic that it conveys, the preference he gives to the hierarchical principle, do not appear to invalidate my reasoning. I shall simply conclude that the hierarchic principle is jointly based on two logical principles—the separation exemplified by the dichotomy of the pure and the impure, and the *maintaining of a balance* between the two sexes through endogamy.

As I have pointed out, it is Célestin Bouglé who has evoked, along with the socio-logical principle ruling the caste system ("hierarchy, hereditary specialization"[30]), the one he calls "repulsion"[31] or "loathing";[32] a principle that seems more psychological but is in fact linked to the logic of the sacred. Particularly, he dwells on the question of "food loathing": is caste a "matter of marriage" or a "matter of meals"? Skirting the psychological or psychoanalytical archeology of repulsion, this controversial anthropologist seeks its anchorage in family organization on the one hand, in the economy of sacrifice on the other. As to family organization, he restricts himself to references to "far away memories of earliest family practices" or to "relics of family religion" (as opposed to the demands of industry); these would account for the traits that cause guild system to resemble caste system.[33] The notion of repulsion is studied neither by Dumont nor by Bouglé, even when Bouglé mentions it in connection with Brahmans and has it spring from the *taboo* that surrounds sacrifice in any society, and which India "merely carried to its highest power." He mentions that the sacrificer is surrounded by taboos because he channels "from the profane world to the sacred world fluid, ambiguous forces, that are at the same time the most dangerous and the most beneficial of all."[34]

HIERARCHY AND NONVIOLENCE

If, on the other hand, one reestablishes Bouglé's outlook in the light of the precise details given by Dumont, one no longer sees the pure/impure opposition that governs Indian hierarchic order as merely encompassing; one also sees it as correlative of marriage rules and religious customs (sacrifices and their evolution). One is then led to conceive of the opposition between pure and impure not as an archetype but as *one* coding of the differentiation of the speaking subject as such, a coding of his repulsion in relation to the other in order to autonomize himself. The pure/impure opposition represents (when it does not function as metaphor) the striving for identity, a difference. It appears instead of *sexual difference* (and in that sense it may seem, as in caste system, parallel to the institutionalizing of bisexuality through endogamic marriage). On that basis, it acts as a *separating value* peculiar to the symbolic function itself (sacrificer/sacrifice/God; subject/thing/meaning). The hierarchy founded on the pure and the impure displaces (or denies) the difference between the sexes; *it replaces the violence of sacrifice with the ritual of purification.*

In the final analysis, the pure/impure opposition would not be a datum in itself but would stem from the necessity for the speaking being to be confronted with sexual difference and the symbolic. The Indian caste system would allow that confrontation to take place smoothly. It would manage it without being

pre-emptive—in the manner of monotheism, for instance—and
with the greatest of care, protecting the subject who, from
abjection to abjection, is confronted with them systematically.
The cost is social immobility and an identification of that which
is elsewhere autonomous subjectivity with the rules of abjection
that pattern the socio-symbolic territory. Hierarchy is indeed
constitutive of Hindu man (and perhaps of any speaking being
if he does not erase his participation in the symbolic), but it is
rooted in two prime shifts: the sign (solemnized by sacrifice),
sexual difference (regulated by marriage). If it be true that the
pure/impure opposition takes in the area that, with us, is governed by the good/evil opposition, the boundary at issue is
related, through the hierarchy of caste and matrimonial regulations that accompany and secure it, to a very deep logic of
the speaking being as separated by sex and language. India has
the incomparable advantage of laying bare the ab-ject logic of
that separation and resolving in its nonviolent fashion the
asymptotic relation between sexuality and symbolism, balancing differences where sexuality is concerned, multiplying and
grading divisions to the utmost in the case of symbolism.

OEDIPUS THE KING OR INVISIBLE ABJECTION

The tragic and sublime fate of Oedipus sums up and displaces
the mythical defilement that situates impurity on the untouchable "other side" constituted by the *other* sex, within the *corporeal border*—the thin sheet of desire—and, basically, within
the mother woman—the myth of natural fullness. To be con-
vinced of this, we would have to follow Sophocles' *Oedipus the
King* and above all his *Oedipus at Colonus*.

A sovereign on account of his *knowing* how to unveil logical
enigmas, Oedipus the king is nonetheless ignorant of his desire.
He *does not know* that he is also the one who kills his father
Laius and marries his mother Jocasta. Had they remained veiled,
that murder as much as that desire would only be the obverse,
quite obviously solidary, of his logical and consequently political power. Abjection breaks out only when, driven to distrac-
tion by a desire to know, Oedipus discovers desire and death

in his sovereign being; when he assigns them to the same, full, knowing, and responsible sovereignty. In *Oedipus the King* the solution remains nonetheless wholly mythical; it proceeds by means of exclusion, as we have seen it at work in the logic of other mythical and ritual systems.

There is, first of all, a spatial exclusion. Oedipus must *exile* himself, leave the proper place of his sovereignty, thrust defilement aside so that the boundaries of the social contract may be perpetuated at Thebes.

At the same time, there is an exclusion from sight. Oedipus blinds himself, so as not to have to suffer the sight of the objects of his desire and murder (the faces of his wife, mother, and children). If it be true that such blinding is equivalent to castration, it is neither eviration nor death. In relation to them, it is a symbolic substitute intended for building the wall, reinforcing the boundary that wards off opprobrium, which, because of this very fact, is not disavowed but shown to be alien. Blinding is thus an image of splitting; it marks, on the very body, the alteration of the self and clean into the defiled—the scar taking the place of a revealed and yet invisible abjection. Of abjection considered as invisible. In return for which citystate and knowledge can endure.

PHARMAKOS THE AMBIGUOUS

Let us emphasize again the tragic development of *Oedipus the King*: does it not sum up the mythic variant of abjection? Entering an impure city—a miasma—he turns himself into *agos*, defilement, in order to purify it and to become *katharmos*. He is thus a purifier by the very fact of being *agos*. His abjection is due to the permanent ambiguity of the parts he plays without his knowledge, even when he believes he knows.[35] It is precisely such a dynamics of reversals that makes of him a being of abjection and a *pharmakos*, a scapegoat who, having been ejected, allows the city to be freed from defilement. The mainspring of the tragedy lies in that ambiguity;[36] prohibition and ideal are joined in a single character in order to signify that the speaking being has no space of his own but stands on a fragile threshold as if stranded on account of an impossible demarcation. If such is the logic of Oedipus as *pharmakos ka-tharmos*, there is no alternative but to note that Sophocles' play derives its effectiveness not only from that mathesis of ambiguity but also from the wholly semantic values it endows opposing terms with. But what "values"?

Thebes is a miasma on account of sterility, disease, and death. Oedipus is *agos* on account of his having, through murder of the father and incest with the mother, interrupted the reproductive chain. Defilement is the stopping of life; (like) sexuality without reproduction (the sons born out of Oedipus' incest will perish, while his daughter will survive only within another logic, that of the contract or symbolic existence, as will be seen in *Oedipus at Colonus*). A certain sexuality, which does not have in Greek tragedy the meaning it has for modern man, which does not even adorn itself with pleasure but with *sovereignty* and *knowledge*, is the equivalent of disease and death. Defilement blends into it: practically, it amounts to tampering with the mother. Defilement is incest considered as transgression of the boundaries of what is clean and proper.

Where then lies the border, the initial phantasmatic limit that establishes the clean and proper self of the speaking and/or social being? Between man and woman? Or between mother and child? Perhaps between woman and mother? The replica of Oedipus-*pharmakos* on the woman's side is Jocasta; she is herself Janus-like, ambiguity and reversal in a single being, a single part, a single function. Janus-like perhaps as any woman is, to the extent that any woman is at the same time a desiring being, that is, a speaking being, and a reproductive being, that is, one that separates itself from its child. Oedipus has perhaps done nothing more than marrying the splitting of Jocasta—the mystery, the enigma of femininity. At the limit, if someone personifies abjection without assurance of purification, it is a woman, "any woman," the "woman as a whole"; as far as he is concerned, man exposes abjection by knowing it, and through that very act purifies it. Jocasta is *miasma* and *agos*— that goes without saying. But Oedipus alone is *pharmakos*. He knows and bounds the mythic universe constituted by the question of (sexual) difference and preoccupied with the separation of the two powers: reproduction/production, feminine/masculine. Oedipus completes that universe by introducing it into the particularity of each individual who then unfailingly becomes *pharmakos* and universally tragic.

But for such interiorization to take place, a transition was needed; from Thebes to Colonus, ambiguity and reversal of differences become *contract*.

PURIFICATION AT COLONUS

Oedipus at Colonus is therefore completely other. The locale has changed. And while divine laws have not lost their harshness, Oedipus, for his part, has modified his stance with respect to them. In point of fact, a transformation of political laws actually took place between the writing of the two plays. Between 42 (*Oedipus the King*) and 402, when *Oedipus at Colonus* was first performed (after Sophocles' death in 406-405), there was a transition from tyranny to democracy. But if in the work of Sophocles' old age the democratic principle appears to hold sway, that is perhaps only *one* of the reasons that explain such a change with respect to divine laws in the dynamics of *Oedipus at Colonus*. In opposition to the sovereign Oedipus, overcome, destroyed, shattered through and within opprobrium, we have here an Oedipus who is *not king*, in other words an Oedipus who is a subject, who proclaims his innocence. Not without hesitations. Having first thought of shaking Theseus' hand and embracing him, he comes to think that he is impure although irresponsible:

But what am I saying? Unhappy as I have become, how could I wish thee to touch one with whom all stain of sin hath made its dwelling, No, not I, nor allow thee, if thou wouldst. (lines 1134 ff.)

And yet he had cried out at the very beginning of that closing in of his fate:

. . . mine acts, at least, have been in suffering rather than doing 268)
stainless before the law, void of malice have I come unto this pass (l. 348)[37]

Let us stop with this acknowledgment. Neither a confession of guilt nor an entreaty of innocence consequent to the suffering that was undergone, that statement marks the slipping from Oedipus the king to Oedipus the subject. "I am innocent before the Law" signifies first, *I do not know the Law, the one who solves logical enigmas does not know the Law*, and that means, *I who knows am not the Law*. Thus a first estrangement is introduced between knowledge and Law, one that unbalances the sovereign. If the Law is in the Other, my fate is neither power nor desire, it is the fate of an estranged person: my fate is death.

The abjection of Oedipus the king was the irreconcilable in knowledge and desire, both all-powerful in man's being.

The abjection of Oedipus at Colonus is the *not known* of the speaking being who is *subject to death* at the same time as to *symbolic union*.

For it is on the threshold of death, while he is making a pact with a foreigner, that Oedipus says he does not know the Law. *Exile*, first desired, then refused by his sons, has become *rejection* before being transformed, for Oedipus, into *choice* and *symbolic handing down*. For it is on foreign soil, and to a foreign hero, Theseus, a symbolic son, that he bequeaths, at the same time as his daughters, the secret of his death. A death that, also in and of itself, without being in any way expiatory or redeeming for Oedipus, is meant for the benefit of others, of foreigners— Theseus and the Atheneans.

Within such a context, it is Ismene, the daughter so often silent but who speaks in order to object to the very Oedipean quarrels of the sons, who also heralds his salvation through the gods: "Yea, for the gods lift thee now, but before they were working thy ruin" (l. 390). Such a lifting will be explained by the innocence of Oedipus before the Law (l. 548); but to make it concrete, he will undergo the purification rites at Colonus (ll. 466–491), rites that provide us with one of the most detailed descriptions of purification in classical literature.

A CHALLENGE TO ABJECTION: THE SYMBOLIC PACT

At Colonus, therefore, the fate of abjection was changed. Neither excluded nor blindly other, it finds its place as his *not known* within a "subject on the verge of death." Abjection is nothing more than a flaw in Oedipus' impossible sovereignty, a flaw in his knowledge. If rituals are called upon to purify it, it is nevertheless in the *sayings* of Oedipus concerning divine Law as well as Theseus that it is assumed. It has nothing to do with confessing a sin; abjection, in a Greece in the process of becoming democratic, is taken over by the one who, through speaking, recognizes himself as mortal (so much so that he leaves no male issue) and subject to the symbolic (one will note the purely nominal handing down of his mortal jouissance to the foreigner, Theseus).

 A bridge has been built toward another logic of abjection: it is no longer defilement to be excluded ritually as the other facet of the sacred (social, cultural, one's own) but *transgression* due to a *misreading* of the Law.

Oedipus the King handed over to Freud and his posterity the strength of (incestuous) desire and the desire for (the father's) death. However abject these desires may be, which threaten the integrity of individual and society, they are nonetheless sovereign. Such is the blinding light cast by Freud, following Oedipus, on abjection, as he invites us to recognize ourselves in it without gouging out our eyes.

But after all, what saves us from performing that decisive gesture? The answer can perhaps be found in *Oedipus at Colonus*, and yet that play does not seem to have preoccupied Freud. The border between abjection and the sacred, between desire and knowledge, between death and society, can be faced squarely, uttered without sham innocence or modest self-effacement, provided one sees in it an incidence of man's particularity as *mortal and speaking*. "There is an abject" is henceforth stated as, "I am abject, that is, mortal and speaking." Incompleteness and dependency on the Other, far from clearing a desiring and murderous Oedipus, allow him only to make his dramatic splitting transmittable—transmittable to a foreign hero, and hence opening up the undecidable possibility of a few truth-effects. Our eyes can remain open provided we recognize ourselves as always already altered by the symbolic—by language. Provided we hear in language—and not in the other, nor in the other sex—the gouged-out eye, the wound, the basic incompleteness that conditions the indefinite quest of signifying concatenations. That amounts to joying in the truth of self-division (abjection/sacred). Here two paths open out: sublimation and perversion.

And their intersection: religion.

Freud did not need to go to Colonus for that. He had Moses, who preceded him in this reversal of defilement in subjection to symbolic law. But it may be that *Oedipus at Colonus* shows, in addition to other modifications of Greek culture, the path by which Hellenism could meet with the Bible.

ᖇ 4

SEMIOTICS OF BIBLICAL ABOMINATION

Thou shalt not seethe a kid in his mother's milk.
Exodus 23:19

See now that I, even I, am he and there is no god with me.
Deuteronomy 32:39

Iudei mente sola unumque numen intellegunt.
Tacitus, *Histories*, 5:5

THE BIBLICAL NEUTRALIZATION OF DEFILEMENT

Interpretations of biblical impurity are, roughly speaking, divided along two lines of persuasion. The first, following up on the ideas of W. Robertson Smith (*The Religion of the Semites*, 1889), considers biblical impurity as a condition internal to Jewish monotheism, intrinsically dependent on divine will, since the impure is what departs from divine precepts. Far from being a demonic force alien to divinity, impurity would then be a kind of *neutralization of taboos* (peculiar to rites of defilement), owing to the fact that it is subordinate to the will of God.[1] The other interpretation, represented by Baruch A. Levine,[2] considers impurity to be indicative of a demonic force, threatening the divinity, acting independently of it and analogous to the autonomous power of a spirit of evil.

I shall try to demonstrate that those two contrary positions, in fact, do no more than unilaterally emphasize the complex dynamics of biblical thought concerning impurity. As I see it, biblical impurity is permeated with the tradition of defilement;

in that sense, it *points to* but does not *signify* an autonomous force that *can* be threatening for divine agency. I shall suggest that such a force is rooted, historically (in the history of religions) and subjectively (in the structuration of the subject's identity), in the cathexis of maternal function—mother, women, reproduction. But the biblical test—and therein lies its extraordinary specificity—performs the tremendous forcing that consists in subordinating maternal power (whether historical or phantasmatic, natural or reproductive) to symbolic order as pure logical order regulating social performance, as divine Law attended to in the Temple. To the extent that the Temple *is* the Law, one is biblically pure or impure only with respect to social order, that is, with respect to the Law or the cult (as Neusner would have it). If, on the other hand, one tries to go back further into the archeology of that impurity, one indeed encounters fear in the face of a power (maternal? natural?—at any rate insubordinate and not liable of being subordinated to Law) that *might* become autonomous evil but *is not*, so long as the hold of subjective and social symbolic order endures. Biblical impurity is thus always already a *logicizing* of what departs from the symbolic, and for that very reason it prevents it from being actualized as demonic evil. Such a logicizing inscribes the demonic in a more abstract an also more moral register as a potential for guilt and sin.

Purity or impurity are thus situated in relation to cult because the latter represents or serves a *logic of distribution* and behavior on which the symbolic community is founded: a Law, a reason. That is what Maimonides says, within a definition of impurity that gives considerable weight not only to reason but also to the subject's initiative:

. . . one who sets his heart on cleansing himself from the uncleannesses that beset men's souls . . . becomes clean as soon as he consents in his heart to shun those counsels and brings his soul into the waters of pure reason.[3]

When Mary Douglas defines impurity as that which *departs from symbolic order* and Neusner sees in it what is *incompatible with the Temple*, they are talking about the same thing according to *two points of view*. The anthropologist must *discover* social order while studying societies that observe it unconsciously, while the historian of religions *stands* before that order, which is not only exhibited but isolated in itself and celebrated as an agency of the Law by that colossal revolution—Hebraic monotheism.

But the question for the analyst-semiologist is to know how far one can analyze ritual impurity. The historian of religions stops soon: the cultically impure is that which is based on a natural "loathing."[4] The anthropologist goes further: there is nothing "loathsome" in itself; the loathsome is that which disobeys classification rules peculiar to the given symbolic system.[5] But as far as I am concerned, I keep asking questions. Why that system of classification and not another? What social, subjective, and socio-subjectively interacting needs does it fulfill? Are there no subjective structurations that, within the organization of each speaking being, correspond to this or that symbolic-social system and represent, if not stages, at least *types* of subjectivity and society? Types that would be defined, in the last analysis, according to the subject's position in language, that is, by the more or less partial use he can make of his potentialities?

A STRATEGY OF IDENTITY

The pure/impure distinction, *tahor/tame*, shows up in the biblical episode of Noah's burnt offerings to the Lord after the flood. "And Noah builded an altar unto the Lord; and took of every clean beast, and of every clean fowl, and offered burnt offerings on the altar."[6] That recognition of the pure/impure difference apparently forces the Lord to defer his judgment—and that entails *clemency* on the one hand, *time* on the other.

I will not again curse the ground any more for men's sake; for the imagination of man's heart is evil from his youth; neither will I again smite any more every thing living, as I have done.

While the earth remaineth, seedtime and harvest, and cold and heat, and summer and winter, and day and night shall not cease.[7]

Neither Cain, although at fault, nor Adam, although wandering (*nad*, and that brings him close to feminine impurity, *niddah*), are defiled. *Tahor / tame*[8] seems to be a specific relation that pertains to setting in order, dependent on a covenant with God. That opposition, even though it is not absolute, is inscribed in the biblical text's basic concern with separating, with constituting strict identities without intermixture. The distance between man and God will be at issue in the elaboration of the theological corpus. One can observe, however, along the complex course followed by Yahwist and Elohist, how that fundamental difference in fact subsumes the others—life and death, vegetal and animal, flesh and blood, hale and ill, otherness and incest. Keeping to the semantic value of those oppositions, one can group them under three major categories of abomination: 1) food taboos; 2) corporeal alteration and its climax, death; and 3) the feminine body and incest. Topologically speaking such variants correspond to one's being allowed to have access or not to a place—the holy place of the Temple. Logically, conformity to the Law is involved, the Law of purity [cleanliness] or Law of holiness, particularly as it is summed up in Leviticus 11–16 and 19–26.

"MATERIAL" OR "ALLEGORICAL" OPPOSITIONS

Commentators have noted that if biblical impurity is from the outset tied to the religious cult since the impure is that which is excluded from the Temple, it deals with matter (food, menses, leprosy, gonorrhea, etc.) having no immediate relation to the sacred place. It is thus in secondary fashion, through a metaphor, that impurity concerns the relation to the Temple, just as, consequently, what is excluded from it—idolatry in particular. Although the pure/impure distinction was already posited earlier, and especially with Isaiah (36–66), it is in fact only at the time of the second Temple, after the return from exile, after Ezekiel, that it becomes fundamental for the religious life of Israel. Nevertheless, and without for that matter undergoing any great change, it now appears even more allegorical or metaphorical, for henceforth there is less stress on the cultic center of purity than on impurity, which has become a metaphor for idolatry, sexuality, and immorality.[9]

It would thus seem that even when the Temple was destroyed, the Temple's function remained as far as the Jews were concerned, and it organized, in "metaphorical" fashion—but what does that mean?—a number of oppositions. I shall try to demonstrate that there is no opposition between material abomination and topo-logical (holy place of the Temple) or logical (holy Law) reference. The one and the other are two aspects, semantic and logical, of the imposition of a *strategy of identity*, which is, in all strictness, that of monotheism. The semes that clothe the process of separation (orality, death, incest) are the inseparable lining of its logical representation aiming to guarantee the place and law of the One God. In other words, the place *and* law of the One do not exist without a *series of separations* that are oral, corporeal, or even more generally material, and in the last analysis relating to fusion with the mother. The pure/impure mechanism testifies to the harsh combat Judaism, in order to constitute itself, must wage against paganism and its maternal cults. It carries into the private lives of everyone the brunt of the struggle each subject must wage during the entire length of his personal history in order to become separate, that is to say, to become a speaking subject and/or subject to Law. In this sense I shall posit that the "material" semes of the pure/impure opposition that mark out the biblical text are not metaphors of the divine prohibition resuming archaic, material customs, but are responses of symbolic Law, in the sphere of subjective economy and the genesis of speaking identity.

As the introduction of the pure/impure opposition coincides, as we have seen, with burnt offerings, this sets up at once the problem of the relations between *taboo* and *sacrifice*. It would seem as though God had penalized by means of the flood a breach of the order regulated by taboo. The burnt offering set up by Noah must then reestablish the order disturbed by the breaking of taboo. Two complementary motions are thus involved.

TABOO FORESTALLS SACRIFICE

The taboo implied by the pure/impure distinction organizes differences, shaping and opening an articulation that we must indeed call metonymic, within which, if he maintains himself there, man has a share in the sacred order. As to sacrifice, it constitutes the alliance with the One when the metonymic order that stems from it is perturbed. Sacrifice thus operates between two heterogeneous, incompatible, forever irreconcilable terms. It connects them necessarily in violent fashion, violating at the same time as it posits it the semantic isotopy of each. Sacrifice is thus a *metaphor*. The question has been raised as to which came first, metonymic taboo or metaphoric sacrifice.[10] All things considered, as sacrifice merely extends the logic of taboo when the latter is perturbed, the anteriority of taboo over sacrifice has been asserted. It seems to me more tenable to say that some collections of religious texts, by stressing taboo, seek protection from sacrificial interference or at least subordinate the latter to the former. Biblical abomination would thus be an attempt to throttle murder. Through sustained abomination, Judaism parts ways with sacrificial religions. And to the extent that religion and sacrifice overlap, biblical abominations perhaps constitute the logical explicitation of the religious (without proceeding to murderous acts—which become unnecessary when the rules of taboo are disclosed and observed). With biblical abomination religion is probably wending its way toward fulfillment.

THE MAN/GOD DISTINCTION: A DIETARY DISTINCTION

From its very beginning, the biblical text insists on maintaining the distance between man and God by means of a dietary differentiation. Thus the Lord (Genesis 3:22), after noting that "man is become as one of us, to know good and evil," decides to prevent this pretentious "scholar" from also becoming immortal. He thus prohibits certain foods by banishing him from the garden of Eden, "lest he put forth his hand, and take also from the tree of life, and eat, and live for ever." If a certain kind of eating, that of the apple of knowledge, could not have been held back from Adam, who was tempted by Eve, herself tempted by the Serpent, another food will be absolutely banned, in order to forestall the chaos that would result from the identification of man with the immortality of God. One should note that it is a feminine and animal temptation that is concealed under the first dietary trespass; for we shall encounter the reference to woman only fortuitously in the later abominations of the Levites.

Thus, as J. Soler points out,[11] food effects an initial division between man and God; to God belong living beings (by way of sacrifice), to man vegetable foods. For, "Thou shalt not kill."

In order to understand, after that first dietary apportionment, the introduction of meat diet, one must assume a cataclysm— for instance, a violation of divine rule and subsequent punishment. It is indeed only *after the Flood* that authorization is granted to eat "every moving thing that liveth" (Genesis 9:3). Far from being a reward, such permission is accompanied by an acknowledgment of essential evil, and it includes a negative, incriminating connotation with respect to man: "For the imagination of man's heart is evil" (Genesis 8:21). As if there had been an acknowledgment of a *bent toward murder* essential to human beings and the authorization for a meat diet was the recognition of that ineradicable "death drive," seen here under its most primordial or archaic aspect—devouring.

And yet, the biblical concern with separating and ordering encounters further on the supposedly previous distinction between vegetable and animal. In the postdiluvian situation such a distinction is brought out again under the guise of the flesh/blood opposition. On the one hand there is bloodless flesh (destined for man) and on the other, blood (destined for God). Blood, indicating the impure, takes on the "animal" seme of the previous opposition and inherits the propensity for murder of which man must cleanse himself. But blood, as a vital element, also refers to women, fertility, and the assurance of fecundation. It thus becomes a fascinating semantic crossroads, the propitious place for abjection where *death* and *femininity, murder* and *procreation, cessation of life* and *vitality* all come together. "But flesh with the life thereof, which is the blood thereof, shall ye not eat" (Genesis 9:4).

Such is the Elohistic covenant agreed upon with Noah for the whole of mankind. The Yahwist, setting up the agreement between Moses and God, valid for a single nation, applies himself to making that system of differences both more rigorous and more precise. "I am the Lord your God, which have separated you from other people. Ye shall therefore put difference between clean beasts and unclean . . ." (Leviticus 20:24–25). The dietary domain will then continue to be the privileged object of divine taboos, but it will be modified, amplified, and even seem to become identified with the most moral, if not the most abstract, statements of the Law. We shall attempt to trace that evolution in chapters 11 to 18 in Leviticus.

LEVITICUS: A PURITY OF PLACE, A PURITY OF SPEECH

Dietary instructions crop up after the burnt offering presented by Moses and Aaron to the Lord Yahweh (as they do after Noah's burnt offering to the Lord Elohim). Two officiants at the sacrifice, having "offered strange fire" to the Lord Yahweh, become "devoured" by the sacred fire (Leviticus, 10.1–2). At that moment, a communication from the Lord seems to indicate that the sacrifice "in itself" cannot assume the status of a divine covenant, unless that sacrifice is *already* inscribed in a logic of the pure/impure distinction, which it would consolidate and enable one to hand down.

Do not drink wine nor strong drink, thou, nor thy sons with thee, when ye go into the tabernacle of the congregation, lest ye die: it shall be a statute for ever throughout your generations:
    And that ye may put difference between holy and unholy, and between unclean and clean;
    And that ye may teach the children of Israel all the statutes which the Lord hath spoken into them by the hand of Moses. (Leviticus 10:9–11)

The sacrifice has efficacy then only when manifesting a logic of separation, distinction, and difference that is governed by admissibility to the holy place, that is, the appointed place for encountering the sacred fire of the Lord Yahweh.

    A *spatial* reference is thus called forth, in a first stage, as criterion of purity, provided that the *blood* of the expiational goat not be brought in (Leviticus 10:18). But such prerequisites for purity (holy space, no blood) seem to have been deemed insufficient, for the following chapter modifies them. The pure will no longer be what is restricted to a *place* but what accords with a *speech*; the impure will not only be a fascinating *element* (connoting murder and life: blood) but any infraction to a *logical conformity*. Thus,

And the Lord spake unto Moses and to Aaron, saying unto them,

Speak unto the children of Israel, saying, These are the beasts which ye shall eat among all the beasts that are on the earth.

Whatsoever parteth the hoof, and is clovenfooted, and cheweth the cud, among the beasts, that ye shall eat.

Nevertheless these shall ye not eat of them that chew the cud, or of them that divide the hoof: as the camel, because he cheweth the cud, but divided not the hoof; he is unclean unto you. (Leviticus 11:1–4)

And so forth.

The list of the occasionally specious prohibitions that make up this chapter becomes clear when it is understood that there is a strict intent of establishing conformity with the logic of the divine word. Now such a logic is founded on the initial biblical postulate of the man/God difference, which is coextensive with the prohibition of murder. As J. Soler has shown,[12] what is involved, as in Deuteronomy 14, is the establishment of a *logical field* preventing man from *eating carnivorous animals*. One needs to preserve oneself from murder, not incorporate carnivorous or rapacious animals, and there is only one prescription for that: eating herbivorous, cud–chewing animals. There are ruminants that do not follow the general rule as to hoofs, and they will be thrust aside. The pure will be that which conforms to an established taxonomy; the impure, that which unsettles it, establishes intermixture and disorder. The example of fish, birds, and insects, normally linked to one of three elements (sea, heaven, earth), is very significant from that point of view; the impure will be those that do not confine themselves to one element but point to admixture and confusion.

Thus, what initially appeared to us as a basic opposition between man and God (vegetable/animal, flesh/blood), following upon the initial contract, "Thou shalt not kill," becomes a complete system of logical oppositions. Differing from burnt offerings, this system of abomination presupposes it and guarantees its efficacy. Semantically controlled, initially at least, by the life/death dichotomy, it becomes in course of time a code of differences and observance of it. It goes without saying that the pragmatic value of those differences (the function of this or that animal in everyday life possibly affecting the pure/impure designation), like their sexual connotations (I shall return to this point), does not detract from the remarkable fact of having a system of taboos constituted like a true formal system—a taxonomy. Mary Douglas brilliantly emphasized the logical conformity of Levitical abominations, which, without a design of "separation" and "individual integrity," would be incomprehensible.

FOOD AND THE FEMININE

A brief and very important chapter of Leviticus, chapter 12, is inserted between those dietary prohibitions and the expansion of their logic to other domains of existence. Between the theme of food and that of the sick body (Leviticus 13–14), the text will deal with the woman in childbed. Because of her parturition and the blood that goes with it, *she* will be "impure": "according to the days of the separation for her infirmity shall she be unclean" (Leviticus 12:2). If she gives birth to a daughter, the girl "shall be unclean two weeks, as in her separation" (Leviticus 12:5). To purify herself, the mother must provide a burnt offering and a sin offering. Thus, on *her* part, there is impurity, defilement, blood, and purifying sacrifice. On the other hand, if she gives birth to a male, "the flesh of his foreskin shall be circumcised" (Leviticus 12:3). Circumcision would thus separate one from maternal, feminine impurity and defilement; it stands instead of sacrifice, meaning not only that it replaces it but is its equivalent—a sign of the alliance with God. Circumcision can be said to find its place in the same series as food taboos; it indicates a separation and at the same time does away with the need for sacrifice, of which it nevertheless bears the trace. Such a comment on circumcision within a text on feminine and particularly maternal impurity, illuminates the rite in fundamental fashion. I agree that it concerns an alliance with the God of the chosen people; but what the male is separated from, the other that circumcision carves out on his very sex, is the other sex, impure, defiled. By repeating the natural scar of the umbilical cord at the location of sex, by duplicating and thus displacing through ritual the preeminent separation, which is that from the mother, Judaism seems to insist in symbolic fashion—the very opposite of what is "natural"—that the identity of the speaking being (with his God) is based on the separation of the son from the mother. Symbolic identity presupposes the violent difference of the sexes.

Let me take a further step. The terms, impurity and defilement, that Leviticus heretofore had tied to food that did not conform to the taxonomy of sacred Law, are now attributed to the mother and to women in general. Dietary abomination has thus a parallel—unless it be a foundation—in the abomination provoked by the fertilizable or fertile feminine body (menses, childbirth). Might it be that dietary prohibitions are a screen in a still more radical separating process? Would the dispositions *place-body* and the more elaborate one *speech-logic of differences* be an attempt to keep a being who speaks to his God separated from the fecund mother? In that case, it would be a matter of separating oneself from the phantasmatic power of the mother, that archaic Mother Goddess who actually haunted the imagination of a nation at war with the surrounding polytheism. A phantasmatic mother who also constitutes, in the specific history of each person, the abyss that must be established as an autonomous (and not encroaching) *place* and *distinct* object, meaning a *signifiable* one, so that such a person might learn to speak. At any rate, that evocation of defiled maternality, in Leviticus 12, inscribes the logic of dietary abominations within that of a limit, a boundary, a border between the sexes, a separation between feminine and masculine as foundation for the organization that is "clean and proper," "individual," and, one thing leading to another, signifiable, legislatable, subject to law and morality.

After that confrontation with the boundary between the sexes, the biblical text continues its journey fully within the image of the body and its limits.

BOUNDARIES OF THE SELF'S CLEAN AND PROPER BODY

Chapters 13 and 14 of Leviticus locate impurity in leprosy: skin tumor, impairment of the cover that guarantees corporeal integrity, sore on the visible, presentable surface. To be sure, leprosy does objectively cause serious damages in a people with a strong community life and, moreover, an often nomadic one. But one may note furthermore that the disease visibly affects the skin, the essential if not initial boundary of biological and psychic individuation. From that point of view, the abomination of leprosy becomes inscribed within the logical conception of impurity to which I have already called attention: intermixture, erasing of differences, threat to identity.

The shift taking place between chapters 12 and 13 seems significant to me; it goes from within the maternal body (childbirth, menses) to the decaying body. By means of what turnabout is the mother's interior associated with decay? I have already noted that turning among split subjects (see pp. 53–55). It is reasonable to assume that the biblical text, in its own way, accurately follows the path of an analogous fantasy. Evocation of the maternal body and childbirth induces the image of birth as a violent act of expulsion through which the nascent body tears itself away from the matter of maternal insides. Now, the skin apparently never ceases to bear the traces of such matter. These are persecuting and threatening traces, by means of which the fantasy of the born body, tightly held in a placenta that is no longer nourishing but devastating, converges with the reality of leprosy. One additional step, and one refuses even more drastically a mother with whom pre-Oedipal identification is intolerable. The subject then gives birth to himself by fantasizing his own bowels as the precious fetus of which he is to be delivered; and yet it is an abject fetus, for even if he calls them his own he has no other idea of the bowels than one of abomination, which links him to the ab-ject, to that non-introjected mother who is incorporated as devouring, and intolerable. The obsession of the leprous and decaying body would thus be the fantasy of a self-rebirth on the part of a subject who has not introjected his mother but has incorporated a devouring mother. Phantasmatically, he is the solidary obverse of a cult of the Great Mother: a negative and demanding identification with her imaginary power. Aside from sanitary effectiveness, that is the fantasy that Levitical abominations aim at cutting back or resorbing. Possibly, one could link to the same rejection of nonconformity with corporeal identity the abjection brought about by physical defect:

For whatsoever man he be that hath a blemish, he shall not approach; a blind man, or a lame, or he that hath a flat nose, or any thing superfluous,
    Or a man that is brokenfooted, or brokenhanded, ...
. . . . he shall not come nigh to offer the bread of his God. (Leviticus 21:18–21)

The body must bear no trace of its debt to nature: it must be clean and proper in order to be fully symbolic. In order to confirm that, it should endure no gash other than that of circumcision, equivalent to sexual separation and/or separation from the mother. Any other mark would be the sign of belonging to the impure, the non-separate, the non-symbolic, the non-holy:

Ye shall not round the corners of your heads, neither shalt thou mar the corners of thy beard.
    Ye shall not make any cuttings in your flesh for the dead, nor print any marks upon you . . . (Leviticus 19:27–28)

Chapter 15 confirms that view: this time it is flow that is impure. Any secretion or discharge, anything that leaks out of the feminine or masculine body defiles. After a reference to sacrifice (chapter 16), we again have a designation of the impurity of blood:

For it is the life of all flesh; the blood of it is for the life thereof: therefore I said unto the children of Israel, Ye shall eat the blood of no manner of flesh: for the life of all flesh is the blood thereof: whosoever eateth it shall be cut off. (Leviticus 17:14)

After the path we have followed, it is easier to understand the various connotations of blood impurity. It takes in the following: prohibition of meat diet (following upon the prohibition against killing), the postdiluvian classification of meat as in conformity or nonconformity with the divine word, the principle of identity without admixture, the exclusion of anything that breaks boundaries (flow, drain, discharge). From food to blood, the loop of prohibitions has no need of being looped, for we are still and from the beginning within the same logic of separation. But we are again led back to the fundamental semanticism of that logic, which persists in positing an agency that is *other* than that of the nutritious, the sanguine, in short, the "natural" maternal.

FROM SEXUAL IDENTITY TO SPEECH AND FROM ABOMINATION TO MORALS

After that firm and clear reminder, the text proceeds anew and henceforth will translate the logical motion of blood and food abomination into contents further removed. In chapter 18, it will be concerned with defining a sexual identity. For that purpose, intercourse between same and same will have to be prohibited—neither promiscuity within families nor homosexuality. Nor can there be contact with another group as constituted by law (human or "natural," that is, always divine): no adultery, no zoophilia. Likewise, in verse 19 of chapter 19,

Ye shall keep my statutes. Thou shalt not let thy cattle gender with a diverse kind: thou shalt not sow thy field with mingled seed: neither shall a garment mingled of linen and woollen come upon thee.

The same condemnation of hybrids and migrant beings can probably be read in the prohibition against leavened bread and the recommendation that azyme be eaten on certain occasions in order to renew ties with the original food of the patriarchs; without the adding of leaven, the elements of such bread have only their own, proper qualities.

We then encounter one of the extreme points of that logic, which masterfully states, after having thus established their foundations, the bases of those separations. It is nothing other but the One God:

Therefore shall ye keep mine ordinance, that ye commit not any one of these abominable customs, which were committed before you, and that ye defile not yourselves therein: I am the Lord your God. (Leviticus 18:30)

And more clearly still, with that emphasis on the divine word as word that is *quoted, transmitted*, always *already prior*:

And the Lord spake unto Moses, saying, Speak unto all the congregation of the children of Israel, and say unto them, Ye shall be holy: for I the Lord your God am holy. (Leviticus 19:1–2)

Henceforth, confronting the "future perfect" of a discourse that is One and transmitted, impurity moves away from the material register and is formulated as profanation of the divine name. At this point in the trajectory, where the separating agency asserts its own pure abstract value ("holy of holies"), the impure will no longer be merely the admixture, the flow, the noncompliant, converging on that "improper and unclean" place, which is the maternal living being. Defilement will now be that which impinges on symbolic oneness, that is, sham, substitutions, doubles, idols. "Turn ye not unto idols, nor make to yourselves molten gods: I am the Lord, your God" (Leviticus 19:4). Similarly,

Ye shall make you no idols nor graven image, neither rear you up a standing image, neither shall ye set up any image of stone in your land, to bow down unto it: for I am the Lord your God. (Leviticus 26:1)

It is moreover in the name of that "I," with whom, through the intermediary of Moses, an entire nation complies, that moral prohibitions, according to the same logic of separation, will follow—those concerning justice, honesty, and truth (Leviticus 19ff).

INCEST TABOO

Deuteronomy takes up again and varies Levitical abominations (14, 22, 32), which in fact underlie the whole biblical text. But the recurrence of a specific trope should be noted; it embodies the asserted logic of separation, and in my view it points to the unconscious foundation of such a persistence: "Thou shalt not seethe a kid in his mother's milk" (Exodus 23:19, 34:26, Deuteronomy 14:21).

A dietary prohibition, therefore, in which there is no question of blood, but in which abomination seems to proceed from another flow that mingles two identities and connotes the bond between the one and the other: milk. A medium that is common to mother and child, a food that does not separate but binds, milk, on account of economic and vital necessities, is nevertheless not prohibited. What is implicated is not milk as food but milk considered in its symbolic value. Abomination does not reside in nourishing but in seething, that is, *cooking* the young goat in its mother's milk; in other words, it amounts to using milk not in terms of a need for survival but according to cultural culinary fancy, which sets up an abnormal bond between mother and child. I agree with J. Soler that this amounts to a metaphor of incest. Such a dietary prohibition must be understood as prohibition of incest, by the same token as prohibitions that enjoin one from taking from a nest the mother with the young or eggs (Deuteronomy 22:6–7), or sacrificing on the same day the cow or ewe with their young (Leviticus 22:28).

Later, when rabbinical legislation strengthens the rules by expanding relations between morals and impurity, the meaning of incestuous impurity seems to subsist. Thus, when we find in the *Midrash Tanhumah* the statement, "In this world I abhor all nations for they are issued of impure seed," the phrase "impure seed" should be understood as "incestuous."

We are thus led to conclude that dietary prohibition, just as the more abstract expressions of Levitical abominations in a logic of differences ordained by a divine "I," are *based upon the prohibition of incest*. Far from being *one* of the semantic values of that tremendous project of separation constituted by the biblical text, the taboo of the mother seems to be its originating mytheme. Not only because psychoanalytic discourse on the one hand and structural anthropology on the other have discovered the fundamental role of incest taboo within any symbolic organization (individual or social); but also and especially because, as we have seen, the biblical text, as it proceeds, comes back, at the intensive moments of its demonstration and expansion, to that mytheme of the archaic relation to the mother. Biblical abjection thus translates a crucial semantics in which the dietary, when it departs from the conformity that can be demanded by the logic of separation, blends with the maternal as unclean and improper coalescence, as undifferentiated power and threat, a defilement to be cut off.

THE PROPHETS, OR INESCAPABLE ABJECTION

If reminders of dietary abomination persist in the Yahwist text, while the Elohist strengthens sociological and moral aspects, this does not prevent the originating "mytheme" from being present everywhere. And yet it is the prophetic strand that carried that "mytheme" into full blossoming. Particularly, through Ezekiel, who inherited from Leviticus the positing of the Law of purity and the Law of holiness, and who wends his way toward a theological distinction between pure and impure. And it is upon the return from exile that the distinction, as Isaiah formulates it, will thoroughly rule the life of Israel. The impure is neither banished nor cut off, it is thrust away but within—right there, working, constitutive.

For your hands are defiled with blood, and your fingers with iniquity; . . . (Isaiah 59:3)

But we are all as an unclean thing, and all our righteousnesses are as filthy rags. (Isaiah 64:6)

A people that provoketh me to anger continually to my face; that sacrificeth in gardens, and burneth incense upon altars of brick;
Which remain among the graves, and lodge in the monuments,

which eat swine's flesh, and broth of abominable things is in their vessels; . . . (Isaiah 65:3–4)

Abjection—dietary, sanguine, and moral—is pushed back within the chosen people, not because they are worse than others, but because in the light of the contract that they alone have entered into, abjection appears as such. The existence and degree of abjection are thus predicated on the very position of the logic of separation. Such at least is the conclusion one can draw from the prophets' insistence upon abjection. As far as the concept of a subjective interiorization of abjection is concerned, that will be the accomplishment of the New Testament.

The logical complicity, the economic inseparability of pure and impure in the Bible, become clear, if need be, thanks to the very word that, in Isaiah, indicates impurity: *t'bh, to'ebah*, an abomination that is also a prohibition (1:13). Henceforth such a notion permeates the entire Bible. On could notice, moreover, as early as Leviticus, for instance, that there was no true opposition between *ṭahor* and *ṭame* since "impure" (see Leviticus 11:7–8, 10, 20) already signified, "impure to you, the faithful to Yahweh" or, "they will make you impure because they are an abomination to Yahweh."[13]

Here we can interpret biblical abomination as the agency of a demoniacal reproduction of the speaking being, whom the compact with God points to, causes to exist, and banishes. Biblical impurity could be "a realized form of demoniacal forces"[14] only to the extent that the prophetic leaven transformed the *dietary abomination* of earlier texts into an inseparable lining, an inherence in the contract or the symbolic condition. Such a demoniacal force (thus not at all autonomous but only intrinsic to and coiled within divine speech) is in fact the *impure*, from which the Temple and the separating divine Speech want to differentiate us, and which appears to the Prophets as non-rejectable, parallel, inseparable from the clean and proper and the identical. What is the demoniacal—an inescapable, repulsive, and yet nurtured abomination? The fantasy of an archaic force, on the near side of separation, unconscious, tempting us to the point of losing our differences, our speech, our life; to the point of aphasia, decay, opprobrium, and death?

One must add, to the prophetic mutation of abjection, the lot the subsequent life of the Jewish nation assigned to it. I shall not go into the details of a history that Neusner has analyzed, particularly in his work on Mishnaic Law.[15] Let me simply recall that the destruction of the Temple transformed rites and beliefs: dietary taboos became even more strict, their moral meaning was strengthened, and the holiness of the Temple extended to the whole of inhabited space. "As long as the Temple remained, the altar was expiatory for Israel, but now each man's table is expiatory for him" (*Berakoth*).

WASTE-BODY, CORPSE-BODY

Contrary to what enters the mouth and nourishes, what goes out of the body, out of its pores and openings, points to the infinitude of the body proper and gives rise to abjection. Fecal matter signifies, as it were, what never ceases to separate from a body in a state of permanent loss in order to become *autonomous, distinct* from the mixtures, alterations, and decay that run through it. That is the price the body must pay if it is to become *clean and proper*. Psychoanalysis has indeed seen that anal dejections constitute the first material separation that is controllable by the human being. It has also deciphered, in that very rejection, the mastered *repetition* of a more archaic separation (from the maternal body) as well as the condition of *division* (high-low), of discretion, of difference, of recurrence, in short the condition of the processes that underpin symbolicity.[16] The biblical abominations, of which we have just seen the oral, dietary anchoring, and which Isaiah (6:5) calls attention to by means of a strikingly condensed statement, "I am a man of unclean lips," are often carried over to waste, dirt—human or animal decay. But allusion to excremental abjection is not lacking either; it is even explicitly mentioned by the Prophets. Thus, Zechariah (3:1–4) presents the high priest Joshua as "clothed with filthy garments" that the Angel orders to be taken away from him, saying, "I have caused thine iniquity to pass from thee"; the word for "filthy" is here *so'im*, excrementious. Or in Ezekiel (4:12), "And thou shalt eat it as barley cakes, and thou shalt bake it with dung that cometh out of man, in their sight." A mouth attributed to the anus: is that not the ensign of a body to be fought against, taken in by its insides, thus refusing to meet the Other? Hence, *logically*, if the priests do not listen to God, "Behold, I will corrupt your seed, and spread dung upon your faces, even the dung of your solemn feasts; and one shall take you away with it" (Malachi 2:3).

But it is the corpse—like, more abstractly, money or the golden calf—that takes on the abjection of waste in the biblical text. A decaying body, lifeless, completely turned into dejection, blurred between the inanimate and the inorganic, a transitional swarming, inseparable lining of a human nature whose life is undistinguishable from the symbolic—the corpse represents fundamental pollution. A body without soul, a non-body, disquieting matter, it is to be excluded from God's *territory* as it is from his *speech*. Without always being impure, the corpse is "accursed of God" (Deuteronomy 21:23): it must not be displayed but immediately buried so as not to pollute the divine earth. Connected nevertheless with excrement and impure on that account ('*erwat davar*, Deuteronomy 24:1), the corpse is to an even greater degree that by means of which the notion of *impurity* slips into that of *abomination* and/or prohibition, *to'ebah*. In other words, if the corpse is waste, transitional matter, mixture, it is above all the opposite of the spiritual, of the symbolic, and of divine law. Impure animals become even more impure once they are dead (Leviticus 11:24–40), contact with their carcasses must be avoided. The human corpse is a fount of impurity and must not be touched (Numbers 19:13ff). Burial is a means of purification: "And seven months shall the house of Israel be burying of [Gog and all his multitude], that they may cleanse the land" (Ezekiel 39:12).

Corpse fanciers, unconscious worshipers of a soulless body, are thus preeminent representatives of inimical religions, identified by their murderous cults. The priceless debt to great mother nature, from which the prohibition of Yahwistic speech separates us, is concealed in such pagan cults.

And when they shall say unto you, Seek unto them that have familiar spirits, and unto wizards that peep and that mutter: should not a people seek unto their God? for the living to the dead? (Isaiah 8:19)

Or again:

[People] which remain among the graves, and lodge in the monuments, which eat swine's flesh, and broth of abominable things is in
their vessels (Isaiah 65:4)

Worshiping corpses on the one hand, eating objectionable
meat on the other: those are the two abominations that bring
about divine malediction and thus point to the two ends of the
chain of prohibitions that binds the biblical text and entails, as
I have suggested, a whole range of sexual or moral prohibitions.

ABOMINATION OF CORPSES WARDS OFF DEATH WISH. TAXONOMY AS MORALS

With the taboo on corpses the assortment of biblical taboos
returns to what we have seen was its point of departure. One
remembers that dietary taboos had been spelled out after Noah's
burnt offerings to God and that, particularly throughout Leviticus, prohibitions accompanied the requirements of sacrifice.
The two logical strands that run through the biblical text to be
joined together at the time of burnt offerings or separated later
on, sacrifice and abomination, reveal their true interdependence
at the moment when the corpse topples from being the object
of *worship* over to being the object of *abomination*. Taboo appears
then as a counterbalance to sacrifice. Strengthening the system
of prohibitions (dietary or other) becomes more and more important to the spiritual scene, and that constitutes the true symbolic covenant with God. *Prohibiting instead of killing*—such is
the lesson of the proliferation of biblical abominations. Separation at the same time as union; taboo and sacrifice partake of
the logic that sets up symbolic order.

But one must stress what differentiates those two currents
beyond their similarity. The killed object, from which I am
separated through sacrifice, while it links me to God it also sets
itself up, in the very act of being destroyed, as desirable, fascinating, and sacred. What has been killed subdues me and
brings me into subjection to what has been sacrificed. To the

contrary, the abjected object from which I am separated through abomination, if it guarantees a pure and holy law, turns me aside, cuts me off, and throws me out. The abject tears me away from the indifferentiated and brings me into subjection to a system. In short, the abominate is a response to the sacred, its exhaustion, its ending. The biblical text does away with sacrifice, particularly human sacrifice: Isaac is not offered to God. If Judaism remains a religion due to the sacrificial act, which persists in order to insure the metaphorical, vertical relation of the officiating priest to the One Alone, that foundation is largely compensated by the considerable expansion of the prohibitions that take over from it and transform its economy into a metonymic, horizontal concatenation. A religion of abomination overlays a religion of the sacred. It marks the exit of religion and the unfolding of morals; or leading back the One that separates and unifies, not to the fascinated contemplation of the sacred, from which it separates, but to the very device that it ushers in: logic, abstraction, rules of systems and judgments. When the victim is changed into an abomination, a deep qualitative change takes place: the religion that ensues, even if it continues to harbor sacrifice, is no longer a sacrificial religion. It tempers the fascination of murder; it gets around its desire by means of the abomination it associates with any act of incorporation and rejection of an ob-ject, thing or living being. What you sacrifice by swallowing, like what you suppress by rejecting, nourishing mother or corpse, are merely pre-texts of the symbolic relation that links you to Meaning. Use them to give existence to the One, but do not make them sacred in themselves. Nothing is sacred outside of the One. At the limit, everything that remains, all remainders, are abominable.

Contrary to accepted interpretation, René Girard maintains that Christian religion breaks with sacrifice as the condition of the sacred and the social contract. Christ, far from being a scapegoat, indeed offers himself to a death-and-resurrection that causes sin to be visited on all members of the community and on each individually, instead of absolving them; it thus prepared them for a (phantasmatic?) society without violence.[17] Whatever interest that argument might or might not have, one thing is clear: it is the Bible, particularly through its emphasis on abominations, that starts the process of going beyond a sacrificial concept of the social and/or symbolic contract. Not only shall you not kill, but you shall not sacrifice anything without observing rules and prohibitions. The tenth chapter of Leviticus brings in as clear consequence all the regulations concerning dietary taboo. The law of purity and holiness that ensues is what replaces sacrifice.

As a lay person, I might ask what that Law is. It is what curtails sacrifice. The law, in other words what restrains the desire to kill, is a taxonomy. Even if it is only after the period of exile, and in place of earlier tribal rules, that homicide becomes the object of a *sacred* law that changes murder into defilement for Israel and establishes rules for atonement, the very idea of homicide as an offense to God is present throughout the biblical text.[18] "Whoso sheddeth man's blood, by man shall his blood be shed" (Genesis 9:6); "So ye shall not pollute the land wherein ye are: for blood it defileth the land: and the land cannot be cleansed of the blood that is shed therein, but by the blood of him that shed it" (Numbers 35:33).

Death drive, in such an adjustment, does not disappear on that account. Checked, it becomes displaced and builds a logic. If abomination is the lining of my symbolic being, "I" am therefore heterogeneous, pure and impure, and as such always potentially condemnable. I am from the very beginning subject to persecution as well as to revenge. The infinite meshing of expulsions and hazings, of divisions and inexorable, abominable reprisals is then thrown into gear. The system of abominations sets in motion the persecuting machine in which I assume the place of the victim in order to justify the purification that will separate me from that place as it will from any other, from all others. Mother and death, both abominated, abjected, slyly build a victimizing and persecuting machine at the cost of which I become subject of the Symbolic as well as Other of the Abject. "Ye shall be holy and made holy, separate (*pureshim*) from the nations of the world and their abominations" (the *Mekhilta* on "And ye shall be unto me a kingdom of priests, and an holy nation"—Exodus 19:6).

∽ 5

. . . QUI TOLLIS PECCATA MUNDI

To breed out of mankind a self-contradiction, an art of self-defilement, a will to lie at any cost, a revulsion, a scorn for all good and upright instincts! [. . .] I call Christianity [. . .] the immortal defiling of mankind.

Nietzsche, The Antichrist

INSIDE/OUTSIDE

It is through abolishment of dietary taboos, partaking of food with pagans, verbal and gestural contact with lepers, as well as through its power over impure spirits that the message of Christ is characterized and, as is well known, compels recognition in a most spectacular manner—superficial perhaps but striking. Those indications should not be construed as simply anecdotal or empirical, nor as drastic staging of a polemic with Judaism. What is happening is that a new arrangement of differences is being set up, an arrangement whose economy will regulate a wholly different system of meaning, hence a wholly different speaking subject. An essential trait of those evangelical attitudes or narratives is that abjection is no longer exterior. It is permanent and comes from within. Threatening, it is not cut off but is reabsorbed into speech. Unacceptable, it endures through the subjection to God of a speaking being who is innerly divided and, precisely through speech, does not cease purging himself of it.

Such an interiorization of abjection, before being effected through the assumption of Christic subjectivity within the Trinity, is brought about through an expedient that takes over Levitical abominations but changes their location. That expedient is *oralization*, which the New Testament will try to rehabilitate, render guiltless, before inverting the pure/impure dichotomy into an outside/inside one.

The New Testament texts of chapters 15 in Matthew and 16 in Mark compress the event that opens out on a new logic. After having noted that the Pharisees' faith is completely centered in appearances (too strongly tied to orality?)—"This people honoureth me with their lips, but their heart is far from me" (Mark 7:6)—Jesus affirms, "Not that which goeth into the mouth defileth a man; but that which cometh out of the mouth, this defileth a man" (Matthew 15:11); and also, "There is nothing from without a man, that entering into him can defile him: but things which come out of him, those are they that defile the man" (Mark: 15).

Other instances give evidence that the emphasis is henceforth placed on the inside/outside boundary, and that the threat comes no longer from outside but from within. "But rather give alms of such things as ye have; and, behold, all things are clean unto you" (Luke 11:41); "Thou blind Pharisee, cleanse first that which is within the cup and platter, that the outside of them may be clean also" (Matthew 23:26); "Woe unto you, scribes and Pharisees, hypocrites! for ye are like unto whited sepulchres, which indeed appear beautiful outward, but are within full of dead men's bones, and of all uncleanness. Even so ye also outwardly appear righteous unto men, but within ye are full of hypocrisy and iniquity" (Matthew 23:27–28). While it is true that reminders of Levitical positions are not lacking (thus, in 2 Corinthians 6:17 to 7:1, "Wherefore come out from among them, and be ye separate, saith the Lord, and touch not the unclean thing, and I will receive you," and so forth), the interiorization of impurity is in progress everywhere: "For, when we were come into Macedonia, our flesh had no rest, but we were troubled on every side; without were fightings, within were fears" (2 Corinthians 7:5).

But let me go back to texts by Matthew and Mark who take more time with that reversal. The already quoted Christic speech, "There is nothing from without a man, that entering

whoa
*

into him can defile him: but the things which come out of him,
those are they that defile the man," and so forth, is in each case
preceded by the reproach, directed at the Pharisees, for hon-
oring God too much and their fathers and mothers too little.
It is thus an appeal to the recognition not so much of a Law
as of a concrete, genetic, and social authority—a natural one,
so to speak—that leads to the interiorization of impurity.
Through re-cognition of your parents, that which is external
threat to you will appear as internal danger. The verses that
follow are even more definite in the invitation to mend the
initial filial relationship.

FROM FOOD TO EARS: A MOTHER

A woman who was "a Syrophenician by nation" (Mark 7:26)
or else a "lost sheep of the house of Israel" (Matthew 15:24)
asks for help in order to "cast forth the devil out of her
daughter" (Mark 7:26). "But Jesus said unto her, Let the children first be filled: for it is not meet to take the children's bread
and cast it unto the dogs" (Mark 7:27). And it is only after the
mother answers, "the dogs under the table eat of the children's
crumbs," that Christ will acknowledge the recovery of her
daughter, the devil having gone out of the child's body. It is
as if the mother had to agree to "fill" her child, give her a
privileged food, distinct from the "crumbs" for dogs, before
the devil would go away and the woman open her heart to the
words of Christ.

The nutritive opening up to the other, the full acceptance of
archaic and gratifying relationship to the mother, pagan as it
might be, and undoubtedly conveying paganistic connotations
of a prolific and protective motherhood, is here the condition
for another opening—the opening up to symbolic relations,
true outcome of the Christic journey. For after the reconciliation
between mother and daughter through the agency of satisfying
nourishment, it is a deaf-mute whom Christ relieves: "And he
took him aside from the multitude, and put his fingers into his
ears, and he spit, and touched his tongue; And looking up to
heaven, he sighed, and said unto him, Ephphatha, that is, Be

Opened. And straightaway his ears were opened, and the string of his tongue was loosed, and he spake plain" (Mark 7:33–35).

As in analytic process, the reader of the New Testament is led, by elaborating on the archaic relation to his parents, particularly the oral relation to his mother, to introject the drive-quality attached to archaic objects. Now, without that introjection, pre-objects and abjects threaten from without as impurity, defilement, abomination, and eventually they trigger the persecutive apparatus. Nevertheless, that introjection, aiming to salve, is not trouble free. For evil, thus displaced *into* the subject, will not cease tormenting him from within, no longer as a polluting or defiling substance, but as the ineradicable repulsion of his henceforth divided and contradictory being.

One can find an exemplary tale of such an interiorization of impurity in the Oxyrhynchus papyrus number 840.[1] Accused by a Pharisee of having entered the Temple without taking a bath, while the Pharisee considers himself pure because he bathed, Jesus answers: " . . . you have cleansed that *outer skin*, the skin that whores and flute players also anoint, bathe, cleanse, and adorn in order to arouse men's lust, whereas *inside they are filled with scorpions* and all kinds of wickedness. As for me (and my disciples), who *did not bathe*, according to you, we did bathe in the *running* (and pure?) *waters* that come from the Father (who is in heaven?). But woe unto them . . ."

THE INTERIORIZATION OF BIBLICAL SEPARATION

Through the process of interiorization, defilement will blend with guilt, which already exists on a moral and symbolic level in the Bible. But out of the merger with the more material, object-like abomination, a new category will be established—Sin. Swallowed up, one might say reabsorbed, Christian defilement is by that token a revenge of paganism, a reconciliation with the maternal principle. Freud moreover stressed the point in *Moses and Monotheism*, revealing that Christian religion is a compromise between paganism and Judaic monotheism. Biblical logic remains nevertheless, even though it is inverted (the inside is to blame, no longer the outside): one uncovers it in the persistence of processes of division, separation, and differentiation.

But this time that logic functions exclusively in the signifying universe of the speaking being, rent between two potentialities, demoniacal and divine. Maternal principle, reconciled with the subject, is not for that matter revalorized, rehabilitated. Of its nourishing as much as threatening heterogeneity, later texts, and even more so theological posterity, will keep only the idea of sinning flesh. On that pivotal point, the New Testament will propose a subtle elaboration of the splitting that contemporary analytic listening discovers in so-called split subjects: the boundary between inside and outside. Before any relation to an other is set up, and as if underlying it, it is the building of that archaic space, the topological demarcation of the preconditions of a subjectivity, qua difference between a sub-ject and an ab-ject in the be-spoken being itself, that takes over from earlier Levitical abominations. "Kill, and eat," says God to an astonished Peter at Joppa (Acts 10:9–16). But that permission, far from being a liberalization, will lead the subject who complies with it to seek no longer his defilement but the error within his own thoughts and speech.

DIVISION AND MULTIPLICATION

It is equally remarkable that Jesus' pronouncement concerning man's defilement by what *emanates* from him, rather than by what enters, is preceded and followed by two tales of multiplication of bread and fishes (Mark 6:38ff. and 8:14ff.). The word for "bread," *artos*, is repeated seventeen times in this section, as if to provide it with unity. Several lines of thought appear to converge on that article of multiplication. If there is, on the one hand, a concern for "satisfying" the hunger of the greatest possible number, it is, once again, to the spirit that the food seems destined, for Jesus does not cease calling upon understanding to decipher the meaning of his action. Satisfied physiological hunger gives way to unsatiable spiritual hunger, a striving for what "it could possibly mean." Ultimately, does not the multiplication of the food, miraculous though it may be, show how petty excessive fixation on *one* object of need can be, that object becoming the *single*, obsessive goal of existence? Even more so, does not that multiplication of dietary objects also constitute (taking into account the inward displacement of emphasis) a sort of invitation to multiply, if not relativize, conscience itself? It is no longer one but polyvalent, as is the entirely parabolic, fictional meaning of the miracle. The interiorization of abomination as sin, in the New Testament, would thus be not only a centering but even more so the condition, on the basis of that center, of pluralizing the object as well as the subject.

The tie between the multiplication of loaves and the Eucharist is well known; it is established by another of Christ's statements, this time bringing together body and bread, "This is my body." By surreptitiously mingling the theme of "devouring" with that of "satiating," that narrative is a way of taming cannibalism. It invites a removal of guilt from the archaic relation to the first pre-object (ab-ject) of need: the mother.

FROM ABOMINATION TO LAPSE AND LOGIC.
FROM SUBSTANCE TO ACTION

Through oral-dietary satisfaction, there emerges, beyond it, a lust for swallowing up the other, while the fear of impure nourishment is revealed as deathly drive to devour the other. A primal fantasy if ever there was one, that theme unremittingly accompanies the tendency toward interiorizing and spiritualizing the abject. It acts as a pedestal for it; man is a spiritual, intelligent, knowing, in short, speaking being only to the extent that he is recognizant of his abjection—from repulsion to murder—and interiorizes it as such, that is, symbolizes it. The *division* within Christian consciousness[2] finds in that fantasy, of which the Eucharist is the catharsis, its material anchorage and logical node. Body and spirit, nature and speech, divine nourishment, the body of Christ, assuming the guise of a natural food (bread), signifies me both as divided (flesh and spirit) and infinitely lapsing. I am divided and lapsing with respect to my ideal, Christ, whose introjection by means of numerous communions sanctifies me while reminding me of my incompletion. Because it identified abjection as a fantasy of devouring, Christianity effects its abreaction. Henceforth reconciled with it, the Christian subject, completely absorbed into the symbolic, is no longer a being of abjection but a lapsing subject.

In consequence of this placement of subjective space, *judgment* henceforth prevails over the preestablished dichotomy between pure and impure: "But let a man examine himself, and so let him eat of that bread, and drink of that cup. For he that eateth and drinketh unworthily, eateth and drinketh damnation to himself, not discerning the Lord's body" (1 Corinthians 11:28–29). A spiritualization of both the purity/impurity distinction and the inside/outside division of subjective space is thus effected. The *understanding* of the disciples is being appealed to, in order to have them comprehend that the outside of man cannot possibly defile him: "And are ye so without *understanding* also? Do ye not *perceive* that whatsoever thing from without entereth into the man, it cannot defile him" (Mark 7:18). The culmination of that interiorization doubtless lies in the proposition that impurity is a matter for the subject himself to decide: "I know, and I am persuaded by the Lord Jesus, that there is nothing unclean of itself; but to him that esteemeth any thing to be unclean, to him it is unclean" (Romans 14:14). Thus subordinated to judgment and dependent upon the subject, the impure (or impious) assumes the status not of a *substance* that is cut off but of an *action* that is indecent. Sin is an action; theologians speak of "peccaminous" acts.

And yet, if it is true that the notion of sin carried that spirituality far, it is nevertheless upon a body that its highest development rests: the body of Christ. Purifying, redeeming all sins, it punctually and temporarily gives back innocence by means of communion. To eat and drink the flesh and blood of Christ means, on the one hand, to transgress symbolically the Levitical prohibitions, to be symbolically satiated (as at the fount of a good mother who would thus expel the devils from her daughter) and to be reconciled with the substance dear to paganism. By the very gesture, however, that corporealizes or incarnates speech, all corporeality is elevated, spiritualized, and sublimated. Thus one might say that if the inside/outside boundary is maintained, osmosis nevertheless takes place between the spiritual and the substantial, the corporeal and the signifying—a heterogeneity that cannot be divided back into its components.[3]

A HETEROGENEOUS BODY—CHRIST

Christ alone, because he accomplished that heterogeneity, is a body without sin. What others must do, because of their fault, is to achieve that sublimation, confess the part of themselves that rebels against divine judgment, a part that is innerly impure.

Because the unrivaled existence of Christ is nevertheless the vanishing point of all fantasies and thus a universal object of faith, everyone is allowed to aspire to Christic sublimation and by the same token know that his sins can be remitted. "Your sins will be forgiven," Jesus keeps telling them, thus accomplishing, in the future this time, a final raising into spirituality of a nevertheless inexorable carnal remainder.

Sin then remains the only token of difference from the sublimity of Christ. In a universe where differences are resorbed through the effort of an ideal identification with the experience of Christ—an impossible one from the very start—Sin, even if its remission is always promised, remains the rock where one endures the human condition as separate: body and spirit, body jettisoned from the spirit; as a condition that is impossible, irreconcilable, and, by that very token, real.

SIN AS DEBT, HOSTILITY, AND INIQUITY

"Confessing sins," "remitting sins"—such phrases are probably liturgic in origin, but in themselves they already define sins as inherent in speech and slated for release; one encounters in them the notions that bespeak the sin-laden act: amartia, debt, and anomia, iniquity.

Clearly Judaic in spirit, debt points to a ruthless creditor and assigns the subject to the place of the debtor whose infinite payment will fill the distance that separates him from God only by means of a faith indefinitely maintained. The parallel between the sins against the Father and our debt to our neighbors is well known. The verbal use of the term is also corroborated. In Matthew 18:21–22 the verb *amartenein* is used to refer to a "sin" against one's brother man, while Paul (Acts 25:8) asserts he has "offended" (*emarton*) "neither against the law of the Jews, neither against the temple, nor yet against Caesar"; and in 1 Corinthians 8:12 he avers that "when ye sin (*amartanontes*) so against the brethren, and wound their weak conscience, ye sin against Christ (*eis Christon amartanete*)."

Especially with Matthew, or it so seems, there is a more specific use of the word *anomia* when referring to sin as general hositility to God. This meaning, peculiar to the Qumran scrolls, often directly refers to the Biblical text itself (Psalms 6:8, 9 for instance). "Depart from me, ye that work iniquity" (Matthew 7:23); "And because iniquity shall abound, the love of many shall wax cold" (Matthew 24:12), and especially: "Even so ye also outwardly appear righteous unto men, but within ye are full of hyprocrisy and iniquity" (Matthew 23:28).

John also wrote that "sin is the transgression of the law" (1 John 3:4), and even if many commentators note that *a-nomia*, in this instance—as elsewhere in the New Testament—should not be connected with *nomos*, it is indeed a transgression of divine jurisdiction, akin to that of the Torah, that is involved in that definition. Is not the sinner the one who places himself under the rule of Satan, by virtue of his breaking away from the new "commandments" (*entole*) of Christ (1 John 4:21)?

On the level of debt and iniquity, even more so than that of impurity, sin is set forth as constitutive of man, coming to him from the depth of his heart, thus recalling the original sin of Adam. "O generation of vipers, how can ye, being evil, speak good things? for out of the abundance of the heart the mouth speaketh" (Matthew 12:34). As *debt* and *iniquity*, breach of duty or injustice, sin is an act and is proven to be within man's jurisdiction, within the scope of his own responsibility. Here then is the list of sins according to the Gospels, which Paul will expand: "For from within, out of the heart of men, proceed evil thoughts, adulteries, fornications, murders, thefts, covetousness, wickedness, deceit, lasciviousness, an evil eye, blasphemy, pride, foolishness" (Mark 7:21–22; in Matthew 15:19 the number of sins is down to seven).

Now it is precisely the sinner and not the righteous whom Christ addresses, and his major role is to drive out evil spirits and devils, to remit sins. The heterogeneity of Christ, Son of both Man and God, resorbs and cleanses the demoniacal. Such heterogeneity does not cease revealing the moral and symbolic existence of infamy; nevertheless, as it is communicated to the sinner by means of his very being, it saves him from the abject.

THE DOORS OF THE INQUISITION

Based in large part on the idea of *retribution*, the notion of sin doubtless leads one to adopt a behavior and speech of conformity, obedience, and self-control under the ruthless gaze of the Other—Justice, Good, or Golden Mean. Basis of asceticism at the same time as it is coiled in judgment, sin guides one along the straitest paths of superego spirituality. It holds the keys that open the doors to Morality and Knowledge, and at the same time those of the Inquisition.

But what will now hold our attention is that sin is also the requisite of the Beautiful. On that plane, through an additional twist, the Law of the Other becomes reconciled with Satan. As a result, the Christian self-contradiction that Nietzsche denounced, once its inimical parts have been reconciled, constitutes the requisite for jouissance. The episode of Christ and the repentant sinner, the woman who "stood at his feet behind him weeping, and began to wash his feet with tears, and did wipe them with the hairs of her head, and kissed his feet, and anointed them with the ointment" (Luke 7:38) conveys that meaning. Contrary to the prophet who, according to the Pharisee, would have recognized impurity in this woman and withdrawn from her, Christ gives himself up to it, deluged with a kind of overflowing—of sin or love? It is, at any rate, the overflow of an interior flux and its ambiguity bursts forth in that scene. Sin, turned upside down into love, attains, on account of the ambivalence, the beauty that Hegel tells us is displayed right here for the one and only time in the Gospels. "Wherefore I say unto thee, Her sins, which are many, are forgiven; for she loved much: but to whom little is forgiven, the same loveth little" (Luke 7:47).

SIN AS REQUISITE FOR THE BEAUTIFUL

Neither debt nor want, sin, as the reverse side of love, is a state of fullness, of plenty. In that sense, it turns around into living beauty. Far from advocating solely a doctrine of limitation and conformity to divine speech, the Christian conception of sin also includes a recognition of an evil whose power is in direct ratio to the holiness that identifies it as such, and into which it can convert. Such a conversion into jouissance and beauty goes far beyond the retributive, legalistic tonality of sin as debt or iniquity. Thus it is that, by means of the beautiful, the demoniacal dimension of the pagan world can be tamed. And that the beautiful penetrates into Christianity to the extent of becoming not merely one of its component parts, but also probably what leads it beyond religion.

AN OVERFLOWING OF DESIRE

The idea of "want" tied to sin as debt and iniquity is therefore coupled with that of an overflowing, a profusion, even an unquenchable desire, which are pejoratively branded with words like "lust" or "greed." *Pleonexia*, greed, is etymologically the desire "to possess always more"; it connotes an appetite that cannot possibly be sated, and that links it, in the writings of Paul for instance, to sexual transgressions and flesh in general; for the cause of this appetite resides in idolatry as disobedience to divine speech. "Wherefore God also gave them up to uncleanness through the lusts of their own hearts, to dishonour their own bodies between themselves: Who changed the truth of God into a lie [. . .] For this cause God gave them up unto vile affections" (Romans 1:24, 26). "Lust," or *epithumia*, depending directly on the biblical text, also covers sexual desires while relating, particularly in the Old Testament, to food as well as to various material goods.

At any rate, those various descriptions of sin converge on the *flesh* or rather on what might be called, by anticipation, an overwhelming release of drives, unrestrained by the symbolic. "This I say then, Walk in the Spirit, and ye shall not fulfill the lust of the flesh. For the flesh lusteth against the Spirit, and the Spirit against the flesh: and these are contrary the one to the other: so that ye cannot do the things that ye would" (Galatians 5:16–17). The outcome, the *telos* of this carnal overflow can only be death ("For the wages of sin is death," Romans 6:23; "For when we were in the flesh, the motions of sins, which were by the law, did work in our members to bring forth fruit unto death," Romans 7:5), which is what sin leads to.

One of the most complex nodes of Christian or at least Pauline theory is precisely centered in that matter of the *flesh*. For on the one hand, the flesh is plainly marked, echoing later Greek thought, as that from which one should be separated ("Therefore, brethren, we are debtors, not to the flesh, to live after the flesh," Romans 8:12). Whereas, elsewhere, we have the following: "For though we walk in the flesh, we do not war after the flesh" (II Corinthians 10:3), and "The life which I now live in the flesh I live by the faith of the Son of God, who loved me, and gave himself for me" (Galatians 2:20). Displaying more than lack of univocity, it is a heterogeneous conception of the flesh that is being set forth.

In opposition to the peaceful Apollonian (not Dionysiac) Greek corporeality, flesh here signifies according to two modalities: on the one hand, close to Hebraic flesh (*basar*), it points to the "body" as eager drive confronted with the law's harshness; on the other, it points to a subdued "body," a body that is pneumatic since it is spiritual, completely submersed into (divine) speech in order to become beauty and love.

These two "bodies" are obviously inseparable, the second ("sublimated") one unable to exist without the first (perverse because it challenges Law). One of the insights of Christianity, and not the least one, is to have gathered in a single move perversion and beauty as the lining and the cloth of one and the same economy.

MASSA DAMNATA AND METANOIA

The two currents of sin interpretation that have buffeted the Church for centuries appear to have been centered in that particular ambiguity of the flesh. Was Adam a sinner to begin with, or did he become one of his own "free will"? Does not sin have a mortgage on the power of the spirit and grace? If God can grant remission of sin, can a man, a priest do the same? What is meant by the sin of angels? Is sin original and hereditary? And so forth. It is a long story, and if it has officially been brought to a close in the institutions that rule society in our time, it is brought to life again every time a man touches on those areas, those nodes, where symbolicity interferes with his corporeality.

Above all, one will recall Augustine's stance, according to which, man, born blind and ignorant, is unable to observe the law after it has been revealed, "because of some unaccountable constraining resistance due to carnal concupiscence."[4] A created being that is always already evil, even if free will gives it responsibility for sin, such would be the ambiguity of the speaking being. Permanence of sin, existence but restriction of the power of free will—these will fit into a different pattern in the later Augustinian writings: man is good, but his offense turns human beings into a *massa damnata*. It is not absurd to consider that such traces of Manicheism doubtless make of Augustine a precursor of Protestantism but especially the first psychological writer (see the *Confessions*). Through his writing, he follows the delightful interlacing of this inextricable heterogeneity, of this seesawing between the excesses of the flesh and the stern though merciful demands of absolute judgment. In so doing, he shows how damnation, because it depends on spirituality, turns not only into humiliated consent but above all into enraptured conversion or, as he writes, into a *metanoia*, a jouissance.

SIN: OWING TO GOD OR TO WOMAN?

The brimming flesh of sin belongs, of course, to both sexes; but its root and basic representation is nothing other than feminine temptation. That was already stated in *Ecclesiasticus*: "Sin originated with woman and because of her we all perish." The reference to Eve's enticement of Adam is clear, but in other respects it is certain that Paul stigmatizes a much more physical corporeality, one closer to Greek notions of it, when he implants the power of sin within the flesh. And yet, the tale of Adam's fall opens up two additional channels of interpretation throwing light on the ambivalence of sin. The one locates it in relation to God's will and in that sense causes it to be not only original but coexistent with the very act of signification; the other places it within the femininity-desire-food-abjection series.

Let me pause and consider the first point of view, which Hegel calls a "marvelous, contradictory feature."[5] On the one hand, according to the narrative, man before the fall, man in paradise, was to live eternally; since it is sin that leads to death, man without sin was in a state of immortality. On the other hand, however, it is stated that man would be immortal if he ate from the tree of life—the tree of knowledge—hence if he transgressed the prohibition, in short if he sinned. Man would thus accede to divine perfection only by sinning, that is, by carrying out the forbidden act of knowledge. Now, the knowledge that would separate him from his natural, animal, and mortal state, enabling him to reach, through thought, purity and freedom, is fundamentally sexual knowledge. It takes only one further step to suppose that the invitation to perfection is also an invitation to sin, and conversely; perhaps official theology does not take that step, but the mystic grants himself the fathomless depravity of doing so. That is so true that only after having sinned does the mystic topple over into holiness, and his holiness never ceases to appear to him as fringed by sin. Such is the cognitive aspect of the narrative of the fall. In that

instance, the fall is the work of God; founding knowledge and
the quest for consciousness, it opens the way to spirituality.

WOMAN OR ABJECTION RECONCILED

Seen from a different viewpoint, the story of the fall sets up
a diabolical otherness in relation to the divine. Adam is no
longer endowed with the composed nature of paradisiac man,
he is torn by covetous desire: desire for woman—sexual covetousness since the serpent is its master, consuming desire for
food since the apple is its object. He must protect himself from
that sinful food that consumes him and that he craves. We know
how the more material, more organic trend of thought of Levitical texts protects itself from abomination; against revulsion—
abjection. Christian sin, tying its spiritual knot between flesh
and law, does not cut off the abject. No more than the sinner
brought by the Pharisees will the adulterous woman be stoned
to death: "He that is without sin among you, let him first cast
a stone at her" (John 8:7): "Neither do I condemn thee: go and
sin no more" (John 8:11). Meant for remission, sin is what is
absorbed—in and through speech. By the same token, abjection
will not be designated as such, that is, as other, as something
to be ejected, or separated, but as the most propitious place for
communication—as the point where the scales are tipped towards pure spirituality. The mystic's familiarity with abjection
is a fount of infinite jouissance. One may stress the masochistic
economy of that jouissance only if one points out at once that
the Christian mystic, far from using it to the benefit of a symbolic or institutional power, displaces it indefinitely (as happens
with dreams, for instance) within a discourse where the subject
is resorbed (is that grace?) into communication with the Other
and with others. One recalls Francis of Assisi who visited le-
proseries "to give out alms and left only after having kissed
each leper on the mouth"; who stayed with lepers and bathed
their wounds, sponging pus and sores. One might also think
of Angela of Foligno.

A source of evil and mingled with sin, abjection becomes the
requisite for a reconciliation, in the mind, between the flesh

and the law. "It is at once what produces the disease, and the source of health, [it is the poisoned cup in which man drinks death and putrefaction, and at the same time the fount of reconciliation; indeed, to set oneself up as evil is to abolish evil in oneself.]"[6]

LAW AND/OR GRACE

Thus, the Gospel's conception seems to distinguish sin from Adam's downfall. For sin, here, subsuming biblical abjection but more closely associated with the passions of the flesh, must carry out the fearsome process of interiorization and spiritualization that I have just discussed. Paul, who was the first to set forth a coherent doctrine of sin as lust and separation from God, seems to distinguish sin from Adam's transgression (see Romans 5:12–21). Was he held back by the paradox of the primitive human condition, as it has just become manifest to us in the narrative concerning Adam? Or by the fully logical conception of that downfall according to the Bible, distinct from abomination? Or is it because there can be no remission for the original misdeed, because no biblical grace has been promised? Christian doctrine, to the contrary, carries the ambiguity to the point of defining sin through its possible remission: "For until the law sin was in the world: but sin is not imputed when there is no law" (Romans 5:13) and "Moreover the law entered, that the offense might abound. But where sin abounded, grace did much more abound" (Romans 5:20).

One could say, in fact, that sin is subjectified abjection. For, always already determined *ad unum* as Thomas Aquinas submits, the created being, subordinated to God and at the same time separated from him by free will, can commit sin only through willful nonobservance of the rule. It is true that Thomism leads to a spiritual, logical excess, subjectifying the doctrine of sin and taking away its Augustinian delights. And yet one must acknowledge that Aquinas goes back to and develops the notion of logical necessity and freedom of knowledge as coextensive with sin—a notion found in the very first narrative of the fall (what I have called its first aspect; see p. 126). Sin as action—as action stemming from will and judgment—is what definitively integrates abjection into logic and language.

Thomist considerations on the sin of angels is one of the masterly demonstrations of such a consequence. If an angel can sin because it is a created being and does so, for instance, by loving its own natural perfection, sin does not reside in the object (which cannot here be an abject) but in "the inordinate willing of a thing good in itself."[7] Neither desire nor abjection, sin is a logical unruliness, an incongruous act of judgment. If defilement was what is impossible within a system, if Levitical taboo was what is excluded from a Law, sin, on the other hand, is a defect in judgment. The biblical conception remained closer to the concrete truth of the sexed and social being. The conception stemming from the New Testament resorbs the guilt of the previous one and, at the risk of cutting itself off from the coarse and intolerable truth of man that Judaism discloses, offers displacements of it that are perhaps elaborations—communital, logical, esthetic ones. On the one hand, we find the truth of the intolerable; on the other, displacement through denial for some, through sublimation for others.

AVOWAL: CONFESSION

Omologeo and *martireo*, *I acknowledge* and *I bear witness*: in those terms Christians *confess*, hence avow their faith in Christ, as they will later their trinitary faith. Already Christ had "confessed" in this way before Pontius Pilate. The avowal of faith is thus from the very start tied to persecution and suffering. This pain, moreover, has wholly permeated the word "martyr," giving it its basic, ordinary meaning, that of torture rather than testimony. Speech addressed to the other, not sinful speech but the speech of faith, is pain; this is what locates the act of *true communication*, the act of avowal, within the register of persecution and victimization. Communication brings my most intimate subjectivity into being for the other; and this act of judgment and supreme freedom, if it authenticates me, also delivers me over to death. Is this to say that my own speech, all speech perhaps, already harbors in itself something that is mortal, culpable, abject?

No dogma predicates it. One will have to wait for Freud to bring out the heterogeneous aspect of drives, or simply the negativity to which any discourse is prey. But the practice of confession, upon the whole, does nothing else but weigh down discourse with sin. By having it bear that load, which alone grants it the intensity of full communication, avowal absolves from sin and, by the same stroke, founds the power of discourse.

We owe that invention, the whirling wherein the Christian cleavage is resolved in the order of discourse, to an Egyptian hermit, Anthony the Abbot—the same one who fascinated Flaubert. In 271, while preaching to his brethren, he declared: "Let everyone of us take note of and write down his acts and feelings, as if he were to apprise other people of them . . . Just as we shall never fornicate in the presence of witnesses, if we write down our thoughts as if to make them known to others, we shall abstain from obscene thoughts for fear of being found out." Foundation of asceticism and very explicitly of sexual repression, the speech addressed to the other ushers in judgment, shame, and fear. Pachomius (290–346) took up the same point: "It is greatly wrong not to let the state of one's soul immediately be known to a man practised in spiritual discernment." Following on bewailing, prayer or atonement, confession, which is often integral to them—especially in the early days of Christianism or in its fervent practices—nonetheless displaces the stress of the act of penance to the needs of an *other*, a wise man. Consequently, the necessity of *speaking* in order to topple sin into the Other becomes more obvious.

First set aside for monks, later spread to Celtic and Frankish lands, the practice is extended to the laity only in the thirteenth century, by decision of the Fourth Lateran Council. There were discussions, divergences, sectarianism. How does one confess? Who may do it? What is forgiven? And so forth. Such questions will not detain me. But I am concerned with the ultimate interiorization of sin within discourses, by the final postulate that does away with an offense because of its enunciation before the One. An enunciation that amounts to a denunciation.

FELIX CULPA: SPOKEN SIN. DUNS SCOTUS

Little by little, acts of atonement, of contrition, of paying one's debt to a pitiless, judging God, are eclipsed by the sole act of speech. One slides over from the judicial to the verbal. Duns Scotus, the logician, is at the heart of this shift, which amounts to a spiritual revolution, as important no doubt as Christ's verdict to the effect that the impure was not outside but inside of man. Acknowledgment and absolution count for everything, sin has no need for actions in order to be remitted. Duns Scotus writes: "One who . . . wishes to receive the sacrament . . . and who at the moment when those words are spoken wherein lies the efficacy of the sacrament (*in quo scilicet est vis sacramenti istius*) offers no obstacle on account of willing a mortal sin, that one shall receive penitential grace, not by virtue of merit . . . but by virtue of the covenant with God who resolved to be present at his sacrament."[8] An acknowledgment, a covenant with the one who absolves, thanks to the words of an other in the name of the Other—and lust, erroneous judgment, fundamental abjection are remitted—not suppressed, but subsumed into a speech that gathers and restrains.

Is this harassment? Or jubilation? It is owing to speech, at any rate, that the lapse has a chance of becoming fortunate; *felix culpa* is merely a phenomenon of enunciation. The whole black history of the Church shows that condemnation, the fiercest censorship, and punishment are nonetheless the common reality of this practice. For only on the fringes of mysticism, or in rare moments of Christian life, can the most subtle transgression of law, that is to say, the enunciation of sin in the presence of the One, reverberate not as a denunciation but as the glorious counterweight to the inquisitorial fate of confession. This marginal potentiality of spoken sin as fortunate sin provides an anchorage for the art that will be found, resplendent, under all the cupolas. Even during the most odious times of the Inquisition, art provided sinners with the opportunity to live, openly and inwardly apart, the joy of their dissipation set into signs: painting, music, words. "And these signs shall follow them that believe; in my name shall they cast out devils; *they shall speak with new tongues*" (Mark 16:17; emphasis added).

On this peak of discourse, power no longer belongs to the judge-God who preserves humanity from abjection while setting aside for himself alone the prerogative of violence—the violence of separation as well as of punishment. Power henceforth belongs to discourse itself, or rather to the act of judgment expressed in speech and, in less orthodox and much more implicit fashion, in all the signs (poetry, painting, music, sculpture) that are contingent upon it. If such signs do not do away with the necessity for confession, they do spread out the logic of speech even to the most inaccessible folds of significance.

CÉLINE: NEITHER ACTOR
NOR MARTYR

To be mistaken about the rhythm of a sentence is to be mistaken about
the very meaning of that sentence.

Nietzsche, Beyond Good and Evil

The world of illusions—the world of religions—brings to light
or embodies the prohibition that has us speak. Thus, it gives
legitimacy to hatred if it does not *invert* it into love. Embodying,
legitimizing—today we are too aware of their techniques to
yield to them. The worlds of illusions, now dead and buried,
have given way to our dreams and deliriums if not to politics
or science—the religions of modern times. Lacking illusions,
lacking shelter, today's universe is divided between *boredom*
(increasingly anguished at the prospect of losing its resources,
through depletion) or (when the spark of the symbolic is maintained and desire to speak explodes) *abjection* and *piercing laughter*.

Conclusively and publicly—for a broad audience—Céline
anchors the destiny of literature in the latter territory, not that
of the Death of God but a reassumption, *through style*, of what
lies hidden by God.

We are thrown into a strange state when reading Céline.
What is involved goes beyond the content of the novels, the
style of the writing, the author's biography or his indefensible
political stands (fascist, anti-semitic); the true "miracle" of
Céline resides in the very experience of one's reading—it is
fascinating, mysterious, intimately nocturnal, and liberating by
means of a laughter without complacency yet complicitous.
Nearly twenty years after his death, close to half a century after

the publication of *Journey to the End of the Night*, how, where, and why does this Célinian universe challenge us so vigorously?

I do not find within it the delightful interlacing of Proustian sentences, which unfold my memory and that of my language's signs down to the silent, glowing recesses of an odyssey of desire deciphered in and through the fashionable wordliness of his contemporaries. I do not come out of it shaken to the point of exaltation, of dizziness (a torment that some flatten into monotony), as happens when the Sadean narrative machine unveils, beneath the power of terror, the playful reckoning of sexual drive coiled up in death. I do not draw from it the stainless, serene, nostalgic beauty of Mallarmé's always already antiquated arabesque; of Mallarmé who could convert the paroxysms of a funereal psalm into the elliptic markings of a convoluted language. I do not encounter in it the black, romantic rage of Lautréamont who chokes classicism in a fiendish laugh; nor the volleys of Artaud's rhythmical suffering where style performs its function of metaphysically transporting the body to the place of the Other, both being ransacked, but leaving a trace, a gesture, a voice.

Céline's effect is quite other. It calls upon what, within us, eludes defenses, trainings, and words, or else struggles against them. A nakedness, a forlornness, a sense of having had it; discomfort, a downfall, a wound. What people do not acknowledge but know they have in common; a base, mass, or anthropological commonality, the secret abode for which all masks are intended. Céline has us believe that he is true, that he is the only authentic one, and we are ready to follow him, deeply settled in that end of night where he seeks us out; we forget that he can show it to us only because he stands elsewhere—within writing. Actor or martyr? Neither one nor the other, or both at the same time, like a true writer who believes in his wiles. He believes that death and horror are what being is. But suddenly, and without warning, the open sore of his very suffering, through the contrivance of a word, becomes haloed, as he puts it, with "a ridiculous little infinite"[1] as tender and packed full of love and cheerful laughter as it is with bitterness, relentless mockery, and a sense of the morrow's impossibility. Even your cherished abjection belongs to the realm of a puppet show's gang [guignol's band] and the enchantment is postponed until some other time . . . [féerie pour une autre fois] As for jouissance, be it of language, meaning, or transcendence grasped from within, in pure literary style, you are barking up the wrong tree . . . All that remains is the tune, without notes . . . Not even the worship of Death . . . The three dots . . . Less than nothing, or more . . . Something else . . . The consuming of Everything, of Nothing, through style . . . The greatest homage to the Word that was not made flesh in order to hoist itself up into Man with a capital letter but to join, body and language being mingled, those intermediate states, those non-states, neither subject nor object, where *you* is alone, singular, untouchable, unsociable, discredited, at the end of a night that is as particular as it is incommensurable.

When reading Céline we are seized at that fragile spot of our subjectivity where our collapsed defenses reveal, beneath the appearances of a fortified castle, a flayed skin; neither inside nor outside, the wounding exterior turning into an abominable interior, war bordering on putrescence, while social and family rigidity, that beautiful mask, crumbles within the beloved abomination of innocent vice. A universe of borders, seesaws, fragile and mingled identities, wanderings of the subject and its objects, fears and struggles, abjections and lyricisms. At the turning point between social and asocial, familial and delinquent, feminine and masculine, fondness and murder.

We have already traveled through such areas—with *defilement, abomination*, and *sin*—beneath other skies, under other protections. For the contemporary reader, they seem more poignant in Céline than in the reminiscences, archaeological upon the whole, that I cited earlier; this is due no doubt to the fragility, with Céline, of the ideal or prohibiting judging agency, which, in other times and cultures, borders on abjection or indeed causes it to come into being. Here, that agency becomes ambiguous, grows hollow, decays, and crumbles; it is a fleeting, derisory, and even idiotic illusion, which is yet upheld. Neither divinity nor morality, it is the watermark that remains in the darkness and horror of night, allowing such a night, nevertheless, to be written. Agency of exploded, thunder-blasted meaning, and yet sparkingly there: a scription. Neither revolutionary challenge, which would assume belief in a new morality, class, or humanity; nor skeptical doubt, which always takes shelter, in the last resort, within the self-satisfaction of a critical stance that leaves the doors of progress open. It is rather a black explosion, having the power of a devastating implosion, an anarchic one if you wish, provided one rectifies at once: there is no anarchy of writing, since writing orders, regulates, and legislates. What? Nothing, perhaps, and perhaps not. What object? Could it be the ab-ject?

Is it vice? Is it playacting or possibly perversion? Better than that. A yearning after Meaning together with its absorption, ingestion, digestion, and rejection. Power and sin of the word. Without God, without any One other than that which lies under the polylogue of the Célinian symphony—a music, a web, a lacework. A *whirl* of abjection that can be borne, that can be written only if it can *also* provide itself with *objects*, hateful of course, the most stable ones, the most archaic, ensuring the most precise, the most certain jouissance.

His adhering to Nazism, ambivalent and paltry as that action was, is not one that can be explained away. It becomes integrated as an internal necessity, as an inherent counterweight, as a massive need for identity, a group, a project, meaning; thus it crystallizes the *objective* and *illusory reconciliation* between, on the one hand, an ego that drowns in the whirl of its objects and its language and, on the other, the identifying prohibitions—an unbearable, untenable, disintegrating one, which causes him to be. His fascination with Jews, which was full of hatred and which he maintained to the end of his life, the simple-minded anti-Semitism that besots the tumultuous pages of the pamphlets, are no accident; they thwart the disintegration of identity that is coextensive with a scription that affects the most archaic distinctions, that bridges the gaps insuring life and meaning. Céline's anti-Semitism, like political commitment, for others—like, as a matter of fact, any political commitment, to the extent that it settles the subject within a socially justified illusion—is a security blanket. A delirium, to be sure, but one whose social unfolding and multiple rationalizations are well known; a *delirium* that literally prevents one from going mad, for it postpones the senseless abyss that threatens this passing through the identical, which is what scription amounts to.

His novels are realistic out of social constraint and, to some extent, out of hatred;[2] or rather they are legends, but also music, dance, emotions, notes edged with silence—Céline's texts, and this has been said only too often, are in bad form. Obviously, one could read them by following the meanderings of the narrative, which, similar to those of well-known storytellers, is picaresque or biographical at the beginning (*Journey to the End of the Night, Death on the Instalment Plan*), then bursts its shell and veers toward the polyphony of *North* and *Rigadoon* after going through the carnival of *Guignol's Band* and *Le Pont de Londres* ["London Bridge"]. And yet a more specifically Célinian feature is the drowning of narrative in a style, which, from the *Journey* to *Rigadoon*, is gradually decanted; more and more incisive, precise, eschewing seduction in favor of cruelty, it is nevertheless haunted by the same concern—to touch the intimate nerve, to grab hold of emotion by means of speech, to make writing oral, in other words, contemporaneous, swift, obscene. If that scription is a struggle, it is not won through the expedient of Oedipal identifications generated by narrative but through much deeper, more remote, and riskier probes. Such probings, which tamper with vocabulary and syntax, relate the Célinian experience not to the novelist's verisimilitude but to the inhumanity of the poet. An inhumanity that resides in his very words; it is hence most radical, affecting mankind's ultimate guarantee—language. In the wake of a black lineage where Lautréamont or Artaud is inscribed, inhumanity discovers its appropriate themes, contrary to all lyrical traditions, in horror, death, madness, orgy, outlaws, war, the feminine threat, the horrendous delights of love, disgust, and fright.

Those are the themes, then, that I am, *seemingly*, going to deal with in Céline. My reading, however, will not be a thematic one, first because of the very themes involved, but mainly because, with Céline, such themes always assume at least a double stance between disgust and laughter, apocalypse and carnival.

Any *fictional theme* is, by definition, a challenge to the *single* signified since it is a polyvalent signified, a "blasting of selfhood" (Georges Bataille). This is no doubt so because the fantasies that nourish such a theme converge on that impossible focus, that unthinkable "origin" constituted by the scene of scenes, the so-called primal scene.[3] In another connection, Bakhtin has shown that there is a fundamental dialogism, a basic bivalence in any speech, word, or utterance in novels stemming from carnivalesque tradition (Dostoyevsky's novels, for instance).[4] Céline brings to its paroxysmal climax this technique, which constitutes a way of being. Can one tell whether the bombing of Hamburg, as written by Céline, represents the height of tragedy or the most cavalier mockery of mankind? Does Titus van Claben's combination of orgy, murder, and fire express the horror of a sickening human condition, or is it an extravagant farce about a few cookies who are more or less smart? To the carnival's semantic ambivalences, which pair the high and the low, the sublime and the abject, Céline adds the merciless crashing of the *apocalypse*. And end-of-the-world flavor exudes from that disgust for mankind in the midst of the Second World War—and this with or without politics. An invisible sword of judgments weighs on Céline's universe more heavily than God (a permissive one, upon the whole) did on medieval carnival and its altogether Christian sequels, Dostoyevsky included. It is the invisible sword of a non-existent God— neither transcendency nor Man, no capital letters, save the place, "Nothing shall have taken place but the place" (Mallarmé). A sword that is perhaps not even an instance but a distance—an ideal and a superego, a being-removed, which cause horror to exist and at the same time take us away from it, grip us with fear and by that very fright change language into a quill, a fleeting and piercing one, a work of lace, a show of acrobatics, a burst of laughter and a mark of death.

. . . *one has to be more than somewhat dead in order to be truly a wisecracker!* That's it! You have to have been *removed* from the spot.[5]

As for me, alas, all I have is a kind of cavalier outlook on instincts and life—I am neither overindulgent nor sensual. I am "removed," serious, classic in my delirium—constructive—That is perhaps where I come close to the great—but that's all . . .[6]

ᔥ 7

SUFFERING AND HORROR

One can be a virgin with respect to Horror as one is virgin toward
Voluptuousness.*

Céline, Journey to the End of the Night

THE NARRATIVE AS CACHE FOR SUFFERING

"In the beginning was emotion . . . ," Céline often repeated
in his writings and interviews. Reading him, one has the impression that in the beginning was discomfort.

Suffering as the place of the subject. Where it emerges, where
it is differentiated from chaos. An incandescent, unbearable
limit between inside and outside, ego and other. The initial,
fleeting grasp: "suffering," "fear," ultimate words sighting the
crest where sense topples over into the senses, the "intimate"
into "nerves." Being as ill-being.

Céline's narrative is a narrative of suffering and horror, not
only because the "themes" are there, as such, but because his
whole narrative stance seems controlled by the necessity of
going through abjection, whose intimate side is suffering and
horror its public feature.

This much is becoming known after so much "Russian for-
malism" but also after so many biographies confided on the
couch: a narrative is, all in all, the most elaborate attempt, next
to syntactic competence, to situate a speaking being between
his desires and their prohibitions, in short, within the Oedipal
triangle.

But not until the advent of twentieth-century "abject" lit-

---

*On est puceau de l'Horreur comme on est puceau de la Volupté.

erature (the sort that takes up where apocalypse and carnival left off) did one realize that the narrative web is a thin film constantly threatened with bursting. For, when narrated identity is unbearable, when the boundary between subject and object is shaken, and when even the limit between inside and outside becomes uncertain, the narrative is what is challenged first. If it continues nevertheless, its makeup changes; its linearity is shattered, it proceeds by flashes, enigmas, short cuts, incompletion, tangles, and cuts. At a later stage, the unbearable identity of the narrator and of the surroundings that are supposed to sustain him can no longer be *narrated* but *cries out* or is *descried* with maximal stylistic intensity (language of violence, of obscenity, or of a rhetoric that relates the text to poetry). The narrative yields to a *crying-out theme* that, when it tends to coincide with the incandescent states of a boundary-subjectivity that I have called abjection, is the crying-out theme of suffering-horror. In other words, the theme of suffering-horror is the ultimate evidence of such states of abjection within a narrative representation. If one wished to proceed farther still along the approaches to abjection, one would find neither narrative nor theme but a recasting of syntax and vocabulary—the violence of poetry, and silence.

"DECAY IN ABEYANCE . . ."

Everything is already contained in the *Journey*: suffering, horror, death, complicitous sarcasm, abjection, fear. And the pit where what speaks is a strange rent between an ego and an other—between *nothing* and *all*. Two extremes that moreover change places, Bardamu and Arthur, and give an aching body to that endless synthesis, that journey without end; a narrative between apocalypse and carnival.

It all began just like that. I had said *nothing*. I hadn't said a word. It was Arthur Ganate who started me off. (J, 3)

Everything was mine that evening; it all belonged only to me. I had the moon to myself and the village and a tremendous sense of *fear*. (J, 34)

It is of men, and of them only, that one should always be *frightened*. (*J*, 11)

Did none of them [the letters from the general to the colonel] contain the order to put an immediate stop to this *abomination*? Was he not being told by HQ that there was some misunderstanding, some *abominable* mistake? (*J*, 10; emphasis added in all four excerpts)

Obviously the atrocities of war are given as the true cause of *fear*. But its violent, quasi-mystical permanence raises it from the level of political or even social contingency (where it would be due to oppression) to another level; fear becomes a *token of humanity*, that is, of an appeal to *love*.

Don't imagine it's as easy as all that to fall asleep once you have begun to disbelieve everything, mostly because of all the times you have been frightened. (*J*, 199–200)

. . . you'll surely finish up by finding out what it is that frightens all these bloody people so, and it's probably somewhere at the farther end of the night. (*J*, 218–219)

. . . an emotion of exceptional trust, which in timid people takes the place of love. (*J*, 227)

And also:

Fear can't be cured, Lola. (*J*, 61)

Just as,

When one's in this world, surely the best thing one can do, isn't it, is to get out of it? Whether one's mad or not, frightened or not. (*J*, 56)

Or the mother who is nothing but sorrow stuffed with fear:

It was as if she was afraid of this cause for sorrow; it was full of sinister things that she did not understand. (*J*, 93)

And finally, quite as expected, this definition of outmoded art, the kind that Céline breaks away from in order to assert the truth of art as unacknowledged fear:

Happiness on earth would consist of dying with pleasure, in the midst of pleasure . . . The rest amounts to nothing at all, it's a fear one daren't confess to, it's just so much Art. (*J*, 378)

In the beginning was a war that caused me to be in a state of fear. In that original state, "I" am weak, frightened in the face of awesome threats. Are there any means of defense? Scouring is the only one; by a reduction, not a transcendental but a mystical one. Mystical: a word that Céline uses (in connection with Lola's body he speaks of "a mystical adventure in anatomical research" (*J*, 50); as to the people one fears, "Their actions no longer have that foul mystical power over you, weakening you and wasting your time" (*J*, 59)). It amounts to setting up not a beyond but two terms, face to face, each judging the other, in turn, and both reducing in the end to the same abjection. On one side, what is base; on the other, the speech that I hold forth and that has me in its hold. Nature, the body, the inside. Facing the spirit, others, appearances. Truth being on the base side; a barren side, without makeup, without seeming, rotten and dead, full of discomfort and sickness, horror.

And the truth of this world is to die. (*J*, 199)

. . . but she [his mother] remained a good deal short of the dog's level because she believed what they told her when they took me away. The dog at least believes only what it knows by sense of smell. (*J*, 92)

Entirely naked, all you have in front of you is really only a wretched, pretentious beggar swollen with conceit, with difficulty getting out its inane babble in one style or another. (*J*, 334)

It didn't matter that it was really Nature; she considered me just as disgusting as Nature herself, and that's what was such an insult to her. (*J*, 395)

And this, about a writer:

. . . a man, whether he's a relation of theirs or not, is nothing but arrested putrescence. (*J*, 425)

And yet what brings into existence this truth of horror and

sickness, of weakness and downfall, is its confrontation with the other term—the powerful, rich, and feared: "There are two of you together."

But when one's weak, the thing that gives one strength is stripping those one fears of the slightest prestige that one may still tend to accord them. One must teach oneself to see them as they are, as worse than they are, that is. One should look at them from all points of view. This detaches you, sets you free and is much more of a protection than you can possibly imagine. It gives you another self, so that there are two of you together. (J, 59)

Nevertheless, in this fascinating confrontation during a merciless war, both end up on the same side, united in abomination; then language turns into slobber, conversation into defecation, it is the end of the night.

When you consider, for instance, the way in which words are formed and uttered, human speech fails to stand up to the test of all these appalling trappings of spittle. The mechanical effort we make in speaking is more complicated and arduous than defecation. (J, 334–335)

Is there not some solution, some salvation on account of this equal sign between the elevated and the base? Céline's universe is provided, in spite of it all, with an *outside*, intermittently and held in compassionate mockery. Sometimes women are the ones who, for their part, do not experience repulsion, but only imagine it, perhaps. Another solution sometimes crops up— impossible, condemned, and just as antiquated—which would amount to keeping to the Idea, a single idea, guarantee and counterweight to overbearing abjection. And finally, the path that Céline chose for himself; to stay within horror but at a very slight distance—an infinitesimal and tremendous one, which from the very heart of Céline's essential abomination, distinguishes and inscribes sublime love for a child or, in a space beyond sexuality and analogous to it, writing as sublimation.

The brink: women.

Women are all housemaids at heart. But perhaps she imagines this repulsion rather than feels it; that is my remaining consolation. Perhaps all that I suggest to her is that I am filthy. Perhaps I am an artist in that line. (J, 74)

Redemptive Unity: an Idea that is one, picayune, and impossible.

My own ideas, the ideas I had, roamed loose in my mind with plenty of gaps in between them; they were like little tapers, flickering and feeble, shuddering all through life in the midst of a truly appalling, awful world. [. . .] but even so there was never any chance of my managing, like Robinson, to fill my head with a single idea, some really superb idea that was definitely stronger than death . . . (*J*, 504–505)

Finally the sublime, with its two modest faces. On the one hand:

Clearly Alcide could rise to sublime heights without difficulty, could feel at home there; there was a fellow who hobnobbed with the angels and you would never have guessed it. . . . Almost without noticing he had given three years of hardship, the annihilation of his wretched life in this tropical monotony, . . . (*J*, 160)

On the other, the musical sublimation that most people miss and that Céline will aim at throughout his writing:

There was nothing left for him to sublimate; he just wanted to go away, to take his body somewhere else. There was no harmony in him, so that to be through with it all he had to upturn everything like a bear. (*J*, 426)

Being sorrowful isn't all; there ought to be some way of starting up the music again, of discovering a further poignancy . . . (*J*, 504)

ACCOUNTS OF DIZZINESS

But the most normal solution, commonplace and public at the same time, communicable, shareable, is and will be the narrative. Narrative as the recounting of suffering: fear, disgust, and abjection crying out, they quiet down, concatenated into a story.

In the shooting sharpness of *his* suffering, Céline will look for a story, a verisimilitude, a myth. That is how we get the famous story of his head wound suffered during the First World War, a wound whose gravity, most biographers agree, was greatly exaggerated by Céline who lays stress on it both when speaking to newspapermen and in his writings. Aching in his head, his ear, his arm. Dizziness, noises, buzzings, vomitings. Even attacks, the onslaughts of which make one think of drugs or epilepsy. Already in *Death on the Instalment Plan*:

I've had it since the war. Madness has been hot on my trail . . . no exaggeration . . . for twenty-two years. That's quite a package. She's tried a million different noises, a tremendous hullabaloo, but I raved faster than she could, I screwed her, I beat her to the tape. [. . .] My great rival is music, it sticks in the bottom of my ear and rots . . . it never stops scolding . . . [. . .] I am the organs of the Universe . . . I provide everything, the ham, the spirit, and the breath . . . Often I seem to be worn out. My thoughts stagger and sprawl . . . I'm not very good to them. I'm working up to the opera of the deluge. [. . .] I am the Devil's stationmaster. [. . .] The gate of hell in your ear is a little atom of nothing.[1]

Suffering speaks its name here—"madness"—but does not linger with it, for the magic of surplus, scription, conveys the body, and even more so the sick body, to a beyond made up of sense and measure. Beyond the narrative, dizziness finds its language: music, as breath of words, rhythm of sentences, and not only as metaphor of an imaginary rival where the voice of the mother and of death is hiding:

A beautiful shroud embroidered with tales—that's what the Pale Lady wants. (*D*, 41)

The narrative, on the other hand, is always umbilicated to the Lady—fascinating and abject object of the telling.

Triggered by the mother, moreover, on the rough seas of the English Channel, one of literature's most abominable scenes of abjection or nausea is unleashed. We are far removed here from buzzing pain that rises musically. The body is turned inside out, sent back from deep within the guts, the bowels turned over in the mouth, food mingled with excretions, fainting spells, horrors, and resentments.

Mama collapses against the rail . . . She vomits herself up again, all she's got . . . A carrot comes up . . . a piece of fat . . . and the whole tail of a mullet . . . (*D*, 124)

We're half drowned in the flood. We're squashed into the toilet bowl
. . . But they never stop snoring . . . I don't even know if I'm dead
or alive. (*D*, 126)

Human beings caught flush with their animality, wallowing
in their vomit, as if to come closer to what is essential for
Céline, beyond all "fancies": violence, blood, and death. Never
perhaps, not even with Bosch or the blackest aspect of Goya,
have human "nature," on the other side of the "sensible," the
"civilized human," or the divine been opened up with so much
cruelty, and with so little satisfaction, illusion, or hope. This
is the horror of hell without God: if no means of salvation, no
optimism, not even a humanistic one, looms on the horizon,
then the verdict is in, with no hope of pardon—the sportful
verdict of scription.

Le Pont de Londres ("London Bridge") is no less revealing of
that war with the bowels, promoted this time to manly rank
(general Des Entrayes has already appeared in *Journey*), of suffering within:

It's a dizzy spell! . . . A sickly feeling! . . . I am a prey to fever!
. . . I sit down! . . . I close my eyes hard . . . I can still see . . . red
and white . . . colonel Des Entrayes! . . . raised on his stirrups! . . .
That's a show from my memories . . . I am back in the war! . . .
Jesus! . . . I'm a hero again! . . . So is he! Aren't memories beautiful!
. . . Just for that I stretch out on the sofa . . . I'm having my attack!
. . . Again I see Des Entrayes, my beloved colonel! . . . Mad he sure
wasn't! . . . He was raised on his stirrups! . . . his cavalry sword ready
for action . . . raised! . . . flashing in the sun . . .[2]

In short a Schreberian suffering, which only humor and style
cause to tilt out of the accounts of the Freudian neuropath into
one of the most suggestive pages of contemporary literature.

SUFFERING AND DESIRE: A DEBILITY

There is no glory in this suffering; it is not an ode: it opens up
only onto idiocy. *Debility* is that ground, a permanent one with
Céline, where "intimate" suffering, both physical and psychic,
joins with sexual excesses. There is nothing pornographic,

nothing attractive or exciting in such a baring of instincts. Caught on the black slope where desire founders in drive or affect, where representations are blurred, where significations vanish, this form of sex is an inebriation, another word for debilitated suffering.

I had reached the limits . . . [. . .] Mimine! . . . no more hallucinations for me . . . I knew how they got to me . . . I had some experience now . . . just a small bit of liquor . . . just a small glass was enough . . . and then a friendly discussion . . . there's someone who contradicted me . . . I'd get excited . . . and that was it! . . . Always on account of my head, it was written on my deferment card! . . . (P, 335)

All my aches are catching up with me . . . piercing me through and through! . . . my forehead, my arms, my ears . . . I hear the trains that are heading for me! . . . filling my head with whistling and roars! . . . I've had it, fuck that shit! . . . I'm going down! . . . I've got hold of the railing . . . Just a bit dizzy . . . And here I am, quaking, in front of her . . . Oh what a scare! . . . what a thrill! . . . [. . .] Does she love me a little? . . . I'm asking myself . . . I ask myself again and again when I'm with her . . . I'm getting so emotional! . . . I really don't know where I'm setting my feet! . . . I'm stumbling all over . . . I can't see where I'm going . . . neither store windows or people . . . not even sidewalks, I trip and bump . . . I pick myself up, I am ecstatic . . . in the enchantment of her presence . . . [. . .] I don't see the GI who's hollering at me 'cause I'm stamping all over his plates . . . or the conductor who's shaking me . . . who's pestering me in my day-dream . . . (P, 137–138)

SCATOLOGY TURNED COMMONPLACE

The no man's land of dizziness that links suffering and sex gives way to a disgust for decay or excretion; Céline talks about it in the same neutral tone, in the same seemingly natural fashion, as when he describes suffering or debility. Granted that his medical practice has something to do with it. But one detects a cold glee, an aloof taming of abjection that remind one less of (sadomasochistic) perversion than of certain moments in the painful life of the fortified castle (see above, pp. 53–55) as well as of the most "borderly" rites of basic religions.

It is as if Céline's scription could only be justified to the extent that it confronted the "entirely other" of signifiance; as if it could only be by having this "entirely other" exist as such, in order to draw back from it but also in order to go to it as to a fountainhead; as if it could be born only through such a confrontation recalling the religions of *defilement, abomination,* and *sin.* As for the narrative, put out of joint by the workings of that device, it is both shattered and punctuated in its simply biographical and logical continuity by such clusters of fascination; what is disconnected regains its coherence in the permanence of abjection.

That obsession refers back to decay, whether it be recalling the excrement discovered by the unhappy father as the other side of his child's success in school (*D,* 76) or else the anal dirtiness that fixates Ferdinand's interest in the swarming interior of a body, about which he will not have to ask whether it is male or female.

I never wiped myself properly, I always had a sock coming to me . . . and hurried to avoid it . . . I left the can door open so as to hear them coming . . . I shat like a bird between two storms . . . (*D,* 69)

Decay: privileged place of mingling, of the contamination of life by death, of begetting and of ending. Its high point may perhaps be found in an apocalyptic description of earth rotted away by the maggots of the scholar Courtial des Pereires: the scientific experiments of the inventor of Genitron, far from perpetuating life, succeed only in transforming a food, potatoes, into an unbearable stench ("corpses or potatoes"), and in rotting the very stones.

One big desert of rot! . . . [. . .] OK, OK, the spirit's fermenting! [. . .] You want to know what putrefaction is? You want me to tell you? It's all the shit we have to put up with . . . (*D,* 515–516)

And yet it is the human corpse that occasions the greatest concentration of abjection and fascination. All of Céline's narratives converge on a scene of massacres or death—the *Journey,* beginning with the First World War, had pointed the way, *Rigadoon* and *North,* spread out over a Europe laid waste by the Second, deepen and sustain the fixation. It is true that contemporary times are conducive to such representations, rife with slaughter as they are, and Céline remains the greatest hyper-realist of the period's massacres. But we are far removed from news accounts of war, even of the most horrible kind. Céline tracks down, flushes out, and displays an ingrained love for death, ecstasy before the corpse, the other that I am and will never reach, the horror with which I communicate no more than with the other sex during pleasure, but which dwells in me, spends me, and carries me to the point where my identity is turned into something undecidable. There is a vertiginous, apocalyptic, and grotesque evocation of ecstasy before death in one of the final scenes of *Death on the Instalment Plan*. Father Fleury, having become mad, dismembers Courtial's corpse:

He sticks his finger into the wound . . . He plunges both hands into the meat . . . he digs into all the holes . . . He tears away the soft edges . . . He pokes around . . . He gets stuck . . . His wrist is caught in the bones . . . Crack! . . . He tugs . . . He struggles like in a trap . . . Some kind of pouch bursts . . . The juice pours out . . . it gushes all over the place . . . all full of brains and blood . . . splashing . . . (*D*, 560)

INGRAINED CARNAGE

The scription of Céline draws its night and its ultimate support from death as the supreme location of suffering, from the aggressivity that provokes it, from the war that leads to it. Abjection is edged with murder, murder is checked by abjection.

Men don't have to be drunk to make havoc of heaven and earth. *With them carnage is ingrained!* It's a miracle they survive when you consider the time they have spent cutting themselves down to nothing. They think only of nothingness, lousy customers, future criminals! They keep seeing red everywhere! Might as well skip it, or that would be the end of poetry . . . (*P*, 406)

Certainly, but not of Céline's texts, quite the contrary.

One is reminded of attempted murders, of many killings—of the old Henrouille, of Robinson (in the *Journey*); of constant brushes with death in "London Bridge" where "scientific" ex-

[margin, handwritten] this is how I want to write

periment is mixed, as in a baleful carnival, with deadly risks and murderous violence in taverns, orgies, and subways. Think of Titus' death rattle in *Guignol's Band*; the heinous outcries over his dying body, struggling between the bodies of two women, the customer and the maid, tokens of an impossible orgy that has shifted into murder:

He's lying there in his silks full of his filth . . . his vomit . . . he's still gurgling! . . . his eyes are swiveling . . . they get rigid . . . revulse . . . Ah! it's horrible to watch! . . . and then poof! He turns crimson! So livid just a second ago! . . . He's swelling up with big gobs . . . his mouth's full . . . he makes an effort . . .[3]

Like a crisis in his illness, his asthma.

When that got him! what a panic! . . . Should've seen his eyes then! . . . the horror that seized him! (G, 155)

The apocalyptic murder scene reaches its climax when drugs are added to the orgy, as in the fire sequence of *Guignol's Band*.

I see a big battle scene! . . . It's a vision! . . . a movie! . . . Ah! it's going to be something out of the ordinary! . . . in the darkness above the tragedy! . . . There's a dragon munching them all! . . . tearing their behinds out . . . their guts . . . their livers [. . .] I can see you, you pain in the ass! [. . .] I'm going to slit the skunk's nostrils! . . . I don't like homos! . . . What if I cut off his organs? . . . ah, that'd be something! I'm thinking about it! . . . I'm thinking about it! . . . (G, 172–173)

And then the vision of murder turns sublime, the murderous apocalypse shows its lyrical side before everything founders into vomit, money swallowed as ultimate food, reincorporated excrement; and fire, actually apocalyptic, devastates everything, after Claben's murder by Boro and Céline-the-pain:

. . . and everything starts turning around the globe! like a merry-go-round . . . the water lamp . . . I'm seeing things inside it! I see garlands . . . I see flowers! I see daffodils! [. . .] I tell Boro! . . . He belches at me! . . . He's between Delphine and the old guy! . . . They're still at their dirty game! . . . there in the big bed! . . . They're making me sicker! . . . The guy who guzzled all his dough! . . . He doesn't feel sick! . . . all the money in his bag! . . . he's satisfied . . . (G, 178)

FERDINAND THE PAIN: A MURDERER

Ferdinand the Pain, the one who speaks in the first person, is here one of the main protagonists of the murder. It is he again, "I," who, in *Guignol's Band*, throws his persecutor, Matthew, under the subway. That scene sets in motion the merry-go-round of persecutor and persecuted and changes the previous sequence's visionary representation of murder into a more dynamic X-ray of the murderous process. A true underground kingdom ruled by death drive finds its natural place in the bowels of the subway, the Célinian equivalent of Dante's hell. Murder as underground lining of the unclean-thinking being.

My blood turns! . . . I stop breathing! . . . I stop moving! . . . I stand there hypnotized . . . he looks at me! . . . I look at him! Ah! but I'm thinking! . . . I'm thinking fast! . . .It's the midget! there against me! . . . It's him! [. . .] It's getting ready by itself! . . . my scheme . . . I concentrate . . . concentrate . . . Not a word . . . calm and collected . . . [. . .] We hear the train roaring . . .it's coming! . . . there in the darkness . . . in the hole . . . at my right . . . Good! . . . Good! . . . Good! . . . the train's approaching. It's roaring fiercely, crashing in, swelling up . . . Brrr! Brrroom . . . Good! Good! Good! . . . It's near . . . I look at Matthew opposite . . . [. . .] Bop! I hit him with my ass! the midget! up in the air! . . . The thunder lets loose, passes over him! (G, 219–220)

THE SECOND WORLD WAR

It is in war, however, that the apocalyptic unfurling of aggressivity and death matches and goes beyond what is found in Goya or Bosch. An abominable war in the *Journey* but one soon traveled through; a sinister and carnivalesque war in "London Bridge" and *Guignol's Band*.

I'm the murderer, doc! . . . I killed ten of 'em! . . . I killed a hundred! . . . I killed a thousand! . . . I'll kill all of 'em next time! . . . Doc, send me back! . . . I belong at the front! . . . a-off to war! (G, 229)

Without the war it is hard to imagine a Célinian scription; the war appears to trigger it off, to be its very condition; it plays the role of Beatrice's death, which leads to the *Vita Nuova*, or of Dante's avoidance of death, which initiates the first canto of the *Divine Comedy*. The trilogy in which the Second World War's horror unfolds, *From Castle to Castle, North,* and *Rigadoon,* best captures the wound that Céline never ceases to palpate, from the individual's to society's. In the political and social fresco, overflowing with rejections and sarcasms directed against a political position that in other respects Céline seems to endorse (a point I shall return to), with betrayals, escapades, massacres, bombings, and destruction, the most destructive aggressivity suddenly shows its abominable, sickly side, within an infernal jouissance—History's abject motive. The site of Céline's scription is always that fascinating crest of decomposition-composition, suffering-music, and abomination-ecstasy.

. . . let them rot, stink, ooze, end up in the sewer . . . they keep wondering what they can do in Gennevilliers . . . easy! fertilize the fields! . . . [. . .] the true sense of History . . . and what we've come to! jumping this way! . . . whoops! and that way! . . . the death dance! impalements! purges! vivisections! . . . twice tanned hides, smoking . . . spoiled, skulking voyeurs, let it start all over again! guts ripped out by hand! let's hear the cries, the death rattles . . . a national orgasm![4]

Let me recall, in connection with the apocalyptic music of the trilogy, the bombing of Hamburg where, amidst the din, the stench, and the chaos, the frenzy of abjection turns into sinister beauty:

these green and pink flames were dancing around . . . and around . . . and shooting up at the sky! . . . those streets of green . . . pink . . . and red rubble . . . you can't deny it . . . looked a lot more cheerful . . . a carnival of flames . . . than in their normal condition . . . gloomy sourpuss bricks . . . it took chaos to liven them up . . . an earthquake . . . a conflagration with the Apocalypse coming out of it! (*R*, 130)

I've told you what it was like, three four times the size of Notre Dame . . . [. . .] the light came from up top . . . the crater hole . . . the effect, I repeat, was like an enormous nave of solid clay . . . [. . .] Hamburg had been destroyed with liquid phosphorus . . . the Pompei deal . . . the whole place had caught fire, houses, street, asphalt, and

the people running in all directions . . . even the gulls on the roofs
. . .(R, 191)

The sacred and history, Notre Dame and Pompei, meaning
and law, in the tremendous unveiling of suffering and death of
the Second World War, give birth to their gruesome hidden
side. And the all-powerful obverse of a fragile culture is, in the
eyes of Céline, the truth of the human species; for the writer,
it is the point of departure of scription as the laying bare of
meaning. Granted that Céline's vision is an apocalyptic one,
that it bears mystical strains in its fixation on Evil as the truth
of impossible Meaning (of the Good, of the Law). And yet, if
apocalypse means, etymologically, a vision, it must be understood as the contrary of revelation of philosophical truth, as the
contrary of *aletheia*. There is no apocalyptic *being*, scored, fainting, forever incomplete, and incapable of setting itself up as a
being, bursting among the flames or reverberating amid the
clamors of universal collapse. Céline does not exhibit a philosophical "evil." Moreover, no ideological interpretation can be
based on his revelation: what principle, what party, what side,
what class comes out unscathed, that is, identical to itself, from
such a thorough critical conflagration? Suffering, horror, and
their convergence on abjection seem to me more adequate as
marks of the *apocalyptic* vision constituted by Céline's scription.

A NARRATIVE? NO, A VISION

It is indeed a vision, to the extent that sight is massively sum-
moned to play a part in it, broken up by the rhythmic sound
of the voice. But it is a vision that resists any representation,
if the latter is a desire to coincide with the presumed identity
of what is to be represented. The vision of the ab-ject is, by
definition, the sign of an impossible ob-ject, a boundary and
a limit. A fantasy, if you wish, but one that brings to the well-
known Freudian primal fantasies, his *Urfantasien*, a drive ov-
erload of hatred or death, which prevents images from crys-
talizing as images of desire and/or nightmare and causes them
to break out into sensation (suffering) and denial (horror), into

a blasting of sight and sound (fire, uproar). Apocalyptic vision could thus be the shattering or the impossibility not only of narrative but also of *Urfantasien* under the pressure of a drive unleashed by a doubtless very "primal" narcissistic wound.

When Céline locates the ultimate of abjection—and thus the supreme and sole interest of literature—in the birth-giving scene, he makes amply clear which fantasy is involved: something *horrible to see* at the impossible doors of the invisible—the mother's body. The scene of scenes is here not the so-called primal scene but the one of giving birth, incest turned inside out, flayed identity. Giving birth: the height of bloodshed and life, scorching moment of hesitation (between inside and outside, ego and other, life and death), horror and beauty, sexuality and the blunt negation of the sexual.

> . . . and I've delivered babies, fascinated, I might say, by difficult passages, visions of the narrows . . . those rare moments when nature lets you observe it in action, so subtle, the way it hesitates, then makes up its mind . . . life's critical moment, as it were . . . all our theater and literature revolve around coitus, deadly repetition! . . . the orgasm is boring, the giants of the pen and silver screen with all the ballyhoo and the millions spent on advertising . . . have never succeeded in putting it across . . . two three shakes of the ass, and there it is . . . the sperm does its work much too quietly, too intimately, the whole thing escapes us . . . but childbirth, that's worth looking at! . . . examining! . . . to the millimeter! (*R*, 195–196)

At the doors of the feminine, at the doors of abjection, as I defined the term earlier, we are also, with Céline, given the most daring X-ray of the "drive foundations" of fascism. For this indeed is the economy, one of horror and suffering in their libidinal surplus-value, which has been tapped, rationalized, and made operative by Nazism and Fascism. Now neither theoretical reason nor frivolous art, stirred by epiphenomena of desire and pleasure, has been able to touch that economy. Such desiring art could only offer a perverse negation of abjection, which, deprived in other respects of its religious sublimation (especially considering the state of bankruptcy of religious codes between the two wars, most particularly in Nazi and Fascist circles), allowed itself to be seduced by the Fascist phenomenon.

Drieu La Rochelle provides us with the very epitome of such a literature. Its solidary reverse is an art of the repressed, traditionally versified and patriotic, that of moral resistance, resolute and limited at the same time. But is any realist (or socialist-realist) literature up to the horrors of the Second World War? Céline, for his part, speaks from the very seat of that horror, he is implicated in it, he is inside of it. Through his scription he causes it to exist and although he comes far short of clearing it up, he throws over it the lacework of his text: a frail netting that is also a latticework, which, without protecting us from anything whatsoever, imprints itself within us, implicating us fully.

❧ 8

THOSE FEMALES WHO CAN WRECK THE INFINITE

It would be hard to find a woman who is neither a bitch nor a ninny—
if so, she will be witch and fey.

Céline, Letter to Milton Hindus

THE TWO-FACED MOTHER

The mother takes up her place, so it goes once again, at the central location of the writer's feminine showroom. But here, explicitly and in very significant fashion, she is split in two.

Ideal, artistically inclined, dedicated to beauty, she is, on the one hand, the focus of the artist's gaze who admits he has taken her as a model.

I am the son of a woman who repaired ancient lace. It so happens that I have a collection of it, quite rare, the only thing that I have left, and I am one of the rare men who can tell cambric from Valenciennes, Valenciennes from Bruges, and Bruges from Alençon. I can tell fine quality very well. Very very well. I don't have to be trained. I know. And likewise I recognize the beauty of women and also that of animals. Very well. I am an expert in this.[1]

Or, in more allusive fashion, but still linking writing, women, and lace:

I am not an artist but I have a good memory for flowers . . . Janine . . . Marie-Louise . . . [. . .] what's written plain, that isn't much, it's transparency that counts . . . the lace-work of Time as they say . . .[2]

And yet, neither mother nor grandmother, as Céline's novels

conjure them up, are characters whose splendor is without shadows. Writing, for instance, originates in the grandmother—"she taught me to read a little," "she herself wasn't very good at it," and even, "I can't say she was tender or affectionate, but she didn't talk much, and that was really great" (D, 63). The love that he bears her is an awkward, modest love, tinged with a chaste and guilt-laden reserve, contrasting with the excess and horror characteristic of Célinian feeling. Moreover, it is at the moment of death that, embarrassed by his childlike clumsiness, he dares to manifest his love.

> We felt kind of ashamed . . . kind of guilty . . . We didn't dare to move . . . for fear of spoiling his grief . . . Mama and all of us cried with our heads on the table . . . (D, 100)

The other maternal image is tied to suffering, illness, sacrifice, and a downfall that Céline, so it seems, readily exaggerated. This kind of motherhood, the masochistic mother who never stops working is repulsive and fascinating, abject.

> As long as it was lousy work, as long as there was plenty of sweat and heartache, she was satisfied . . . That was her nature . . . [. . .] She was really attached to her horrible fate . . . (D, 295)

We had already encountered that in the *Journey*:

> It was as if she was afraid of this cause for sadness; it was full of sinister things which she did not understand. She believed really that small fry like herself were meant to suffer all the time, that that was their role on earth, . . . (J, 93)

It is a wretched representation, degraded even by the relentlessness with which her limping leg was emphasized, "It was my mother's legs, the skinny one and the fat one" (D, 54), and by the exceeding poverty Céline would have us believe prevailed in Passage Choiseul. To what end is castration embodied in the mother? Is it the representation of an abiding blame, the appeasement of a precocious narcissistic wound? Or a way of expressing a love that only the weak can receive without those who utter it being threatened?

The theme of the two-faced mother is perhaps the representation of the baleful power of women to bestow mortal life.

As Céline put it, the mother gives us life but without infinity:

She did all she could to keep me alive, I just shouldn't have been born. (D, 55)

. . . those females can wreck the infinite . . . (D, 46)

I have already mentioned that birth-giving is, for Céline, the privileged object of scription. In its miscarriage, too, in abortion, the writer discovers, quite naturally, the basic fate and abominable tragedy of the other sex. He evokes this insuperable drama in the *Journey* when sexual pleasure is drowned in a pool of blood during a confrontation between the sensual daughter and her jealous, deadly mother (J, 259ff).

LIFE? A DEATH

Let me recall that Céline devoted his doctoral dissertation (1924) on Ignaz Semmelweis to the infection that develops during childbirth—puerperal fever. Very much unlike what one would expect in a medical treatise, quite novelistic, this work can be deciphered as Céline's identification with the Hungarian doctor practicing in Vienna. A foreigner, a solitary, on the fringe of the profession, insane in the end, persecuted by everyone, the inventor of obstetric hygiene had what it takes to fascinate not only those suffering from obsessions but, more deeply, those who fear decay and death at the touch of the feminine. He advocated that a doctor wash his hands after having been in contact with corpses in order not to contaminate the women whose deliveries he might be attending to—and this during the Napoleonic era, before the discovery of microbes. Semmelweis noted, in fact, that puerperal fever is the result of the female genitalia being contaminated by a corpse; here then is a fever where what bears life passes over to the side of the dead body. Distracting moment when opposites (life/death, feminine/masculine) join in order to constitute what is probably more than a defense fantasy against the persecuting power of the mother: a panic hallucination of the inside's destruction, of an interiorization of death following the abolishment of limits and differences. The remedy?—Once more it involves separating, not touching, dividing, washing. The third party, the doctor, must be an agent not of communication but of isolation, thus providing the lay counterpart to religious abominations, excisions, and purifications. It is an impossible role: prey to violent hallucinations, Semmelweis rushes to a corpse, cuts, cuts himself, and becomes infected. Like a woman giving birth? The agent turning victim? The doctor failing to escape the fate of the sick mother, pledged to death? Céline follows step by step the painful experience of the doctor poet who was, too, the author of a dissertation written in quite literary style ("The life of plants"—"twelve pages of poetry"); he comments, as if he were not referring to the Viennese doctor but to himself, the novelist to be, "the world and dance were leading him to femininity." This dissertation is in fact a journey to the dark portals of life, where the woman in childbed succumbs to infection, life to death, women's fever to the delirious hallucinations of man, reason to enigma. What attracts Céline, of all the old enigmas of science, is the one lying at the way out or the way in for woman, confusing inside and outside, life and death, feminine and masculine—and that is certainly more than a metaphor. His dissertation is a preparation for the *Journey to the End of the Night* in that it discusses in nearly explicit fashion, although within the constraint of "scientific" repression, the enigma constituted, for reason, by the feminine. It will have been necessary, so it seems, for Céline's reason to come up against that obstruction to make it possible, beyond the foulness of abjection, for his two unyielding protagonists to appear—death and words.

The Célinian universe remains dichotomous; without a third party, or because of the latter's failure, two terms rise up, facing each other, Woman and Lover, Sex and Corpse, Woman in childbed and Doctor, Death and Words, Hell and the Writer, the Impossible and Style.

Beyond those few colorful embellishments, there were on the path of infection only death and words . . .[3]

. . . hell begins at the doors of our Reason.[4]

One does not explain everything with facts, ideas, and words. There is, in addition, everything we do not know and shall never know.[5]

As for the writer, his task is to be more than a doctor—he is to be not only the one who separates, a father, as it were, but also the one who touches, the son and the lover, even taking the place of the feminine. The One and the Other and by that very token neither the One nor the Other, a person Removed. This is a very particular solution to the Oedipal situation; the subject does not become normalized through triangulation of the neurosis; he does not appear in the dual fear of narcissistic relationship in the absence of a third party; he covers the three positions at the same time—trinity, three dots, from one identity the other, no identity, rhythm, rotation, rigadoon.

Giving life—snatching life away: the Célinian mother is Janus-faced, she married beauty and death. She is a condition of writing, for life given without infinity aspires to find its supplement of lacework within words; she is also the black power who points to the ephemeral nature of sublimation and the unrelenting end of life, the death of man. The paranoid woman, another Célinian character, is perhaps a projection of the danger of death prompted within the speaking being by his perception of that part of himself he fantasies as maternal and feminine. Let me point out that the double aspect of the mother in Céline's writing defines it as scription of death on the one hand, and as revenge on the other. It is a being pledged to death who narrates stories to the Lady, but by the same token he rehabilitates his mother. For everyday reasoning, things seem reversed; but in Céline's text, it is she who wants him dead, he who causes her to live.

A beautiful shroud embroidered with tales—that's what the Pale Lady wants. (*D*, 41)

My teeth are gone! but I remember a few ditties . . . mother! A tiny second all life long . . . a lustful woman mother wasn't . . . it passed her by . . . like myself, her son . . . what a sacrifice! [. . .] Oh but I'll write, I will, full of hatred as I am, I'll avenge everyone, ass riven to my seat, their historical names engraved in gold . . . in the Sainte

Chapelle! . . . the writer's power is so weak! weak poet, weaker than anything! Look out, all you bulky Herculeses wearing togae! I'll see that your names are written in gold! (*F*, 301)

COURTLINESS AFFRONTED

There is courtly code in the amorous code of Céline. Explicit at times, it is above all constantly present in the background as modesty and lyricism. Without it abjection could not exist, could not be spoken as our other, as the nocturnal reverse of the magnificent legend. The enchantments of the Célinian ballets ("without music, without anybody, without anything" as the subtitle [to *Féerie pour une autre fois*] makes clear) are an ineffectual attempt at staging an archaizing idealization where the feminine ideal persists, no matter what the personality of the female characters, in the sublime body of the ballerina. But one remembers, more abruptly yet, those pages in *Death on the Instalment Plan* where Ferdinand confesses to Gustin Sabayot his intention of writing a thoroughly chivalrous legend about the adventures of Gwendor the Magnificent. Immediately afterward he relates that enchanted knightly romance to a perverted minor, Mireille, before she becomes the object of his hardly courtly pornographic and sadistic desires. (*D*, 136ff). This episodic character and the isolated sequence set apart from the thread of a narrative without continuity are nevertheless symptomatic. The conjunction of opposites (courtliness-sadism) is again encountered in all of Céline's feminine characters. To varying degrees, such ambivalence seems to show that genital fear can be kept within bounds by idealization as well as by the unleashing of partial drives (sado-masochistic, voyeurist-exhibitionist, oral-anal).

Molly, the most sublime, does not escape such a pattern. Doubtless a prostitute, dispensing her charms in a "clandestine whorehouse," she nevertheless has none of the destitution that is the lot of Joyce's Molly Bloom—one without illusions and commonplace to the point of sickly obscenity. To the contrary, Céline's Molly benefits from angelic idealization; the modesty and lyricism of his writing endow her with the enchanted existence of the great white-draped priestesses of ancient Phallic myths. Could the devalorization of sex, dissociated, parcelized, marginalized, and in the final analysis degraded, as we saw it in the theme of suffering-horror, be the condition for a phallic idealization of Woman? There is at any rate in Céline a precise place where abjection vanishes and becomes veneration:

Good, admirable Molly, I should like her, if she ever reads these lines of mine, to know for certain that I have not changed towards her, that I love her still and always shall, in my own way; that she can come to me here, whenever she may care to, and share my bread and my furtive destiny. If she is no longer beautiful, ah, well, no matter! The more's the pity, we'll manage somehow, I've kept so much of her beauty with me still, so warm, so much alive, that I've enough for both of us, and it will last another twenty years, long enough to see us through. (*J*, 235)

Elisabeth Craig, to whom the *Journey* is dedicated, seems to be the main referent for that confession touched with emotion; Céline wrote Milton Hindus about her:

What a genius that woman had! I never would have amounted to anything without her. What a mind! what subtlety . . . What pantheism, at the same time painful and mischievous.[6]

MY CHILD, MY SISTER

The aura of amorous idealization seems to appear as soon as one can ward off the fear aroused by the sexual desire that women are assumed to have for a man. This perhaps explains why those the writer allows himself to win over, or even to love, are either lesbians or women playing the role of a sister. Molly is probably the most dazzling representation of a sisterly friendship-love. A variant of it, more openly incestuous or perverse, is provided by Virginia in "London Bridge." But *Guignol's Band* already gave us an angelic foretaste of it, to a rhythm of dancing harlequins:

Pert brisk little girl with golden muscles! . . . Keener health! . . . whimsical leap from one end of our troubles to the other! At the very beginning of the world the fairies must have been young enough to have ordained only extravagance . . . The world at the time was all whimsical marvel and peopled with children, all games and trifles and whirls and gewgaws! A spray of giggles! . . . Happy dances! . . . carried off in the ring! (G, 33)

A carnivalesque counterpart to Lewis Carroll's Alice, Virginia is the child who enables one to imagine angels in the feminine. This has the phantasmatic advantage of deferring the abject encounter with feminine sex, for in the body of a child-dancer thus presented to one's gaze, touch, hearing, and scent, the sexual component being everywhere is actually nowhere.

I'd like to talk to her about quicksilver again . . . [. . .] She can't stay put . . . she leaps, pirouettes like an imp . . . in the room all around me . . . What beautiful hair! . . . what gold! . . . what a filly! . . . [. . .] She speaks to me . . . it's bird-language . . . I don't understand everything . . . [. . .] I wouldn't have eaten! . . . I would have died a dainty person! . . . preferring it all for Virginia's sake! . . . (P, 36)

Even more significant is this paradisiacal vision in the midst of a world of vagrants and orgies, of drunken revels and demons:

. . . I touch, I brush against the fingers of my pixie! of the adored marvel . . . Virginia! . . . I no longer dare, everywhere about us . . . a thousand flakes of fire are flying . . . flitting . . . graceful fire streamers all over the trees! . . . from one branch to the next . . . Joyful sparkling daisies, corollas showing . . . blazing camellias . . . scorching wistaria . . . to be tossed to the skies! . . . among the blasts of music . . . the fairies' chorus . . . the tremendous humming of their voices . . . the secret of the smiles' charm . . . That's the way of the feast of fire in Paradise! (P, 111)

That mischievous child evocation is also a link between Ferdinand and the girl's uncle, a character both feared and cheated by the narrator; one can thus locate within denied homosexuality the giddying reality of the relation to the girl where Ferdinand, from one identity to another, from one sex to the other, ends up losing his mind.

I'm a bit dizzy . . . I am again in front of her, shaking all over . . . Ah, what a fright! . . . what a thrill . . . (P, 138)

. . . before childplay is swallowed up in a loving embrace, in the rain

. . . I cover her with caresses, I lick her like a dog . . . I lap her up
. . . I suck the water from the tip of her nose . . . [. . .] from time
to time there's an awful taste! A behavior worthy of a lout! Hooligan's
jumble, obscenity! . . . debauchery! I would've layed my Virginia!
(*P*, 163)

The pixie's loving brother is on the verge of becoming an
incestuous father; all that holds him back is the fear of others
and the circumstances, always somewhat persecutive.

One will note the twisted aspect of incest: the sister becomes
her brother's daughter, and that allows the man, in this context,
to be a brother or father but to keep his mother untouched and
to continue his war with the other man, the real brother of the
object of his desire. Finally, pregnant Virginia obviously prof-
fers the very image of the undecidable situation within such a
carnivalesque world. A feeling of compassion and a desire to
escape henceforth accompany, for the narrator, a paternity that
is as magical as it is grotesque. "I am in the cage of her happiness" (*P*, 367) contrasts with "I was fed up with my destiny!
[. . .] Stolen destiny! Another name for God" (*P*, 290). And
now it turns out that the "satyr for little girls" behaves like a
hero. "My pregnant daughter, my angel! my cherub! my life!
Oh I wouldn't want them to touch her! . . . I would kill them
all! shit!" (*P*, 466). Next he surrenders to another character,
female this time, a Delphine out of the London slums. She takes
up the end of the novel, conjuring up Lady Macbeth and murder, while all the participants in the carnival sail off on an
indefinite journey, in a book that abruptly comes to an end at
London Bridge with the confession of the brother-father's buf-
foonery: "I'm the buffoon at present! A whole way of life! Me
that's got care and circumspection!" (*P*, 490). Carnival covers
up incest. From one identity to an other, unfinished like the
novel itself, abjection is resorbed in the grotesque: a way of
living it from the inside.

THE PHALLUS' VOYEUR

Idealization of the child's form is in fact only one aspect of
Céline's pagan enthusiasm for femininity separated from rea-

son, language, and the symbolicity that, in his eyes, alters, socializes, and sexualizes it. If he is fond of women on occasion, he is so as sensualist-voyeur of a pure form, a beauty that lets itself be conquered only by the gaze, one made up of lines, muscles, rhythm, and health. A ballerina is the most perfect example of it, preferably a foreigner—the opposite of the mother language, without language if need be, all sensitivity and acrobatics.

And a pagan on account of my absolute adoration of *physical beauty*, of *health*—I hate sickness, penance, morbidity—[. . .] madly *in love*— I say, *in love*—with a four-year-old girl at the height of gracefulness and blond beauty and health—[. . .] America! the feline nature of its women! [. . .] I would give all of Baudelaire for an olympic swimmer! There's not a penny's worth of the rapist in me—but I am a voyeur to the death![7]

And again:

I have always liked women to be beautiful and lesbian—very pleasing to look at, I wouldn't get tired out by their sexual summonses! [. . .] me, a voyeur—that suits me! [. . .] and an enthusiastic consumer, just a bit but very quiet.[8]

American dancers, who find their clearest phantasmatic expression in the comedy *L'Eglise*, best embody that absolute phallus of unaltered beauty: a feminine body in the purest state of nature, free from any other (man or language). *L'Eglise* is a play with neither stylistic nor dramatic value, but it is interesting in that it stages the Célinian fantasy of feminine nature, which is here the object of a strong endorsement and contrasts with the extreme poverty of blacks and the bureaucracy of the Jews. "Long live American women who despise me"—such is the basic message of that feminine worship, which is less suggestive of satyrism than of morbid relish.

There remains for the playwright confronted with the enchantment of dance the jouissance of being the waste cut off the phallus. Janine performs that transposition of parts that allows Bardamu to be more than passive, threatened with death: she shoots at him with a revolver while the splendid Elizabeth is dancing.

It is not reason but phallic instinct that writes the law; Woman is its representative in a life where henceforth, in spite of enchantment, murder dominates. The end of religion is no doubt worship of Woman, and also penal colony. "Life, kiddo, is not a religion, Janine [. . .]: it's a penal colony! Mustn't try to deck the walls like a church."⁹

CARNIVAL—IN HYSTERICAL FASHION, SOCIETY—IN PARANOID FASHION

After it has forsaken the veil of childhood and femininity without other (sex), beauty is no longer pleasing in Céline's eyes. An unbridled woman then arises, eager for sex and power, nevertheless a grotesque and sorry victim in her raw violence that extends from drunken revels to murder. As early as the *Journey*, Céline displayed her colors by means of a seemingly harmless series of women who turned into farce the tragedy experienced by soldiers in the war. One remembers Lola and her apple fritters, Musyne and her violin, tough and bloodthirsty nurses—"War goes straight to their ovaries . . ." (*J*, 87). But it is especially with prostitutes and nymphomaniacs, who are nevertheless tackled with fascination if not with a certain amount of sympathy, that we are presented with a wild, obscene, and threatening femininity. Their abject power is none the less kept in the background owing to a shift in the narrator's vision, which simultaneously gives of that power an image of downfall, abject poverty, and senseless masochism. One will recall Sosthene's wife, in "London Bridge," nymphomaniac and battered. Even though demoniacal, such femininity is nonetheless in the position of a fallen demon who finds being only with reference to man:

War! war! always war! There was nothing except bang bang bang that could awaken them just a bit . . . It had to keep going, the whole shebang, shaking heaven and earth . . . so as to open up their peepers again . . . a whore without men is a flabby thing. (*P*, 428)

The pinnacle of this compound of abomination and fascination, sex and murder, attraction and repulsion, is probably

Gioconda, the prostitute in *Guignol's Band*, who makes good use of her name by defiling it in her hysterical spells, with the bleeding sore of her loving body reduced to a wound in the ass.

Ah, it's a big challenge! . . . And stamps her heel! . . . she's a fury! . . . it's a dance! . . . a trance! . . . her fingers all nerves! . . . her hands quivering all over! crackling, spluttering! . . . small . . . small . . . tiny . . . still smaller . . . [. . .] The devil's tail! . . . the tail's caught! . . . trr! . . . rebounds! (G, 82–83)

She trips! . . . Tumbles! sprawls! It's Gioconda! in a package! . . . in her cotton . . . bandages! . . . she gets up, she screams, she's awful! . . . starts blaming right away! . . . there it goes . . . she hoists herself up, clings to the bar! . . . A fury! She's choking with effort . . . she's suffocating . . . she ran through the whole neighborhood . . . looking for us! (G, 114)

She was pulling at her dressings, she was chucking them all around, all over the floor, cotton, bandages, shreds . . . Boy, what laughing in the joint! (G, 115)

A dark, abominable, and degraded power when she keeps to using and trading her sex, woman can be far more effective and dangerous when socialized as wife, mother, or career woman. The unbridling is then changed into crafty reckoning, hysterical spells turn to murderous plots, extreme masochistic poverty becomes a commercial triumph. While hysterical woman is merely a carnival puppet, under a law she perversely attempts to get around, the paranoid woman becomes successful by making of herself the expression of a murderous sociality. The whole procession of wives, or, better still, of more or less overbearing widows, controlling the circulation of wealth, children, and loves, in the *Journey* or in *Death on the Instalment Plan*, contributes to such a view of the feminine. And yet we find in the two Henrouilles, the daughter-in-law murdering her mother-in-law (through an intercessory man, of course) and the mother-in-law profiteering until the end of her unscathed life, the best embodiment, in the *Journey*, of calculated abjection; they represent the feminine that saves, hoards, foresees, settles down wretchedly, living from hand to mouth, but doing it all through extreme measures of hatred and murder. One would have to rate the two Henrouille women close to Lady Macbeth—who, under the apparent narcissistic essence of the feminine, bares death drive. They are derisive and ghoulish representations of a feminine paranoia that is the more unbridled, the more coldly calculated, as they have given up on all sexual satisfactions.

Gioconda and Henrouille, in brief, are shown as the two facets of an otherness that cannot be sublimated—the sexual and the repressed, the marginal and the social. They are the prototypes of an abject femininity that, for Céline, is capable of neither music nor beauty; instead, mistress and victim, it breaks out into the world of instincts where, as a naturally successful paranoid, it craftily rules the social institutions (from families to small businesses) where puppet-men, shabby men are living.

The capable woman, the intellectual, does not escape being grotesque either. If she does not share in the sordid craftiness of an Henrouille or an Henrode, she is fated to prove the absurdity of reason (a masculine element) when it is sheltered in a body that is feminine to boot. Such is the woman inventor, the railroad company accountant: an unusual person who "decomposed water from the Seine with a diaper pin" (D, 423), but in fact she thought only of getting married—and got fleeced by fancied suitors. There is thus only decay in this fallen, heartrending, murderous, dominating, and derisive femininity.

Women, you know, they wane by candle-light, they spoil, melt, twist, and ooze! [. . .] The end of tapers is a horrible sight, the end of ladies, too, . . . (F, 16)

And there you have the muse just as she is after two thousand years of art and religion. A muse in the true tradition of the lowly genres—apocalyptic, Menippean, and carnivalesque. The pitiful power of the feminine, however, be it drive or murder, is in fact unleashed only with the help of masculine degradation or bankruptcy—a bankruptcy of the father and manly authority. Does that mean that this is the feminine from which scription withdraws? Or, if you wish, is it from this feminine, defined as the other of sublimatory area, that scription, in a more ambiguous fashion, draws its inspiration?

A CARTOON-LIKE FATHER

Auguste, the father, emerges out of a conjuring up of the primal scene at the beginning of *Death on the Instalment Plan*, and all through the novel he stands out as both the opposite and the other self of the writer.

Later they closed the door . . . the door to their bedroom . . . I slept in the dining room. The missionaries' hymn came in over the walls . . . And in the whole rue Babylone there was only a walking horse . . . clop clop . . . that late cab . . . (D, 54)

Family quarrels, the most intimate and doubtless essential elements in Célinian family life, reveal a petty clerk embittered by unfulfilled dreams of becoming a merchant marine captain; an artist on occasion, he draws, but he also tells stories in a manner both fierce and harping. When mother and son argue over the father's values, the polarity of this tragicomic figure of a clown is clearly stated: "He was an artist at heart," and "There was no lousier bastard in the whole universe" (D, 46, 47). Overwhelmed with fear ("He was building up to the next outburst, the Deluge that wouldn't be long in coming," D, 64–65), obsessed with the passing of time ("He was always in a temper anyway, because the time wouldn't pass," D, 62–63) and with cleanliness (see D, 75–76), Auguste actually possesses Clemence by beating her up (D, 67), demonstrates his manhood by shooting off his revolver (D, 77), and cannot help imagining persecutions and plots directed at himself in his mother-in-law's talk (D, 79). While none of all that is basically alien to Ferdinand, what brings them closest together is probably the art of story-telling. Auguste can describe the enchantment of the World's Fair (D, 82), but he also keeps them breathless when telling about the journey to England (D, 129–130).

My father had style, elegance came natural to him. (D, 54)

But also:

My father distrusted his imagination. He talked to himself in corners. He was afraid of being carried away . . . He must have been steaming inside . . . (D, 59)

In the context of this ambivalent portrait, which definitely leans toward caricature, it is quite significant that Céline would ascribe to Auguste anti-Masonic and anti-Semitic feelings while seeming to repudiate them (if only through the Oedipal context of *Death on the Instalment Plan*) and accept responsibility for them later on.

. . . he'd be stringing the beans . . . why wouldn't we turn on the gas and all commit suicide? . . . My mother just sat there . . . He blamed it all on the Freemasons . . . and Dreyfus! . . . and all the other criminals who were out to get us. (D, 101–102)

He was being persecuted by a whole carnival of demons . . . He really revved it up . . . He dragged everybody into it . . . Jews . . . schemers . . . social climbers . . . And most of all the Freemasons . . . (D, 152)

Auguste-Laius reaches the utmost in degeneracy during his scrap with Ferdinand, the violent and jerky description of which is almost explicitly sexual:

He starts trembling again, his whole carcass is quaking, he's beside himself . . . He clenches his fists . . . His stool is creaking and dancing . . . He's winding up, he's going to lunge . . . He comes back blowing up my nose . . . more insults . . . more and more of them . . . I feel things coming up in me too . . . And the heat besides [. . .] I lift up the big heavy machine . . . I lift it way up. And wham! . . . I give it to him full in the face! . . . [. . .] I stumble, I charge with it . . . I can't contain myself anymore . . . That does it, I've got to finish the stinking bastard! (D, 316)

Is not this tale of the father's murder what Ferdinand is day-dreaming about as he lifts his eyes to the ceiling and attempts to find his way through a very personal narrative?

I see Thibaud the Minstrel . . . He's always in need of money. He's going to kill Joad's father . . . Well, at least that will be one father

less in the world . . . I see splendid tournaments on the ceiling . . .
I see lancers impaling each other . . . (D, 44)

If the murder of the father provides a key to enchantment,
it is accompanied not only by guilt but also by a tremendous
sense of panic before a woman thus freed of any curb, hold,
or master. One of the sources of Célinian abjection no doubt
lies in the bankruptcy of the fathers. They represent a seeming
of power barely sufficient for the frightened son who is writing
to rise up against a universe forsaken by infinity, which only
thus appears true to him. The writer-son does not spare Auguste, including even his illness—attacks, nightmares, exhaustion, delirious states, cold towels wrapped around his head; the
reader knows that Ferdinand, too, is going through the same
hell. The father, moreover, is from the beginning a mixture of
childishness and ridiculous manhood:

. . . with a chubby round nose like a baby's over an enormous mustache. He rolled his eyes ferociously when he was angry. He never
remembered anything but vexations. (D, 53)

The ideal figure is nevertheless not completely absent; it is
the uncle—the maternal one, of course; it is Edouard, the devil's
own Luck, the hope of righteous families. But the positive
glimmer that filters in, ironical as it may be, among men that
are mere marionettes, is not without danger. There we have
Courtial des Pereires, who solidly embodies manhood, paternity, and science combined; identifying the paternal with the
rational, he leads them together to the pinnacle of grotesque-
ness, to the heart of catastrophe. A universalist, familialist,
collectivist, and rationalist, Des Pereires, as his name suggests,
speaks to the "Anguished Fathers of France" and establishes the
"Renovated Familistery for the Creation of a New Race" (D
989). He is, of course, a disciple of Auguste Comte in whose
wake he founds "The Friends of Pure Reason"; for fairgound
carnivals he substitutes the "Agricultural Revolution"; he even
includes astronomy in his "Explanations for Families"; he is an
inventor, to be sure, and head of a *Genitron*, a genetic research
institute, as it were, before anything of the sort existed; he i
a Utopian on occasion, having devised his Polyvalent Cottage

a house that is flexible, expanding, adapted to any size family; with all this, Des Pereires clearly represents the modernistic, socializing, and rationalistic excesses of social conformism, which, in the final analysis, is always familial. In less sociological fashion, he embodies the castration of modern man, of the technocratic father, universal dummy and ultimate token of a world lacking in jouissance and able to find being only in abjection. In this sense, Des Pereires and Gioconda, like the Henrouille women, are perhaps the privileged representations of contemporary post-Catholic destiny for mankind bereft of meaning. Representations of the paternal and the maternal, of the masculine and the feminine, in a society on the threshold of fascist totalitarianism.

§➣ 9

"OURS TO JEW OR DIE"

Enthusiasm involves a lot of mad raving—Alas! Freud certainly raved a great deal—but our ravings now seem to involve solely political fanaticism—that's even more ridiculous—I know. I was caught up in it.

Céline, Letter to Milton Hindus

LOGICAL OSCILLATIONS: AN ANARCHISM

Doubtless contradictory, hotheaded, "raving" if you wish, Céline's pamphlets (*Mea Culpa*, 1936, *Bagatelles pour un massacre*, 1937, *L'Ecole des cadavres*, 1938, *Les Beaux Draps*, 1941), in spite of their stereotyped themes, carry on the wild beauty of his style. Isolating them from the whole of his writings constitutes a defense or a claim on the part of the political left or right; it is at any rate an ideological stance, not an analytic or literary position.

The pamphlets provide the phantasmatic substratum on which, in another connection and another place, the novelistic works were built. Thus, very "honestly," the person who signs novels and pamphlets with his grandmother's first name, Céline, remembers his father's name, the one on his birth certificate, Louis Destouches, in order to acknowledge the thoroughly existential, biographical paternity of the pamphlets.
• Where my identity is concerned, "I" have no other truth to tell save my delirium: my paroxysmal desire under its social guise. Where that other who writes and is not my familial ego is concerned, "I" go beyond, "I" shift, "I" am no longer, for the end of the night is without subject, rigadoon, music, or enchantment. Destouche and Céline: biography and thanatogra-

phy, delirium and scription—the distinction surely exists, but it is never complete; like Janus who avoids the trap of an impossible identity, the texts, novels or pamphlets, also display two faces.

Céline can thus at the same time *attack the collapse of ideals and the reduction of the masses to the satisfaction of their basest needs while extolling those who foster such a situation,* beginning with Hitler. For instance, he writes in *Les Beaux Draps*:

The masses have no ideals, all they have is needs. And what are those needs? [. . .] It's a platform with nothing but material things, a swell feed, and a gold brick. They're an embryonic bourgeoisie that hasn't yet negotiated its contract.[1]

Or else:

The downtrodden of the earth on the one side, the bourgeois on the other, they have basically only one idea, to become rich or to stay rich, it's the same thing, the lining has the same value as the cloth, the same currency, the same coin, no difference in their hearts. It's all guts, incorporated. Everything for the belly. (*BD,* 89)

And in *L'Ecole des cadavres*:

Who is the true friend of the people? Fascism is. / Who has done the most for the working man? the USSR or Hitler? / Hitler has. / All you have to do is look, keeping all that red shit away from your eyes. / Who has done the most for the small businessman? Not Thorez but Hitler![2]

This does not prevent him from attacking Hitler violently—though after the war, it is true:

Hitlerite clamors, that howling neo-Romanticism, that Wagnerian satanism, always seems to me obscene and unbearable—I am for Couperin, Rameau—Jaquin [. . .], Ronsard . . . Rabelais.[3]

Backing Hitler there was nothing, or almost nothing, I mean from the spiritual point of view, a horde of petty bourgeois, greedy swine rushing in for the spoils.[4]

(And that, as Céline saw it, is what made the Nazis unfit for Nazism.)

He can *lash out at and inveigh against Freemasons, academics, and other secular elites, and at the same time attack no less violently, with Nietzchean overtones, the Catholic church.* Thus, on the one hand:

France is Jewish and Masonic [. . .] It's the Hydra with a hundred and twenty thousand heads! Siegfried can't get over it! (*BD*, 78)

The French Masonic Republic is no longer anything but a very disgusting electoral rip-off, a fantastic organization for gulling very naive Frenchmen. (*EC*, 31)

The profligate Masonic Republic, so-called French, which is completely at the mercy of secret societies and Jewish banks (Rothschild, Lazare, Baruch, etc.), is feeling the pangs of agony. More gangrened than one would think possible, it is rotting away scandal by scandal. All that's left are puss-laden scraps from which, in spite of all, the Jew and his Freemason dog tear away a few new goodies each day, cadaverous snatches; they stuff themselves, what a blow-out! thrive on them, gloat, exult, they go delirious on carrion. (*EC*, 31)

And on the other:

Having spread to the manly races, to the hated Aryan races, "Peter and Paul's" religion performed admirably; as early as the cradle it reduced to beggars, to a lower form of man, the subjected people, the hordes intoxicated by Christianic literature; it hurled them, bewildered and besotted, to the conquest of Christ's Sindon, the magic hosts, forever forsaking their Gods, their exalting religions, the Gods of their blood, the Gods of their race. (*BD*, 81)

The most shameless gambling joint for corn-holed Christianese the kikes have ever laid hands on . . . [. . .] Christianic religion? Judeo-Talmudo-communism? A gang! The apostles? Jews. All of them! Gangsters all! The first gang? The Church! The first racket? The first people's commissariat? The Church! Peter? Al Capone of the Canticles! A Trotsky for Roman muzhiks! The Gospel? A code for racketeers . . . (*EC*, 270)

The Judeo-Christian connivance serves as prelude to the great Judeo-Masonic rushing for the spoils . . . (*EC*, 272)

He can *shoot down in flames communism and the "Middling Revolution," but he can do the same to Charles Maurras.* Thus, for instance, in *Mea Culpa* or in other texts:

Communism without poets as it is practiced by Jews, scientists, rational reasoners, materialists, Marxists, bureaucrats, skunks, louts, at the rate of six hundred kilos per sentence, is a very boring process of prosaic tyranny, absolutely unable to take wings, an absolutely atrocious, Jewish satrapal imposture, unedible and inhuman, a very sickening forcing house for slaves, a hellish wager, a remedy worse than the disease. (*EC*, 133)

And at the same time on the other side:

But what is Maurras getting at? I don't understand a thing about the cunning, the dosulage, the high-sounding hare and hounderies of his most Latin doctrine. (*EC*, 252)

And his style! His famous style! Sticky, stumbling, tendentious, fake, Jewish . . . (*EC*, 189)

And against the bourgeois:

As for the Bourgeois, he doesn't give a damn, what he wants is to keep his lettuce, his "Royal Dutch" stock, his privileges, his situation, and the Lodge where he meets such fine people, the kind who have a pipe-line to the government. In short he is Jewish, seeing that the Jews have got the gold . . . (*BD*, 70)

In similar fashion, he flies into a *black rage against the schools, which are reductive of animal spontaneity and are based on abstract, paternal reason*, a reason that constrains and maims (A "hatcher of symbols,"[5] the school, in *Les Beaux Draps*, is a "devourer" of the "mischievous liveliness" of children; by means of reason, it inflicts false and fake values upon them, as opposed to spontaneous, innate, animal beauty), and he *feverishly defends the true family, the solid dictatorship of the father* ("I go by another Family code, one that is much hardier, more ample, a lot more generous, not a code for shrivelled up argumentative preservers. Of course not! Not at all! A real code, one that would include everything, animals, goods and people, children and the aged, all of France in the same family, Jews excluded of course, a single family, a single dad, dictator and respected" *BD*, 172).

One has to admit that out of such logical oscillations there emerge a few striking words of truth. Such words present us with harsh X-rays of given *areas* of social and political experience; they turn into fantasies or deliriums only from the moment when reason attempts to *globalize, unify,* or *totalize.* Then the crushing anarchy or nihilism of discourse topples over and, as if it were the reverse of that negativism, an *object* appears— an object of hatred and desire, of threat and aggressivity, of envy and abomination.

That object, the Jew, gives thought a focus where all contradictions are explained and satisfied. The function of the Jew in the economy of Célinian discourse will perhaps be better understood after I have called attention to at least *two common features* that structure the fluctuations of the pamphlets.

AGAINST THE SYMBOLIC LAW: A SUBSTITUTE LAW

The first is *rage against the Symbolic,* which is represented here by religious, para-religious, and moral establishments (Church, Freemasonry, School, intellectual Elite, communist Ideology, etc.); it culminates in what Céline hallucinates and knows to be their foundation and forebear—Jewish monotheism. When one follows his associations of ideas, his anti-Semitism—virulent and stereotyped but impassioned—appears as the simple outcome of a fully secular rage; anti-Semitism would be a diehard secularism sweeping away, along with its number one enemy, religion, all its secondary representatives: abstraction, reason, and adulterated power, considered emasculating.

The second is the attempt to substitute *another Law* for the constraining and frustrating symbolic one, a law that would be absolute, full, and reassuring. The wishes of Céline, as Fascist ideologue, call for that law, seen as mystic positivity:

There is an idea that can lead nations. There is a law. It stems from an idea that rises toward absolute mysticism, that rises still without fear or program. If it flows in the direction of politics, that is the end of it. It falls lower than mud and we with it [. . .] we need an idea, a harsh doctrine, a diamond-like doctrine, one even more awesome than the others, we need it for France.[6]

Beyond politics, and yet taking it into account, ⌈*material positivity,*⌋ a full, tangible, reassuring, and happy substance, will be embodied in the Family, the Nation, the Race, and the Body.

The novelist Céline has only too deeply explored the abomination that such entities are prey to. But the pamphleteer wants them; he fantasies them as capable of being full, without other, without threat, without heterogeneity; he wants them harmoniously to absorb their differences into a kind of sameness that would be obtained by means of a subtle drifting, a scansion, a punctuation that would relay but without interrupting—a replica of primary narcissism. Without Master, this universe has rhythm; without Other, it is Dance and Music; without God, it has style. Against the ternary economy of a Transcendence, Céline proclaims the immanence of substance and meaning, of the natural/racial/familial and the spiritual, of the feminine and the masculine, of life and death—a glorification of the Phallus that does not speak its name but is communicated to the senses as Rhythm.

One should again learn to dance. France remained happy up to the rigadoon. One will never dance in the factories, nor will one ever sing again. If one no longer sings, one passes away, one no longer conceives children, one locks oneself up in a movie theater just to forget that one exists. (*BD*, 148)

Oh, what delightful impertinence! Caught in the whirlwind [. . .] For heavens' sake! amid a thousand flippancies! cat-like, on their toes, by fits and starts! they're making fun of us! Ta! ta! ta! . . . [. . .] where the melody has led us . . . a summons in F! . . . everything evaporates! . . . two trills again! . . . an arabesque! . . . an échappée! Good Lord, here they are! . . . F . . . E . . . D . . . C . . . B! . . . Saucy girls of heaven enchant us! Since we are to be damned anyway, what's the difference! (*BD*, 221–222)

Céline's style shows that such a dual enchantment between the "not yet one" and the "not quite another" can be written. He convinces us that the jouissance of so-called primary narcissism's immanence can be sublimated in a signifier that has been recast and desemanticized into music (see p. 188).

Furthermore, it is impossible not to hear the liberating truth of such a call to rhythm and joy, beyond the crippling constraints of a society ruled by monotheistic symbolism and its political and legal repercussions.

And yet, both the enchantment of the style and libertarian spontaneity bear within themselves their own *limit*; at the very moment that they seek to escape the oppression of the thinking, ethical, or legislative Unity, they prove to be tied to the deadliest of fantasies. The negated and frightened desire for the One as well as for the Other produces a symptom of destroying hatred directed toward both.

At that point the image of the Jew will concentrate negated love become hatred for Mastery on the one hand, and on the other and jointly, desire for what mastery cuts out: weakness, the joying substance, sex tinged with femininity and death.

Anti-Semitism, for which there thus exists an object as phantasmatic and ambivalent as the Jew, is a kind of parareligious formation; it is the sociological thrill, flush with history, that believers and nonbelievers alike seek in order to experience abjection. One may suppose, consequently, that anti-Semitism will be the more violent as the social and/or symbolic code is found wanting in the face of developing abjection. That, at any rate, is the situation in our contemporary world, and it is also, for more personal reasons, that of Céline. Do not all attempts, in our own cultural sphere at least, at escaping from the Judeo-Christian compound by means of a unilateral call to return to what it has repressed (rhythm, drive, the feminine, etc.), converge on the same Célinian anti-Semitic fantasy? And this is so because, as I have tried to explain earlier (see pp. 90ff.) the writings of the chosen people have selected a place, in the most determined manner, on that untenable crest of manness seen as symbolic fact—which constitutes abjection.

In this sense, Céline's pamphlets are the avowed delirium out of which the work emerges to venture into obscure regions at the limits of identity. If delirium is indeed involved, and Céline himself suggests that it is,[7] that is also the nature of all anti-Semitism, the daily banality of which surrounds us; Nazi excesses or Célinian outbursts, which are cathartic upon the whole, give us a warning while we thirst for sleep and jouissance.

BROTHER . . .

What fantasies can the Jew thus precipitate in Céline, in order to be the exemplar of all hatred, of all desire, of all fear of the Symbolic?

How common it is for the hateful to view the oppressed as the reason for their suffering.

All powerful at first, he stands as a *hero*. Not so much as father than as preferred son, chosen, availing himself of paternal power. Freud had noted that every hero is a patricide. Céline does not go so far perhaps as to think of that kind of heroism, although he implicitly takes it for granted when he deems that, beyond comparison, over all other sons, "the Jew is a man more than anyone else" (*BM*, 270).[8]

Such a brother, superior and envied, is essentially active as opposed to the "grotesque unconcern" of the Aryan (*BM*, 128). Such a one is Yubelblat, in *Bagatelles pour un massacre*:

He's a top-notch go-getter . . . Not a minute of interruption . . . He promises . . . Promises . . . flatters while delineating . . . rousing ardor or hatred . . . that tarry, weaken, become lost . . . He goes and badgers them again! What a hustle . . . Looking out for squalls! Skimming through! . . . Skimming through [. . .] pirouettes, nimble dodges, acrobatics . . . stealthy conferences, international mysteries and legerdemain, the frail Yubelblat. (*BM*, 102)

And what is more, contrary to accepted stereotypes, Céline depicts him as fearless, "The Jew, he's afraid of nothing . . ." (*BD*, 136) as long as he can reach his goal—power. "He always has to be the one who gives orders" (*BD*, 141).

It is by means of full anal mastery ("the future is his, he's got the dough," *BM*, 327), which involves *having* the primordial object, that the Jew makes certain of *being*, of being *everything* and *everywhere*, totaling the world as a flawless unity under his absolute control.

The Jews, you know, they're all camouflaged, disguised, chameleon-like, they change names like they cross frontiers, now they pass themselves off for Bretons, Auvergnats, Corsicans, now for Turandots, Durandards, Cassoulets . . . anything at all . . . that throws people off, that sounds deceptive. (*BM*, 127)

He's mimetic, he's a whore, he would have dissolved long ago, after assimilating to others so much, if it weren't for his greed, his greed saves him, he has worn out all races, all men, all animals, the earth is now done with [. . .] He's still hassling the universe, heaven, God, the Stars, he wants everything, he wants more, he wants the Moon, he wants our bones, he wants our guts as hair-curlers to celebrate the Sabbath, to deck the Carnival. (*BD*, 142)

Secretive, privy to mystery ("The Jew is mysterious, he has alien ways . . ." *BD*, 119), he holds elusive power. His ubiquity is not limited to space, he is not only on our land and under our skin, the very closest neighbor, the nearly same, the one we do not differentiate, the *dizziness of identity*, "we don't know what mugs they have, or could have, what manners they've got" (*BM*, 127); it also takes in the totality of time, he is *heir*, scion, enhanced by issue, by a kind of nobility that guarantees him the opportunity to amass traditions as well as goods of the family and social group:

Any little Jew, at birth, finds in his cradle all the possibilities of a fine career . . . (*BM*, 127)

Blessed by the father and by reliable families, he artfully manipulates the networks of social reality, and he does it even better if he can be accepted by the aristocracy.

And yet, this position of power has nothing in common with the cold and majestic mastery proper to classic domination. In the anti-Semitic fantasy, Jewish power does not arouse respect as does paternal authority. Edged with fear, to the contrary, it unleashes the excitement brought on by sibling rivalry; the Aryan who engages in it is then swept into the fire of denied homosexual passion. Indeed, this chosen brother displays too much *weakness* (concerning him Céline calls to mind the small size and features indicative of crossbreeding, when he does not refer directly to the circumcised foreskin: "Lenin, Warburg, Trotsky, Rothschild, they all think alike in this. Not a foreskin of difference, it's one hundred percent Marxism" *BD*, 103), ambivalent lack—which can just as well cause *surplus* or even *jouissance*—for one to be satisfied with obeying him or defying him. Is it possible to give in to a being whose behavior signifies he is an emanation of the Everything Everywhere, if he is so obviously weak and sensual? His weakness will be held against him—he will be considered a usurper, but very soon one will admit that his jouissance is what grates. As if he were that unique being, so different from the pagan, who draws his aura out of his weakness, that is, not out of a full and glorious body but out of his subjectivation to the Other.

It is indeed for an incomprehensible jouissance that Céline upbraids that favored brother by means of a sadomasochistic language that is openly sexual, or homosexual: "Fifteen million Jews will corn-hole five hundred million Aryans" (*BM*, 127). "He just couldn't care less, he comes, he's old enough, he's having fun" (*BD*, 31), is said about Roosevelt but in the context it also applies to Jews. "The Jews, Afro-Asiatic hybrids, quadroons, half-negroes, and Near-Easterners, unbridled fornicators, have no reason to be in this country" (*EC*, 215); or this letter signed "Jewish Salvador" and addressed to the "repulsive Céline," where one reads, among other fantasies, "The kikes stick it up your ass and if you want to be corn-holed just let us know" (*EC*, 17). The anti-Semite who comes up against it finds himself reduced to a feminine and masochistic position, as a passive object and slave to this jouissance, aggressed, sadisticized.

The fantasy of a Jewish threat, weighing against the Aryan world ("we are in the midst of Jewish Fascism," *BM*, 180) in a period when, to the contrary, persecutions against the Jews are beginning, cannot be explained in any other way; it emanates directly out of that vision of the Jew as a being of having, as issuing from the All in which he joys, and especially from the immediate sexualization of that jouissance.

They do you no personal wrong? . . .—They get my goat . . . [. . .] they feel me out in order to corner me . . . they come to size up the crap, at each turn of the page . . . each minute . . . to see how much more I have softened, grown weaker . . . (*BM*, 319)

Please condescend, my darling monster! too discreet crucifier! too seldom as I see it! I adore you! Grant all my wishes! You are keeping me on tenterhooks! You can see that I am weeping! overcome with happiness at the thought that I am at least going to suffer still a lot more . . .(*BM*, 134)

There's always a little Jew there in the corner, crouching, mocking, thinking it over . . . watching the goy, who's seething . . . now heartened he comes closer . . . Seeing the object so fully aflame . . . runs his hand over that lovely cunt! . . . (*BD*, 124)

Through the crescendo of the phantasmatic build up, the Jew ends up becoming a despotic tyrant to whom the anti-Semite submits his anal eroticism, explicitly with Céline, elsewhere in more or less underhanded fashion. Céline describes himself, as he faces this imaginary aggressor, as a "corn-holed figure," "the kikes shit in your kisser" (*EC*, 17); he often seems "the good Aryan [. . .] always ready to make his Jew come" (*BD*, 125).

And yet, if jouissance is something the Jew is supposed to have knowledge of, he appears anxious not to spend (himself) for it. He is master of jouissance, but not an artisan, not an artist. That tyrannical brother thus places himself under the purview of a law that is paternal, in the nature of the superego, dominating drives, the opposite of natural, childish, animal, and musical spontaneity. Anxious to commit himself to a bit of "direct humanity," the Jew "immediately becomes more and more tyrannical" (*BM*, 194). A domineering person, he first gains mastery over himself through cold reason, which deprives him of any access to talent. The Jew is the prototype of the intellectual, the superintellectual, so to speak (the utmost in intellectual frigidity is reached when the university man happens to be Jewish, like Ben Montaigne, the professor in *Les Beaux Draps*); he is incapable of art but he has invented "technix" (which ushers in the artificial world of "flies without pricks! soft sphincters! falsies, all the filthy trickeries" (*BM*, 177)). If he is a writer, he is like the bourgeois writer author of "patched up borrowings, things seen through a windshield . . . a bumper or simply stolen from the depths of libraries . . ." (*BM*, 166). Thus identified with Law, Mastery, Abstraction, and Home, he will drift from the position of desired and envied brother to that of impregnable father against whom all the quite Oedipal attacks of Céline's scription, claiming Emotion and Music as the other of Law and Language, will unceasingly be directed.

At this far point of "delirium" the anti-Semite unveils his denied but fierce belief in the Absolute of Jewish Religion as religion of the Father and of the Law; the anti-Semite is its possessed servant, its demon, its "dibbuk" as someone has said,[9] who provides *a contrario* proof of monotheistic power of which he becomes the symptom, the failure, the envier. Is that why he expresses the traumatic topoi of that religion—like those of abjection—which religion, to the contrary, elaborates, sublimates, or masters? All of which, without being its truth, at least constitutes for the subject its unconscious impact?

. . . OR WIFE

A third step needs to be taken now as I construct anti-Semitic discourse, which is frightened desire for the inheriting brother. If he joys in being under the Law of the Other, if he submits to the Other and draws out of it his mastery as well as his jouissance, is not this dreaded Jew an object of the Father, a piece of waste, his wife as it were, an abjection? It is on account of being such an unbearable conjoining of the One and the Other, of Law and Jouissance, of the one who Is and the one who Has that the Jew becomes threatening. So, in order to be protected, anti-Semitic fantasy relegates that object to the place of the ab-ject. The Jew: a conjunction of waste and object of desire, of corpse and life, fecality and pleasure, murderous aggressivity and the most neutralizing power—"What trow I? I trow that it is 'ours to Jew or die!'" (BD, 57), instinctively then, and uncompromisingly! The Jew becomes the feminine exalted to the point of mastery, the impaired master, the ambivalent, the border where exact limits between same and other, subject and object, and even beyond these, between inside and outside, and disappearing—hence an Object of fear and fascination. *Abjection itself.* He is abject: dirty, rotten. And I who identify with him, who desire to share with him a brotherly, mortal embrace in which I lose my own limits, I find myself reduced to the same abjection, a fecalized, feminized, passivated rot: "the repulsive Céline."

[. . .] dirty bastard, loafer [. . .] Flushed out by Moses he holds his rank of big shit de luxe, pally with none but the other flushed-outs, within the realm of Moses, of the Eternal! He is nothing but decay, decaying. He has but one authentic thing deep in his shitty substance, and that's his hatred for us, his scorn, the fury with which he wants to have us crumble, deeper and deeper, into potter's field. (BD, 113)

The Aryan, lacking the symbolic power of the Jew, is no more than "experimental flesh," a "flesh in the state of decay" (*BM*, 316). The French Republic is "gangrened," the Jews can tear from it only "purulent scraps," "goodies," and "cadaverous fragments" (*EC*, 30). We are now far removed from Louis XIV or Louis XV, to whom Céline compared himself, in an interview after the war, when he tried to account for, even to criticize, his anti-Semitism ("But to the extent that they [the Jews] constituted a sect, like the Templars, or the Jansenists, I was as categorical as Louis XIV [. . .] and Louis XV when he got rid of the Jesuits . . . So, there you have it: I mistook myself for Louis XV or Louis XIV, that was obviously a serious error").[10]. Unless such a megalomania, like Majesty itself, is the final mask behind which is concealed the empty, dilapidated castle of a foul, putrid, crisis-ridden identity.

The anti-Semite is not mistaken. Jewish monotheism is not only the most rigorous application of Unicity of the Law and the Symbolic; it is also the one that wears with the greatest assurance, but like a lining, the mark of maternal, feminine, or pagan substance. If it *removes* itself with matchless vigor from its fierce presence, it also integrates it without complacency. And it is probably such a presence, other but still integrated, that endows the monotheistic subject with the strength of an other-directed being. *In short, when a scription on the limits of identity comes face to face with abjection, it enters into competition with biblical abominations and even more so with prophetic discourse.* Céline alludes to biblical texts, mentions the prophets, vituperates against them. Nevertheless, his text follows their trajectory, jealously and yet differently. For he lacks the Law that belongs to prophetic stance; the abjection that he stages, contrary to that of the prophets, will not be relieved, not through any Name; it will merely be inscribed in enchantment, not for some other time, but here and now, in the text. If Céline, too, like the wandering people, undertakes a journey—the abjection inherent in the speaking being having been duly noted—what is involved for the novelist is a journey without project, without faith, to the end of the night. And yet is it not obvious that for Céline Scription and Style fully occupy the place left vacant by the disappearance of God, Prophet, and Faith? It remains for us to examine how such a scription, as Céline understands and practices it, rather than replacing displaces and therefore modifies transcendence and also reshapes the subjectivity that stirs within.

§~ 10

IN THE BEGINNING AND
WITHOUT END . . .

You know, in the Scriptures it says, "In the beginning was the word."
No! In the beginning was emotion. The Word came later, replacing
emotion like trot replaced gallop, while the natural law of the horse
is gallop; it is forced to break into trot. Man was removed from
emotional poetry and pushed into dialectics, in other words, splat-
tering, isn't that so?

"Louis-Ferdinand Céline vous parle"

FROM CONTENT TO SOUND

If we let Céline's text ring, if we read his professions of faith
as a writer, we discover, toward the end of that night of narratives and historical contentions, Céline the stylist.

I am not a man of ideas. I am a man of style. Style, well, everyone
stops before that, no one really reaches the thing. Because it's very
hard work. It involves taking sentences, as I was saying, and having
them fly off their handle . . .[1]

Toward the end or in the beginning? Undoubtedly a metaphysical question, it is one that worries Céline and precisely in
relation to his confrontation with language.

For his "work" is a struggle, if not full of hatred at least
fascinated and loving, with the mother tongue. With and
against, further, through, beneath, or beyond? Céline seeks to
loosen the language from itself, to divide it and shift it from
itself "but ever so slightly! ever so slightly! because in all that,
if you are heavy-handed, you know, it's putting your foot in
it, it's a howler."[2] Such loving auscultation is imagined essen-

tially as probing a hidden inside, a buried authenticity. For Céline, that is where the unnamable truth of emotion lies; there, too, is the void that he sometimes points to, in a less natural or substantial fashion, and where the rhythm of a music or the gestures of a dance are being woven. Let us first listen to him worshiping the French language at the very moment when he tries to have it "fly off its handle":

Oh, how happy we shall be there together! thousands and thousands of us over there! together and speaking French! Joy! Joy! Joy! how we shall embrace! my own depravity, I confess my only one: the French way of speaking! If my executioner were to speak French to me, I should forgive him almost everything . . . how I hate foreign languages! hard to believe that such gobbledygook exists! What humbug! (F, 95)

The French language is regal! What crappy gobbledygook surrounds it! (F, 154)

I loathe English [. . .] In spite of everything France is doing to me I cannot break away from the French language. It's got me. I can't free myself of it.[3]

Such loving dedication leads the one who writes to an incursion the outcome of which he does not visualize as addition or creation but quite simply as revelation; the point is to bring the depths to the surface, carry emotional identity as far as signifying appearances, raise neural and biological experience up to social contract and communication.

To tell the truth I do not create anything—I clean up a sort of hidden medal, a statue buried in loam—[. . .] Everything is already written outside of man in the sky.[4]

The following definition of style should also be read as worship of the depths, as resurrection of the emotional, maternal abyss, brought up flush with language: "In my emotional subway! I don't leave anything on the surface."[5] Or in more naturalistic fashion:

Not simply to his ear! . . . no! . . . in the intimacy of his fibers! right in his nervous system! in his own mind.[6]

Carried to the extreme, this takes on aspects of reverse racism:

politics, speeches, bullshit! . . . only one truth! biology! . . . in half a century, maybe sooner, France will be yellow, black around the edges . . . (R, 107)

The dizziness Céline gives way to and binds himself to in order to tap emotion from the inside is, as he sees it, the fundamental truth of scription. Such dizziness leads him to the fulfillment of a kind of challenge to abjection; it is only thus that he can, by naming it, both have it exist and go beyond it. "Vulgarity" and "sexuality" are merely stepping stones on the way to the ultimate unveiling of the signifier; at the limit, such themes scarcely matter:

Neither vulgarity nor sexuality have anything to do in this business— They are nothing but stage properties.[7]

His project is to

resensitize language, to have it throb more than reason—SUCH WAS MY AIM . . .[8]

Even though that search for the emotional depths is described in terms of a substantial plunge into the "very intimacy of things," Céline is the first to realize that melody alone reveals, and even holds, such buried intimacy. The worship of emotion thus slips into glorification of sound:

That doesn't happen without imparting to thought a certain melodious, melodic twist, a subway track [. . .] a minor harmonic feat.[9]

I know the music from deep inside of things—I could if need be have alligators dance to the tune of Pan's pipe.[10]

. . . so that once written [. . .] IT SEEMS to the reader that someone is speaking to his ear.[11]

At the precise point where emotion turns into sound, on that articulation between body and language, on the catastrophefold between the two, there looms up "my great rival, music":

I am the organs of the Universe . . . [. . .] I'm working up the opera of the deluge [. . .] The gate of hell in your ear is a little atom of nothing. (D, 40)

In the final analysis, however, that slippage of emotion toward music and dance actually opens out on the *void*. Ultimately, at the end of the journey, there stands revealed the complete trajectory of the mutation of language into style under the impulse of an unnameable otherness, which, passional to begin with, then acquires rhythm before becoming empty:

I am comfortable only in the presence of *the nothing-at-all, the void.*[12]

WRITING HATRED

Before reaching such a hollowing out, and perhaps precisely on purpose of getting there, emotion, in order to make itself heard, adopts colloquial speech or, when it acknowledges its hatred straightforwardly, slang.

Slang is a language of hatred that knocks the reader out very nicely . . . annihilates him! . . . completely in your power! . . . he just lies there like an eightball![13]

The vocabulary of slang, because of its strangeness, its very violence, and especially because the reader does not always understand it, is of course a radical instrument of separation, of rejection, and, at the limit, of hatred. Slang produces a semantic fuzziness, if not interruption, within the utterances that it punctuates and rhythmicizes, but above all it draws near to that emptiness of meaning at which Céline seems to aim.

The "spoken" outcome of emotion is more diversified; it is both semantically and melodically more musical. I must emphasize that the colloquialism of Céline's prose does not only express an ideological position, it is also a stylistic strategy. It allows the signifier itself to hold the overflow of emotion that Céline wishes to exhibit on the plane of language. Thus, when he rebels against "ideas," it is in order to allow the appearance "of *spoken* language's emotion through writing";[14] "emotion can be tapped and transcribed only through *spoken language*";[15] "emotion is encountered in spoken language alone."[16] Even if "in fact there are few *flashes* in spoken language." "I attempt to *tap* them . . . [. . .] I am cornering the market of the living diamonds of *spoken language*."[17]

Céline's plan to smuggle spoken language into writing thus becomes the meeting place of a thematic, ideological commitment with an enunciation that attempts to downgrade the logical or grammatical dominant of written language. The strong counterattack (producing what semioticians would call a "secondary modeling system") of what is, for him, an emotion and is marked in language by the abundance of prosodic and rhetorical operations, accomplishes that downgrading, that reversal.

Such an enunciation strategy obviously entails deep transformations in syntax. In Célinian language they are characterized by two basic devices: sentence *segmentation* (with preposing or postponing), which is typical of the early novels; and *syntactic ellipsis*, more or less recoverable, which appears in the later novels. Thus Céline's music is composed through the work of a syntactician; Céline the musician turns out to be a specialist in spoken language, a grammarian who reconciles melody and logic admirably well.

SEGMENTATION: INTONATION, SYNTAX, SUBJECTIVITY

The particular, colloquial segmentation of the Célinian sentence has been noticed and commented upon by Leo Spitzer.[18] What is involved is cutting up the syntactic unit and displacing one of its constituents, postponing and preposing it. As a consequence, the normally descending modulation of the sentence melody is transformed into an intonation having two centers. There are countless examples of this in the early novels of Céline, particularly in the *Journey*.

I had suddenly discovered, all at once, what the war was, the whole war. I'd lost my innocence. You need to be pretty well alone with it, face to face, as I was then, to see it properly, in the round, *the filthy thing*. (J, 10)

Grief had come to her, in fact, when her words came to an end; she did not seem to know what to do with it, with that *grief* of hers; she tried to wipe it away with her handkerchief, but it came back into her throat, *her grief* did, and tears came too, and she began all over again. (J, 275).

The item displaced from the statement is, in the first instance, *postposed* ("*the filthy thing*"), while in the second quotation it is first *preposed* ("*grief*"). The displaced element is represented in the statement by an anaphoric one ("to see *it* properly"; "what to do with *it* . . . that grief"; "*it* came back . . . her grief"). In such cases of reentries, the displaced item does not have a precise syntactic function in the statement.

If one analyzed those same statements within another framework, not as syntactical *structures* but as *messages* in the enunciation process between a speaking subject and an addressee, one would note that the purpose of the displacement is to *thematicize* the displaced item; the latter then gains the status not of a theme (in other words, that about which the speaker is talking) but of an emphasized rheme (that is, information pertaining to the theme). In such a contrast, *the filthy thing* and *grief* convey the main information, the essential message the speaker stresses. From this point of view also, the displaced element has been desyntacticized.[19]

In short, the informative nucleus is by means of various displacement devices emphasized to the prejudice of the normative syntactic structure. It is as if the *logic of the message* (theme, rheme, support/addition, topic/comment, implied, stated, etc.) modeled, in the last analysis, that of *the syntax* (subject-verb-predicate). Indeed, the end figuration of the rheme (according to the two possible modalities, assertive or interrogative) indicates that the modality of enunciation is in the most fundamental manner based on it. The preponderance of this figuration, coupled with the theme/rheme bipartition, especially during syntax learning by children, or in the emotional, relaxed speech of everyday or colloquial discourse is additional evidence of its being an organizer of enunciation far more deep-seated than syntactic structurations.[20]

Another Célinian phrase betrays similar processes. I refer to the sentence auxiliary *c'est* followed by or not by *qui* or *que*; in French, this provides a possibility of syntacticizing, by means of an identifying predicate, a particular value of the message that selects one of its constituents in an emphatic manner.[21] Thus, with Céline: "*C'est* bien mieux payé et plus artiste les *chœurs* que la figuration simple" (They're better paid and more artistic in the chorus line than those who are just extras). *"C'est"* identifies and emphasizes the entire predicate ("bien mieux payé et plus artiste"); at the same time the subject constituent *"les chœurs"* is, owing to the emphasis on the predicate, displaced but chosen in relation to "la figuration simple." A strictly syntactic analysis could not account for such a turn; one would obviously have to take into account the speaking subject's emotive and logical intent, which imbues the usual syntactic structure subject/predicate with a deeper logic. In a similar fashion, "C'est très compréhensible les gens qui cherchent du boulot" (It's very understandable that people be looking for a job). The sentence auxiliary "c'est" here introduces an inclusive predicate, "très compréhensible," which refers to "les gens qui cherchent du boulot." In this case the determinative item precedes the determined one, the information (or rheme) precedes the object (or theme).

Such a remodeling of normative syntax brings the spoken sentence (and the Célinian sentence closer to those languages whose normal syntactic order is modifier/modified (Hungarian and classical Chinese, for instance). There is a tendency in them to give the main information first rather than start with the less informative element; in other words, they prefer the rheme/recall scheme over the theme/rheme scheme.

This turn, which Spitzer called a "binary turn," is accounted for by the predominance of a *logic of the message or of the enunciation* (with a taking into account of the intention or desire of the speaking subject within the communication act) over the *logic of the statement* (with, in French, the so-called normative syntax Subject-Verb-Object). It is distinguished, in addition to its segmentations, preposings, displacements, or repetitions for emphasis, by *successive surges of the intonational curve*; the latter, instead of being smoothed out in "classic" descending fashion, is slightly delayed, either raised or remaining at mid-intensity, at every boundary between theme and rheme, support and addition. The resulting rhythm in Céline's enunciation is generally a binary one, and in the longer sentences it is often staccato. These starts are, it should be noted, in addition to those marked by commas; as if, with colloquial segmentation, Céline procured, in addition to punctuation, new means of shaping his sentences and imparting rhythm and music to them. "A côté d'Alcide, /rien qu'un muffle impuissant/moi, épais, et vain/j' étais . . ." (Compared with Alcide, I was just a helpless cad, that's what I was, dense and conceited, that's me). "Le printemps qu'ils/les oiseaux/ne reverront jamais dans leurs cages, auprès des cabinets, qui sont tous groupés/les cabinets, là, dans le fond de l'ombre . . ." (Spring, which they, the birds I mean, will never see again in their cages, near the toilets, which are all close together, the toilets I mean, there, way back in the shadows . . .). At every virgule (/) there is a slight tremolo, less than a punctuation, more than a simple linking, and it gives Céline's writings that very particular thrill that connotes what is musical or intimate—in short, what is desirable, sexual.

Finally, what could be the psychological value of such a technique? Spitzer notes that preposing information testifies to too much self-confidence or overestimating the addressee, while repeating the displaced constituent indicates adjustment, a supplement of information that was needed because what was said was not self-evident. From this he concludes, "The two contrary forces that are competing in this writer's segmented sentence are self-assurance and nihilistic self-observation."[22]There would be uneasiness, with Céline, over narrating what he is, blunt, quick, and impulsive, in the face of the other. Consciousness of the other's existence would demand repetition for the purpose of additional clarity and thus lead to segmentation. In that type of sentence the speaking subject would, in short, be in two places: that of his own identity (there he goes straight to the information, the rheme), that of objective expression, for the other (when he goes back, repeats, clarifies). Such a psychological interpretation has the advantage of clarifying certain of Bakhtin's positions with reference to dialogism in a number of novelistic writings, particularly those of Dostoyevsky.[23]

I shall on the other hand take into consideration the prevalence of that type of construction (theme/rheme) in children's first sentences during syntax learning.[24] For this binomial, which is both intonational and logical, coincides with a fundamental stage in the elaboration of the subject—autonomization with respect to the other, establishment of his own identity. If saying *no*, according to studies by Freud and by René A. Spitz, marks man's entry into the symbolic and his distinguishing between pleasure principle and reality principle, one might also posit that the binarity of the message (rheme/theme and conversely) represents one step further, a fundamental step, in the symbolic integration of negativism, rejection, and death drive. One might even call it a decisive step, for with message binarity and before the establishment of syntactic structure, the subject not only differentiates between pleasure and reality, but, quite close to that painful and upon the whole impossible distinction, he asserts, "I state while presupposing" and "I state while making clear," that is to say, "I state what matters to me" and "I state in order to be clear," or again, "I state what pleases me" and "I state for you, for us, so that one might understand one other." The binary message thus effects a shift from the *I* of pleasure to the *you* of the addressee and to the impersonal *one* that is necessary for the establishment of a truly universal syntax. It is thus that the subject of enunciation is born. By calling this trajectory back to mind he may rediscover, if not his origin, at least his originality. Céline's "spoken" writing accomplishes such a remembrance.

The important, integrating, and logico-syntactic role that intonation plays here confirms the hypothesis according to which an archaic structure would be involved. Indeed, recent investigations have demonstrated that intonation, at the same time as being a token of emotivity close to drives, is a syntactic organizer both very precocious and very profound. It allows one, before solid syntactical categories have been established, and wherever there is ambiguity, to identify the true semantico-logical value of the constituents.[25] Straddling two categories in a way, the emotive and the syntactical, intonation *produces* the language system before the latter can be made explicit as such. Before being in his statement, the subject is manifested in the intonational figuration of his enunciation, and such an anteriority is as logical as it is chronological.

One should not conclude, however, that a style where intonation prevails as a factor of logical and syntactic organization and where the structure of the message (theme/rheme or conversely) overshadows that of the sentence (subject-verb-object) corresponds to a simple regression of the speaker to childish stages or to the domain of the *id*. When such strategies turn up in adult usage, in colloquial speech, for instance, and above all intentionally in Célinian style, they operate not on the near side but on the far side of syntactic processes; we are dealing not with a "less" but with a "more" of syntax. The syntactical capacity that is already there, to which "regressive" strategies are superadded, may only be a competence (not necessarily explicit in the performance) of vulgar speakers. It is on the other hand actualized, present, and effective with a writer like Céline, for whom writing "like the common people" is a contrivance, an unwritten provision, the result of stubborn work with and through syntax aimed at "having sentences slightly fly off their handle." "Speak straight out, child"—that seems to have been the message of Céline's grandfather, a famous rhetorician, if we are to believe what his grandson says in *Guignol's Band*. "I do follow emotion with words, but I don't give it time to dress up in flowery language."[26] But this flight of the sentence is in short an over-syntacticism. Enunciation devices, usually repressed, by means of which subject and addressee, in their mutual combat and fascination, discover logical (theme/rheme), spatial (preposing, displacing), and intonational means of revealing themselves in the statement, show up here as an additional charging of syntactical processes. The emotion so dear to Céline is not uttered in any other way except by a return of repressed enunciative strategies; added to normative syntax, they make up a complicated mental machine in which two programs are meshed (enunciation and statement), just as a piano performance results from conjoined playing by two hands.

ELLIPSES: THREE DOTS AND A SUSPENSION

In the later novels, *From Castle to Castle, North,* and *Rigadoon,* Céline's sentence, while maintaining the spoken devices of earlier ones, is especially striking on account of its concision. The famous "three dots," or points of suspension, as well as the exclamation point, already present in previous texts, proliferate here; they assert themselves as external tokens of a staccato rhythm, of syntactical and logical ellipsis. Less pronounced in *Castle to Castle*, the device is accentuated in *Rigadoon*, in keeping no doubt with the apocalyptic and strident theme of a continent and culture that are falling into ruins.

Let us take a closer look at Céline's sentence in *Castle to Castle*. Very frequently the three dots come at the end of complete clauses where no ellipsis is involved. It seems then that their function is to signal that, while the *syntactical structure* is normally complete, the *enunciation*, on the other hand, is not; it continues, becomes displaced, concatenates other clauses. Far from being the mark of a lacuna in the clause, the three dots rather point to the *overflowing of the clause* into a higher unit of enunciation, that of the message; this unit is marked out, in formal terms, by the paragraph, and within it by the lack of capital letters at the beginning of each new clause following the three dots. This technique brings into being a full sentence, very often half a page long, sometimes extending to a page or more. In opposition to the variability of Proustian sentences, Céline's avoid subordination, do not present themselves as logico-syntactic units, and proceed by means of brief statements; clauses that can be uttered in one breath, cutting, chopping, imparting rhythm. Here is an example:

She doesn't know, she doesn't care . . . she turns over . . . she's asleep . . . I'll look all by myself! . . . I've got to tell you that in addition to being a voyeur I'm a fanatic about the movement of harbors, about everything that goes on on the water . . . everything that sails or floats or docks . . . I was on the jetties with my father . . . a week's vacation in Le Tréport . . . Christ, the things we saw! . . . the fishing boats' entrances and exits . . . whiting at the risk of their lives! . . . the widows and the kids imploring the sea! . . . the emotion of those jetties! . . .the suspense! . . . make the Grand Guignol and the billion-dollar thrillers from Hollywood look like a kindergarten! . . . Well, down there the Seine . . . oh, I'm just as fascinated . . . just as nuts about everything connected with water and boats, the way they move, their comings and goings, it's for life . . . there aren't many fascinations that last a lifetime [. . .] either you've got the bug . . . or you haven't . . . [. . .] a measly little yawl puts into shore and down I go . . .on the run! . . . I used to run . . . I don't any more . . . nowadays I'm satisfied with the spyglass . . .[27]

Next to complete clauses that are nonetheless concatenated by the three dots, one notes two kinds of ellipses. On the one hand, the points of suspension cut off a constituent from the main clause or from the predicate; thus isolated, the constituent *loses its identity* as object phrase, for instance, and while it does not gain a truly autonomous value it still floats in a syntactic irresolution that opens a path to various logical and semantic connotations, in short, to daydreaming. Thus, "I'm a fanatic about the movement of harbors, about everything that goes on the water . . . everything that sails or floats or docks." A comma in the place of the three dots would simply have linked "I'm a fanatic" to "everything that sails or floats or docks." Instead, Céline's scription gives to the object phrase ("everything that sails or floats or docks") a relative independence from subject and predicate ("I'm a fanatic"), thus inviting the reader to link it to another subject, another predicate, both indefinite and perhaps more subjective.

The technique of making a constituent autonomous with respect to the basic structure, subject/predicate, leads us to the second type of ellipsis in the Célinian sentence: noun phrases. For instance, "a week's vacation in Le Tréport . . . [. . .] fishing boats' entrances and exits . . . whiting at the risk of their lives! . . ." Two modalities can be distinguished here: the *suspensive noun phrase* [. . .] and the *exclamatory noun phrase* (!). In both cases the predicate relationship has been omitted: "(there was, or, we spent) a week's vacation in Le Tréport"; "(we could see, or, there were) the fishing boats' entrances and exists"; "(they went out for) whiting at the risk of their lives!" One could also interpret these statement as themes whose rhemes are suspended. It is as if the main information that these descriptions contain were hushed up. What replaces it, what thus plays the part of the verb, or what assimilates the attitude of the subject of enunciation is *intonation*. *Suspensive intonation* stresses incompletion and invites the addressee to include himself in the day-dream. The *exclamatory intonation* shows the enthusiasm, the surprise, the fascination of the speaker. As a result, the rheme being included in and impressed upon the theme as intonation does not become detached; on the other hand, the theme is subjectivized. The noun phrase, "a week's vacation in Le Tréport," not only gives information concerning the length and the place of my vacation, it also points to my saying it, since it *indicates*—without making clear—my place, my emotional and logical attitude as a subject who remembers, with melancholy or delight.

The coalescence of theme and rheme, objectal information and strongly subjective information in *exclamatory noun phrases* is more powerful yet: "the widows and the kids imploring the sea! . . . the emotion on those jetties! . . . the suspense! . . ." Whether actual noun phrases or not, those exclamatory utterances carry, through their signification, a deeper *meaning* that is not lexicalized; they reveal an intense, passionate attitude, through which the speaking subject displays his desire and calls upon the reader to embrace it, beyond words, through the archaic configuration of melody—the original mark of syntax and subjective position. "(I am delighted, I am telling you, see how extraordinary it is to watch) the widows and the kids imploring the sea!"

One notices here, contrary to the binary practice of the early novels, a *condensation of the two terms of the message*. Theme and rheme become superposed in a statement that is more and more elliptic, a statement whose lexical precision is matched only by the sparingness of the description. Commentary and logical or psychological expliciting become unstated and are merely *indicated*, present but allusive in intonation alone. Avoiding signification, the speaker chooses not a sign (lexeme), even less a sentence (syntacticological structure), but a *token*: intonation, which bears both *affect* and *subjective position* (to be dressed up semantically later or never).

Céline has compared his style to that of impressionist painters. It is indeed possible to liken to color dots statements in which the binary turn of the early novels is condensed in short units that the blank spaces of the three dots place side by side to form a halo not of descriptions but of subjective impressions.

You know, three dots, the impressionists made three dots. Take Seurat, he would put three dots everywhere; he thought it let air into his paintings, made it fly about. The fellow was right. It didn't start much of a school [. . .] It's too hard.[28]

Rigadoon fully makes use of this device, leading to the greatest condensation where the noun phrase—or simply the missing phrase of an omitted syntactic structure—attains to the eruptive value, as descriptive as it is subjective, of *onomatopeia*. Competing with comic strips, Céline in his writing used onomatopeia more and more frequently. According to Céline himself the infernal rhythm of war was the major cause of his utterly particular style, which thus meshes in its very musicality with a kind of realism, since it reverberates with the war, and a definite contemporariness, since it echoes comic strips.

From this moment on, I warn you, my chronicle is a little jerky, I myself, who lived through what I'm telling you, have trouble getting it straight . . . I was talking about "comics" . . . even in the comics you'd have a hard time finding a sudden break like that in the continuity, balloons, and characters . . . a double-barreled shambles . . . take my word for it! . . . so brutal that all of a sudden nothing was there . . . and I myself . . . I hem and haw, I'm all balled up . . . too many bits and pieces! . . . you'll have to forgive me . . . (*R*, 138)

It is indeed in connection with the bombings that the condensed scription of *Rigadoon* finds its privileged expression.

The whole earth jumps! worse! like it was broken in two! . . . and the air . . . this is it! Restif hadn't been lying . . . *boom!* and another! . . . further away . . . we can see it! the flashes of their cannon! . . . red! . . . green! no! shorter! howitzers! . . . all on the station! . . . I can see them now . . . Oddort! . . . an ocean of flame, as they say . . . big flames from all over, the windows, the doors, the cars . . . and *boom!* another! . . . another! . . . they'll never get out of that station, not one of them! . . . Restif hadn't been lying . . .but where can he be? and those people we'd followed . . . where'd they go? . . . I won't bore you with the shelling . . . dead center . . . all on the

station . . .a furnace! . . . now we can see it plainly . . . the howitzers
and the gunners . . .weird . . . short barrels . . . [. . .] their Mes-
serschmidt . . . we know the sound . . . *rat-tat-tat! rat-tat-tat!* . . . in
bursts . . . like grinding coffee by hand . . . I say to Lili . . . I don't
need to say, she knows . . . down! flatter! and *wham!* . . . *crash!*
. . . a bomb! and flying fragments . . . the death blow! . . . (R,
125–126)

The narrative goes on, nevertheless, through these real
"flying fragments" of the sentence; characters, crowd, setting,
the plan and vicissitudes of the journey—all are there, stated,
narrated if you wish, but barely suggested, in succinct fashion,
to be reconstructed in their duration or their logical clumsiness
by those who will have world and time. Here, on that page,
in that war, which is both the era and the style of the writer,
exclamation marks turn up to score the sentence and punctuate
object noun phrases with affect ("the flashes of their cannon!"
"howitzers!"); they do the same for determinatives ("red!
. . . green!"), subject noun phrases ("and the air!"—and the air
also jumps), elliptic adverbial complements ("all on the station!"—we can see it all on the station, or they have all zeroed
in on the station), noun clauses ("a furnace!"), and complete
sentences ("The whole earth jumps!" and "they'll never get out
of that station, not one of them!"). Let me note that the binary
turn of this last colloquial sentence, with the stressed, elliptic
recall, "not one of them," integrates the dualism of the early
Célinian writings and their exclamatory and elliptic scription
with the shortened statements bearing affects without commentary of the later novels.

One thus reaches that extreme Célinian situation where the
most objectal, the most sparing description is blended with the
most intense affective charge, which, deprived of comment,
holds the unsaid but effective meaning of the text. In short, a
barren description of the objectal world, which practitioners
of the new novel that was to follow should have recognized as
their antecedent. But also—and thereby going beyond the rei-
fying or sexological technocratism of some new novelists—an
overflowing subjectivity that does not identify itself, painfully
modest, that cries out or sings, passionately sure of its right.

If the early novels' binary seesawing is now avoided and replaced with the terseness of noun phrases or clauses, exclamatorily suspended, a certain amount of duality persists nevertheless. Such a duality accounts for the constant tension that makes up Céline's scription, its very being. It specifically involves the inscription of affect, on the near and far side of words, in the movement of the voice as signaled by punctuation signs. Children's holophrases also hold in abeyance, in the motion of the hand or of the entire body, as well as in the intensity or modulation of the voice, the judgment that, later, will signal the position of the speaker with respect to the object of enunciation. But in the later texts of Céline, as in the binary turn of his early ones, what is involved is not simply a regression to the holophrastic level. As they reappear in adult discourse, holophrastic operations emphasize a strategy that comes as a supplement to normative syntactic competence and performance; they perform as markers of a "return of the repressed" at the level of the statement itself (and not at the thematic level that I have discussed in previous chapters).

Once more, the Célinian music proves to be "written affect," thanks to a syntactico-logical overcompetence and to an additional complication of linguistic operations. It is now easier to understand Céline's statements concerning the considerable work that is demanded, in his view, for the elaboration of a style.

Style is a certain way of doing violence to sentences [. . .] of having them slightly fly off the handle, so to speak, displacing them, and thus making the reader himself displace his meaning. But ever so slightly! ever so slightly! Because in all that, if you are heavy-handed, you know, it's putting your foot in it, it's a howler [. . .] Often people come to see me and say, "You seem to write easily." On the contrary! I don't write easily! Only with great difficulty! And writing bores me, on top of that. And it has to be done very shrewdly, very delicately. That means 80,000 pages in order to produce 800 pages of manuscript, where work has been obliterated. One doesn't see it.[29]

In *Rigadoon* the work of the writer is compared to the ant's clever patience, "scurrying around in the filings" (*R*, 29).

An absorption of work, a withholding of effort, a deletion

of abstraction, so that thanks to them but without stating them, and through them, an affect bursts out, in sound and outcry, bordering close on drive and abjection as well as fascination. Bordering on the unnamable.

THE LAUGHTER OF THE APOCALYPSE

The trans-syntactic inscription of emotion as inherent in the elementary structures of enunciation is probably the most subtle manifestation of what we have called abjection in connection with Célinian contents, themes, and myths.

For exclamatory suspension reveals, as I have said, an intense subjective attitude, but an indeterminate, ambivalent one. Being fluid, it can easily occupy both ends of the drive scale, from acceptance to rejection. Excitement and disgust, joy and repulsion—the reader deciphers them very fast on these lines pitted with blank spaces where emotion does not allow itself to be dolled up in flowery sentences. Descriptions of absurdity, stupidity, violence, sorrow, moral and physical degeneracy locate them, as a result, and *also in formal fashion*, in that interspace between abjection and fascination signaled by Célinian exclamations.

Such an affective ambivalence, enclosed in the intonation and marked by suspension or exclamation, enables us to put a finger on one of Céline's essential peculiarities, flush with his style—his horrified laughter: the comedy of abjection. He ceaselessly renders the sound and the image, or even the causes, of the apocalypse. Never anything resembling treatise, commentary, or judgment. Confronting the apocalypse, he exclaims with a horror close to ecstasy. Célinian laughter is a horrified and fascinated exclamation. An apocalyptic laughter.

We are familiar with the genesis and the catastrophic rhetoric of the apocalyptic genre in the Greek oracles, Egyptian or Persian sources, but especially the Hebrew prophets. The great Palestinian apocalyptic movement (between the second century B.C. and the second century A.D.) encodes a seeingness that, contrary to the philosophical revelation of truth, imposes through a poetic incantation that is often elliptic, rhythmic, and cryptogrammic the incompleteness and abjection of any identity, group, or speech. Such a seeingness asserts itself as the premise of an impossible future and as a promise of explosion.[30]

Considering only the New Testament and what is known as the Revelation of Saint John the Divine, whom Céline mentions among his masters ("Everything is in Saint John," *Féerie pour une autre fois* ["Enchantment for Some Other Time"], p. 54), it is around the time of the Christian era that the apocalyptic genre is established; it is broadly inspired by Jewish prophetic literature and other Middle-Eastern ones as well, immersed in a flow of cataclysms, catastrophes, deaths, and ends of the world. An identical sacred horror for the feminine, the diabolical, and the sexual are expounded therein, by means of an incantation whose particular prosody confirms the name of the genre: a discovering, a baring of truth. A vision through sounds hallucinated as images. In no case, thus, is there philosophical unveiling or reasoning demonstration of the hidden.

Carnival, to the contrary, does not keep to the rigid, that is, moral position of apocalyptic inspiration; it transgresses it, sets its repressed against it—the lower things, sexual matters, what is blasphemous and to which it holds while mocking the law.

We are familiar with the sublime laughter, the astral laughter of Dante's comedy in which the body, joying in a "successful" incest, is fully celebrated in the delight of the word incarnate. We are envious of the renascent mirth of Rabelais who gives himself up, trustfully, to the pleasures of a palate where mankind becomes intoxicated, thinking it has found guiltless flesh, mother, and body. We follow attentively Balzac's human comedy, knowing that its monstrous sufferings or absurdities are only freakish and that they establish, *a contrario*, the truth of divine harmony and the luminous project of a mind or providence in which Balzac says he believes.

With Céline we are elsewhere. As in apocalyptic or even prophetic utterances, he speaks out on horror. But while the former can be withstood because of a distance that allows for judging, lamenting, condemning, Céline—who speaks from within—has no threats to utter, no morality to defend. In the name of what would he do it? So his laughter bursts out, facing abjection, and always originating at the same source, of which Freud had caught a glimpse: the gushing forth of the unconscious, the repressed, suppressed pleasure, be it sex or death. And yet, if there is a gushing forth, it is neither jovial, nor trustful, nor sublime, nor enraptured by preexisting harmony. It is bare, anguished, and as fascinated as it is frightened.

A laughing apocalypse is an apocalypse without god. Black mysticism of transcendental collapse. The resulting scription is perhaps the ultimate form of a secular attitude without morality, without judgment, without hope. Neither Céline, who is such a writer, nor the catastrophic exclamation that constitutes his style, can find outside support to maintain themselves. Their only sustenance lies in the beauty of a gesture that, here, on the page, compels language to come nearest to the human enigma, to the place where it kills, thinks, and experiences jouissance all at the same time. A language of abjection of which the writer is both subject and victim, witness and topple. Toppling into what? Into nothing more than the effervescence of passion and language we call style, where any ideology, thesis, interpretation, mania, collectivity, threat, or hope become drowned. A brilliant and dangerous beauty, fragile obverse of a radical nihilism that can disappear only in "those bubbling depths that cancel our existence" (R, 261). Music, rhythm, rigadoon, without end, for no reason.

POWERS OF HORROR

All the great monstrosities, all of them are in Saint John! Kirghiz
librarians can cook up the damnest tricks!

Céline, *Féerie pour une autre fois, I*

Throughout a night without images but buffeted by black
sounds; amidst a throng of forsaken bodies beset with no longing but to last against all odds and for nothing; on a page where
I plotted out the convolutions of those who, in transference,
presented me with the gift of their void—I have spelled out
abjection. Passing through the memories of a thousand years,
a fiction without scientific objective but attentive to religious
imagination, it is within literature that I finally saw it carrying,
with its horror, its full power into effect.

On close inspection, all literature is probably a version of the
apocalypse that seems to me rooted, no matter what its socio-
historical conditions might be, on the fragile border (borderline
cases) where identities (subject/object, etc.) do not exist or only
barely so—double, fuzzy, heterogeneous, animal, metamor-
phosed, altered, abject.

The work of Céline, which draws on the contemporary for
its destructive, if not analytical, obstinacy, and on the classical
for its epic capability together with its plebeian, if not vulgar,
breadth, is upon the whole only one possible example among
others of the abject. Baudelaire, Lautréamont, Kafka, Georges
Bataille, Sartre (*Nausea*), or other contemporaries could have
guided, each in his own way, my descent into the hell of naming, that is to say of signifiable identity. But perhaps Céline is
also a privileged example and hence a convenient one to deal
with. For his coarseness, issuing from the global catastrophe

of the Second World War, does not, within the orb of abjection, spare a single sphere: neither that of morality, or politics, or religion, or esthetics, or, all the more so, subjectivity or language. If in that process he shows us the ultimate point that can be reached by what a moralist would call nihilism, he also testifies to the power of fascination exerted upon us, openly or secretly, by that field of horror. I have sought in this book to demonstrate on what mechanism of subjectivity (which I believe to be universal) such horror, its meaning as well as its power, is based. By suggesting that literature is its privileged signifier, I wish to point out that, far from being a minor, marginal activity in our culture, as a general consensus seems to have it, this kind of literature, or even literature as such, represents the ultimate coding of our crises, of our most intimate and most serious apocalypses. Hence its nocturnal power, "the great darkness" (Angela of Foligno). Hence its continual compromising: "Literature and Evil" (Georges Bataille). Hence also its being seen as taking the place of the sacred, which, to the extent that it has left us without leaving us alone, calls forth the quacks from all four corners of perversion. Because it occupies its place, because it hence decks itself out in the sacred power of horror, literature may also involve not an ultimate resistance to but an unveiling of the abject: an elaboration, a discharge, and a hollowing out of abjection through the Crisis of the Word.

If "something maternal" happens to bear upon the uncertainty that I call abjection, it illuminates the literary scription of the essential struggle that a writer (man or woman) has to engage in with what he calls demonic only to call attention to it as the inseparable obverse of his very being, of the other (sex) that torments and possesses him. Does one write under any other condition than being possessed by abjection, in an indefinite catharsis? Leaving aside adherents of a feminism that is jealous of conserving its power—the last of the power-seeking ideologies—none will accuse of being a usurper the artist who, even if he does not know it, is an undoer of narcissism and of all imaginary identity as well, sexual included.

And yet, in these times of dreary crisis, what is the point of emphasizing the horror of being?

Perhaps those that the path of analysis, or scription, or of a painful or ecstatic ordeal has led to tear the veil of the communitarian mystery, on which love of self and others is set up, only to catch a glimpse of the abyss of abjection with which they are underlaid—they perhaps might be able to read this book as something other than an intellectual exercise. For abjection, when all is said and done, is the other facet of religious, moral, and ideological codes on which rest the sleep of individuals and the breathing spells of societies. Such codes are abjection's purification and repression. But the return of their repressed make up our "apocalypse," and that is why we cannot escape the dramatic convulsions of religious crises.

In the end, our only difference is our unwillingness to have a face-to-face confrontation with the abject. Who would want to be a prophet? For we have lost faith in One Master Signifier. We prefer to foresee or seduce; to plan ahead, promise a recovery, or esthetize; to provide social security or make art not too far removed from the level of the media.

In short, who, I ask you, would agree to call himself abject, subject of or subject to abjection?

Nothing preordains the psychoanalyst to take the place of the mystic. Psychoanalytic establishments seem even less suited to this, so much does their intrinsic perversion consign them to mummifying transference in the production of mini-paranoids if not merely stereotyped besotments. And yet, it would perhaps be possible for an analyst (if he could manage to stay in the only place that is his, *the void*, that is, the unthinkable of metaphysics) to begin hearing, actually to listen to himself build up a discourse around the braided horror and fascination that bespeaks the incompleteness of the speaking being but, because it is heard as a narcissistic crisis on the outskirts of the feminine, shows up with a comic gleam the religious and political pretensions that attempt to give meaning to the human adventure. For, facing abjection, meaning has only a scored, rejected, ab-jected meaning—a comical one. "Divine," "human," or "for some other time," the comedy or the enchantment can be realized, on the whole, only by reckoning with the impossible for later or never, but set and maintained right here.

Fastened to meaning like Raymond Roussel's parrot to its

chain, the analyst, since he interprets, is probably among the rare contemporary witnesses to our dancing on a volcano. If he draws perverse jouissance from it, fine; provided that, in his or her capacity as a man or woman without qualities, he allow the most deeply buried logic of our anguish and hatred to burst out. Would he then be capable of X-raying horror without making capital out of its power? Of displaying the abject without confusing himself for it?

Probably not. Because of knowing it, however, with a knowledge undermined by forgetfulness and laughter, an abject knowledge, he is, she is preparing to go through the first great demystification of Power (religious, moral, political, and verbal) that mankind has ever witnessed; and it is necessarily taking place within that fulfillment of religion as sacred horror, which is Judeo-Christian monotheism. In the meantime, let others continue their long march toward idols and truths of all kinds, buttressed with the necessarily righteous faith for wars to come, wars that will necessarily be holy.

Is it the quiet shore of contemplation that I set aside for myself, as I lay bare, under the cunning, orderly surface of civilizations, the nurturing horror that they attend to pushing aside by purifying, systematizing, and thinking; the horror that they seize on in order to build themselves up and function? I rather conceive it as a work of disappointment, of frustration, and hollowing—probably the only counterweight to abjection. While everything else—its archeology and its exhaustion—is only literature: the sublime point at which the abject collapses in a burst of beauty that overwhelms us—and "that cancels our existence" (Céline).

NOTES

1. APPROACHING ABJECTION

1. Francis de Sales, *Introduction to a Devout Life*, Thomas S. Kepler, tr. (New York: World, 1952), p. 125. [Modified to conform to the French text, which reads, "l'abjection de soy-mesme."]

2. Fyodor Dostoyevsky, *The Devils*, David Magarshack, tr. (London: Penguin Books, 1953), p. 512.

3. Dostoyevsky, pp. 586–587.

4. Dostoyevsky, pp. 418–419.

5. Marcel Proust, *Swann's Way*, C. K. Scott-Moncrieff, tr. (New York: Random House, 1922), 2:141.

6. Proust, *Cities of the Plain*, Frederick A. Blossom, tr. (New York: Random House, 1934), p. 9.

7. James Joyce, *Ulysses* (New York: Vintage Books, 1961), pp. 738–739.

8. Jorge Luis Borges, *A Universal History of Infamy*, Norman Thomas Di Giovanni, tr. (New York: Dutton, 1979), pp. 23–25.

9. Antonin Artaud, "Suppôts et supplications," in *Œuvres Complètes* (Paris: Gallimard, 1978), 14:14.

10. Artaud, p. 72.

11. Artaud, p. 203.

12. Artaud, p. 155.

13. Jacques Lacan, *Télévision* (Paris: Seuil, 1974), p. 28.

14. In connection with catharsis in the Greek world, see Louis Molinier, *Le Pur et l'impur dans la pensée des Grecs* (Paris: Klincksieck, 1952).

15. See A. Philonenko, "Note sur les concepts de souillure et de pureté dans l'idéalisme allemand," *Les Etudes Philosophiques* (1972), 4:481–493.

2. SOMETHING TO BE SCARED OF

1. See particularly D. W. Winnicot, *The Maturation Processes and the Facilitating Environment* (New York: International Universities Press, 1965), and *Playing and Reality* (New York: Basic Books, 1971).

2. Sigmund Freud, *Analysis of a Phobia in a Five-Year-Old Boy*, in *The Complete Psychological Works of Sigmund Freud* (London: Hogarth Press,

1953–1974), 10:83. Later, when he referred to "the enigmatic phobias of early childhood," Freud explicitly defined them as "reactions to the danger of object loss." He suggests that the reactions are (phantasmatically?) very archaic when he considers the possible connections between childish phobia of small animals or storms, for instance, and "the atrophied remainders of congenital preparation for real dangers that are so clearly developed in other animals." He nevertheless concludes that, "in the case of man, the only portion of that archaic inheritance to be appropriated is what pertains to object loss" (*Inhibitions, Symptoms, and Anxiety,* in *Complete Psychological Works,* 20:160). That clearly locates the reflection on phobia within the problematic scope of object relation. What remains to be clarified is the latter's dependency on symbolic function, particularly on language, on which rest not only its very existence but all of its variants.

3. "It may well be that before its sharp cleavage into an ego and an id, and before the formation of a super-ego, the mental apparatus makes use of different methods of defense from those which it employs after it has reached these stages of organization." Freud, *Inhibitions, Symptoms, and Anxiety,* p. 164. To begin with, Freud had pointed out that the word "defense," in opposition to the more precise term "repression," included all the protective devices of the ego against the demands of drives; with the statement I have just quoted, Freud seems to proceed to areas where, without the ego existing as such, modalities of defense other than repression are at work. Does this have to do with defensive capabilities that are elaborated along with primal repression? With the power of the symbolic alone, always already present but working within its pre-sign, pre-meaning (trans-sign, trans-meaning) modality, which I call "semiotic"? Would not the phobic "object," and the abject as well, be located on that trail, which was blazed by Freud?

4. Freud, *Analysis of a Phobia,* p. 83.

5. See Anneliese Schnurmann, "Observation of a Phobia" (contribution to Anna Freud's seminar, 1946), in *Psychoanalytic Study of the Child,* 3/4:253–270.

6. Freud, *Analysis of a Phobia,* p. 139.

7. Freud, *Papers on Metapsychology,* in *Complete Works,* 14:122. Emphasis mine.

8. "Voyeurism is a normal moment of evolution during pregenital stages; if it remains within limits, it allows a very sophisticated approach to the Oedipal conflict. Paradoxically, it becomes a perversion as a result of its failure to provide assurance against the possible destruction of the object." Michel Fain, "Contribution à l'analyse du voyeurisme," *Revue Française de Psychanalyse* (1954), 18:177–192.

9. Jacques Lacan, *Ecrits/A Selection* (New York: Norton, 1977), pp. 156–157.

10. André Green, *Le Discours vivant* (Paris: Presses Universitaires de France, 1973).

11. Hanna Segal, "Notes on Symbol Formation," *International Journal of Psychoanalysis* (1957), 38:381–397.

12. See Freud's first book, *Aphasia* (*Zur Auffassung der Aphasien*, 1891).

13. See *The Interpretation of Dreams* (1900; New York: Random House, 1950).

14. See *Negation* (1925), in volume 19 of the *Complete Works*.

15. One might compare that definition with what André Green says concerning the trauma-object: "Thus, within the series, precocious trauma-defense (this set establishing fixation)-latency-breaking out of neurosis-partial return of the repressed, I should like to emphasize the *confusion between drive* (*represented by affect*) *and object*, for the danger stems from the violence done to sexuality in the Ego as well as from violence done to the object. Consequently it will be understood that the problem involving relationship between Ego and object is that of their limits, their coexistence. [. . .] When I speak of trauma-object I basically refer to the threat that the object holds for the Ego, to the extent that it forces the Ego to modify its operation through its presence alone." André Green, "L'Angoisse et le narcissisme," *Revue Française de Psychanalyse* (1979), 1:52–53 and 55.

16. Freud, "Draft G. Melancholia" (1895), in vol. 1 of *Complete Works*; J.-B. Pontalis comments, "not a *lacuna* but a *hole*, not a *want* but an *overflow*," in *Entre le rêve et la douleur* (Paris: Gallimard, 1977), p. 248.

3. FROM FILTH TO DEFILEMENT

1. In *Totem and Taboo* (1913), in vol. 13 of *Complete Works*. References will be to the Vintage Book edition published by Random House.

2. *Totem and Taboo*, p. 170.

3. *Totem and Taboo*, p. 185.

4. See René Girard, *Des Choses cachées depuis la fondation du monde* (Paris: Grasset, 1978).

5. Freud quoted from T. W. Atkinson's *Primal Law, Totem and Taboo* (London, 1903); see p. 184n.

6. *Totem and Taboo*, pp. 85–86—although the translation used is that of the *Complete Works*, 13:64.

7. *Totem and Taboo*, p. 86n; quoted from the *Complete Works*, 13:65.

8. *Totem and Taboo*, p. 207.

9. *Totem and Taboo*, pp. 115–116.

10. See Georges Bataille, "L'Abjection et les formes misérables," in *Essais de sociologie, Œuvres complètes*, (Paris: Gallimard, 1970), 2:217ff.

11. Mary Douglas, *Purity and Danger* (London, Boston, and Henley: Routledge and Kegan Paul, 1969), p. 121.

12. Douglas, p. 113.

13. Douglas, p. 113.

14. See Douglas, pp. 149ff.

15. "For the Lele evil is not to be included in the total system of the world, but to be expunged without compromise" (Douglas, p. 171).

16. V. S. Naipaul, *An Area of Darkness* (London: Deutsch, 1964), as quoted by Douglas, p. 124.

17. Louis Dumont, *Homo Hierarchicus* (Chicago: University of Chicago Press, 1970), pp. 139ff.

18. See Charles Malamoud, "Observations sur la notion de "reste" dans le brahmanisme," *Wiener Zeitschrift für die Kunde Südasiens* (1972), 16:5–26.

19. See K. Maddock, "Dangerous Proximities and Their Analogues," *Mankind* (1974), 5(3):206–217.

20. See K. Gouph, "Nuer Kinship: A Re-examination," in T. O. Beidelman, ed., *The Translation of Culture* (London: Tavistock, 1971), p. 91.

21. See L. N. Rosen, "Contagion and Cataclysm: A Theoretical Approach to the Study of Ritual Pollution Beliefs," *African Studies* (1973), 32(4):229–246.

22. See S. Lindenbaum, "Sorcerers, Ghosts, and Polluting Women: An Analysis of Religious Belief and Population Control," *Journal of Geography* (1972), 11(3):241.

23. Dumont, pp. 137–138.

24. M. B. Emenau, "Language and Social Forms. A Study of Toda Kinship Terms and Dual Descent," in *Language, Culture, and Personality*, Essays in Memory of Edward Sapir (Menasha, Wis.: Sapir Memorial Publication Fund, 1941), pp. 158–179.

25. Dumont, "Hierarchy and Marriage Alliance in South India Kinship," *Occasional Papers of the Royal Anthropological Institute* (1957), 12:22.

26. Dumont, *Homo Hierarchicus*, p. 120.

27. Dumont, p. 53.

28. Dumont, p. 53.

29. Dumont, p. 120.

30. Célestin Bouglé, *Essai sur le régime des castes* (Paris: Presses Universitaires de France, 1969), p. 3.

31. Bouglé, pp. 3, 25, etc.

32. Bouglé, p. 18.

33. Bouglé, pp. 36–37.

34. Bouglé, p. 64.

35. J.-P. Vernant has analyzed that logic in "Ambiguïté et renversement. Sur la structure enigmatique d'Œdipe roi," in J.-P. Vernant and P. Vidal-Naquet, *Mythe et tragédie* (Paris: Maspéro, 1973), pp. 101ff.

36. See Vernant and Vidal-Naquet and also the publications of L. Gernet.

37. R. C. Jebb's translation has been used; it comes somewhat closer than more recent ones to the French translation by Jean Grosjean quoted by Julia Kristeva [trans.].

4. SEMIOTICS OF BIBLICAL ABOMINATION

1. See Jacob Neusner, *The Idea of Purity in Ancient Judaism* (Leiden: Brill, 1973), p. 9.

2. Baruch A. Levine, *In the Presence of the Lord. Aspects of Ritual in Ancient Israel* (Leiden: Brill, 1974).

3. *The Code of Maimonides. The Book of Cleanness*, Herbert Danby, tr. (New Haven: Yale University Press, 1954), p. 535.

4. Neusner, p. 12.

5. Mary Douglas, "Critique and Commentary," in Neusner, pp. 138–139.

6. Genesis 8:20.

7. Genesis 8:21–22.

8. There are other words, with different origins and semantic variants, that are used to signify purity and impurity at various points and stages of the biblical text. See H. Cazelles, "Pureté et impureté dans l'Ancien Testament," in *Supplément au dictionnaire de la Bible* (Paris: Letaizey et Ané, 1965), pp. 491–508.

9. See Neusner, "The Idea of Purity in Ancient Judaism," *Journal of the American Academy of Religion* (1975), 43(1):15–26.

10. See E. M. Zuesse, "Taboo and the Divine Order," *Journal of the American Academy of Religion* (1974), 42(3):482–504.

11. See the excellent article, J. Saler, "Sémiotique de la nourriture dans la Bible," *Annales*, July–August 1973, pp. 93ff.

12. *Ibid.*

13. See Cazelles, *Supplément.*

14. According to B. Levine, as quoted in Neusner's "The Idea of Purity in Ancient Judaism."

15. Jacob Neusner, *A History of the Mishnaic Law of Purities* (Leiden: Brill, 1974).

16. See Melanie Klein, "On the Importance of Symbol Formation in the Development of the Ego," in *Contributions to Psychoanalysis 1921–1945* (London: Hogarth Press, 1948).

17. René Girard, *Des choses cachées depuis le commencement du monde*, pp. 203ff.

18. See H. McKeating, "The Development of the Law on Homicide in Ancient Israel," *Vetus Testamentum* (1975), 25(1):46–68.

. . . . *QUI TOLLIS PECCATA MUNDI*

1. See J. Jeremias, *Les Paroles inconnues de Jésus* (Paris: Cerf, 1970), pp. 50–62.

2. "If Man is not by nature what he should be, then he is implicitly rational, implicitly Spirit. [. . .] in the state of nature he is not what he ought to be"; "it is reflection of knowledge which makes him evil"; "knowledge or consciousness is just the act by which separation [. . .] comes into existence"; "Man regarded in accordance with his conception or notion [. . .] is consciousness, and consequently he enters into this state of disunion"; G. W. F. Hegel, *Lectures on the Philosophy of Religion*, E. B. Speirs and J. Burdon Sanderson, tr. (New York: Humanities Press, 1962), 3:50, 52, and 55.

3. Such osmosis of separate terms, such heterogeneity, appears to have been glimpsed by Hegel when he considered "sin" as inseparable from "remission of sins" and concluded, "Between sin and its forgiveness there is as little place for an alien thing as there is between sin and punishment. Life has severed itself from itself and united itself again." *The Spirit of Christianity and its Fate* in *Early Theological Writings*, T. M. Knox, tr. (Chicago: University of Chicago Press, 1948), p. 239.

4. *De libero arbitrio*, 3, 19, 53, col. 1,256.

5. The Speirs translation of *Lectures on the Philosophy of Religion* reads, "This is the extraordinary combination which directly contradicts the Understanding" (3:76). It corresponds to the text of the *Sämtliche Werke* (Stuttgart, 1959), 16:286: ". . . diese ungeheure Zusammensetzung ist es, die dem Verstande schlechthin widerspricht." See "Translator's Note" in this volume.

6. The passage within brackets appears neither in the Speirs translation (3:53) nor in the *Sämtliche Werke* (16:265). See "Translator's Note."

7. Jacques Maritain, *The Sin of the Angel*, William L. Rossner, S. J., tr. (Westminster, Md.: Newman Press, 1959), p. 50.

8. *Sententia* 4, 14, 4, 7. Duns Scotus indeed posits "the absolution of penitent man accomplished by certain words," *Sententia* 4, 14, 4, 2. See Joseph Turmel, *Histoire des dogmes* (Paris: Rieder, 1936), pp. 449–450.

6. CÉLINE: NEITHER ACTOR NOR MARTYR

1. Louis-Ferdinand Céline, *Journey to the End of the Night*, John H. P. Marks, tr. (Boston: Little, Brown, 1934), p. 213. Subsequent references to this work, abbreviated as *J*, will appear in the body of the text.

2. Letter to Milton Hindus, dated May 29, 1947, in *Louis-Ferdinand Céline II, Les Cahiers de l'Herne* (1965), 5:76.

3. See Julia Kristeva, "L'Expérience et la pratique," in *Polylogue* (Paris: Seuil, 1977), pp. 107–136.

4. See Mikhail Bakhtin, *Problems of Dostoyevsky's Poetics* (Ann Arbor, Mich.: Ardis, 1973) and *Rabelais and His World* (Cambridge: M.I.T. Press, 1968).

5. Céline, *Entretiens avec le professeur Y.* (Paris: Gallimard, 1954), p. 67.

6. Letter to Hindus, March 31, 1948, *L'Herne*, 5:107.

7. SUFFERING AND HORROR

1. Louis-Ferdinand Céline, *Death on the Instalment Plan*, Ralph Manheim, tr. (New York: New Directions, 1966), pp. 39–40. Subsequent references to this work, abbreviated as *D*, will appear in the body of the text.

2. Louis-Ferdinand Céline, *Le Pont de Londres* ("Guignols's Band II"; Paris: Gallimard, 1964), p. 137. Subsequent references to this work, abbreviated as *P*, will appear in the body of the text.

3. Louis-Ferdinand Céline, *Guignol's Band*, Bernard Frechtman and Jack T. Nile, tr. (New York: New Directions, 1969), p. 135. Subsequent references to this work, abbreviated as *G*, will appear in the body of the text.

4. Louis-Ferdinand Céline, *Rigadoon*, Ralph Manheim, tr. (New York: Dell, 1974), p. 179. Subsequent references to this work, abbreviated as *R*, will appear in the body of the text.

8. THOSE FEMALES WHO CAN WRECK THE INFINITE

1. "Entretiens avec A. Zbinden," in Céline, *Romans II* (Paris: Gallimard, 1974), p. 945.

2. Louis-Ferdinand Céline, *Féerie pour une autre fois* (Paris: Gallimard, 1952), p. 144. Subsequent references to this work, abbreviated as *F*, will appear in the body of the text.

3. Louis-Ferdinand Céline, *La Vie et l'œuvre de Philippe Ignace Semmelweis* (Paris: Denoël et Steele, 1936), p. 588.

4. Céline, *Semmelweis*, p. 617.

5. Céline, *Semmelweis*, p. 621.

6. On September 10, 1947, *L'Herne*, 5:96.

7. Letter to Hindus, August 23, 1947, *L'Herne*, 5:92.

8. Letter to Hindus, February 28, 1948, *L'Herne*, 5:104.

9. Louis-Ferdinand Céline, *L'Eglise* (Paris: Denoël et Steele, 1933), p. 488.

9. "OURS TO JEW OR DIE"

1. Louis-Ferdinand Céline, *Les Beaux Draps* (Paris: Nouvelles Editions Françaises, 1941), p. 90. Subsequent references to this work, abbreviated as *BD*, will appear in the body of the text.

2. Louis-Ferdinand Céline, *L'Ecole des cadavres* (Paris: Denoël, 1938), p. 140. Subsequent references to this work, abbreviated as *EC*, will appear in the body of the text.

3. Letter to Hindus, September 2, 1947, *L'Herne*, 5:94.

4. Letter to Hindus, April 16, 1947, *L'Herne*, 5:72.

5. Louis-Ferdinand Céline, *Bagatelles pour un massacre* (Paris: Denoël, 1937), p. 144. Subsequent references to this work, abbreviated as *BM*, will appear in the body of the text.

6. From an interview with Ivan-M. Sicard published in *L'Emancipation Nationale*, November 21, 1941.

7. It would not only seem that, to the end of his life, he never clearly renounced anti-Semitism ("I disown nothing at all . . . I have not at all changed my mind . . . I simply put in a modicum of doubt, but people will have to prove that I was wrong rather than me showing that I was right"— "Entretien avec A. Zbinden," *Romans II*, p. 940), but even when he entertains the idea of a reconciliation with Jews (he specifies, "not a *Defense of the Jews*

but a *Reconciliation*") he is led to advocate a new racism, a decidedly permanent feeling of love/hatred for the other: "We must create a new racism upon biological bases" (letter to Hindus, August 10, 1947, *L'Herne*, 5:90).

8. Catherine Francblin has presented a very lucid analysis of Céline's anti-Semitism in an unpublished master's essay entitled "Céline et les Juifs." I am indebted to her for the following development.

9. See A. Mandel, "D'un Céline juif," *L'Herne* (1963), 3:252–257, and "L'Ame irresponsable, ou Céline et le Dibbouk," *L'Herne* (1965) 5:207–209.

10. "Entretiens avec A. Zbinden," *Romans II*, p. 939.

10. IN THE BEGINNING AND WITHOUT END . . .

1. "Louis-Ferdinand Céline vous parle." in *Romans II*, p. 934.
2. "Céline vous parle," p. 933.
3. Quoted in Pierre Monier, "Résidence surveillée," *L'Herne* (1963), 3:76.
4. See letter to Hindus, December 15, 1947, *L'Herne*, 5:103.
5. *Entretiens avec le professeur Y.*, p. 104.
6. *Entretiens*, p. 122.
7. See letter to Hindus, May 15, 1947, *L'Herne*, 5:76.
8. Same letter, p. 75.
9. Same letter, p. 75.
10. Letter to Hindus, March 30, 1947, *L'Herne*, 5:72.
11. Letter to Hindus, May 15, 1947, *L'Herne*, 5:75.
12. Letter to Hindus, May 29, 1947, *L'Herne*, 5:76.
13. *Entretiens avec le professeur Y.* p. 72.
14. *Entretiens*, p. 23.
15. *Entretiens*, p. 28.
16. *Entretiens*, p. 35.
17. Letter to Hindus, October 17, 1947, *L'Herne*, 5:99.
18. Leo Spitzer, "Une Habitude de style, le rappel chez Céline," *Le Français Moderne* (1935), 3:193–208; reprinted in *L'Herne*, 5:153–164.
19. With respect to segmentation in contemporary French, see Jean Perrot, "Fonctions syntaxiques, énonciation, information," *Bulletin de la Société de Linguistique de Paris* (1978), 73(1):85; Mario Rossi, "L'Intonation et la troisième articulation," *BSLP* (1977), 72(1):55–68; Claude Hagège, "Intonation, fonctions syntaxiques, universaux," *BSLP* (1977), 72(1):1–47.
20. See Ivan Fonágy, "Prélangage et régressions syntaxiques," *Lingua* (1975), 36:163–208.
21. See Jean Perrot, "Fonctions syntaxiques."
22. Spitzer, *L'Herne*, 5:162.
23. See Bakhtin, *Problems of Dostoyevsky's Poetics*.
24. See Fonágy, "Prélangage et régressions syntaxiques."
25. See Rossi, "L'Intonation et la troisième articulation, and Hagège, "Intonation, fonctions syntaxiques, universaux."

26. Letter to Hindus, April 16, 1947, *L'Herne*, 5:73.

27. Louis-Ferdinand Céline, *Castle to Castle* (New York: Delacorte, 1968), p. 80.

28. "Louis-Ferdinand Céline vous parle," in *Romans II*, p. 934.

29. *Ibid.*, pp. 933–934.

30. See H. Sterlin, *La Vérité sur l'Apocalypse* (Paris: Buchet-Chastel, 1972); R. P. Boismard, "L'Apocalypse ou les apocalypses de Saint Jean," *Revue Biblique*, October 1949; J. Lévitan, *Une Conception juive de l'apocalypse* (Paris: Debresse, 1966); etc.